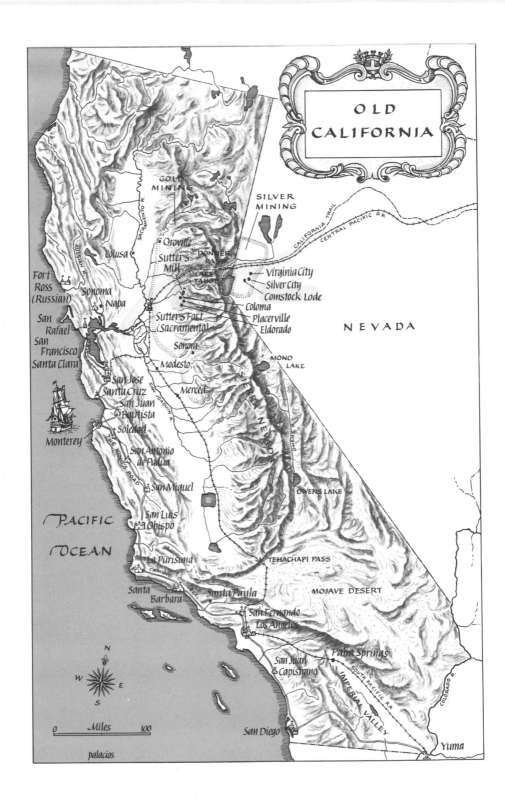

OLD CALIFORNIA

GOLD MINING

SILVER MINING

CALIFORNIA TRAIL

CENTRAL PACIFIC RR

Oroville

Colusa

Sutter's Mill

DONNER PASS

LAKE TAHOE

Virginia City

Silver City

Comstock Lode

Coloma

Placerville

Eldorado

NEVADA

SACRAMENTO R.

RUSSIAN R.

Fort Ross (Russian)

Sonoma

Napa

San Rafael

San Francisco

Santa Clara

Sutter's Fort (Sacramento)

Sonora

Modesto

Merced

SAN JOAQUIN R.

SIERRA NEVADA

MONO LAKE

San Jose

Santa Cruz

San Juan Bautista

Soledad

Monterey

THE KINGS ROAD

San Antonio de Padua

San Miguel

San Luis Obispo

OWENS R.

OWENS LAKE

PACIFIC OCEAN

La Purisima

EL CAMINO REAL

Santa Barbara

Santa Paula

TEHACHAPI PASS

MOJAVE DESERT

San Fernando

Los Angeles

San Juan Capistrano

Palm Springs

SOUTH PACIFIC RR

IMPERIAL VALLEY

COLORADO R.

N
W E
S

0   Miles   100

palacios

San Diego

Yuma

CALIFORNIA RICH

STEPHEN BIRMINGHAM

Simon and Schuster
New York

Published by Simon and Schuster
A Division of Gulf & Western Corporation
Simon & Schuster Building
Rockefeller Center
1230 Avenue of the Americas
New York, New York 10020
SIMON AND SCHUSTER and colophon are
    trademarks of Simon & Schuster
Designed by Carole Stephens
Photo editor: Vincent Virga
Manufactured in the United States of America

1 2 3 4 5 6 7 8 9 10

Library of Congress Cataloging in Publication Data

Birmingham, Stephen.
    California rich.

    Bibliography: p.
    Includes index.
    1. California—Social life and customs.
    2. Millionaires—California—Biography.
    3. California—Biography. I. Title.
F861.B57   979.4   80-15377

ISBN 0-671-24127-3

The excerpt from *Run River* by Joan Didion
is reprinted by permission of the author.

Contents

ACKNOWLEDGMENTS

A BOOK is many people, and the list of those who have offered to help with this one—giving false leads, unexpectedly supplying surprising bits of information—would be long indeed. But there are some who have been especially helpful and supportive and each is due a special word of thanks.

In northern California, I would like particularly to thank Mr. and Mrs. John N. Rosekrans, Jr., of San Francisco for the hospitality of their houses and for supplying books, letters, and documents pertaining to the Spreckels family. In San Francisco, I am additionally grateful to Mr. Rosekrans' brother, Adolph Spreckels Rosekrans; to their mother, Mrs. Alma E. Spreckels; and to their late grandmother, Mrs. Adolph B. Spreckels, of whom I have delightful memories. For other Spreckels memorabilia, as well as many photographs, I am indebted to Mr. and Mrs. William R. Phillips, Jr., of Yountville,

California, who also offered the warm hospitality of their Napa Valley house. In San Francisco, I would also like to thank my old friend, Mr. Thomas Carr Howe, as well as Mr. Ian White and Mr. Earl Anderson, for access to the archives of the California Palace of the Legion of Honor. In Sacramento, I am indebted to Mr. C. K. McClatchy.

In southern California, I am indebted to Mrs. Thelma Irvine for Irvine family recollections, as well as to her daughter, Mrs. Linda Irvine Gaede, both of Newport Beach. Additionally, Irvine family and corporate information, as well as photographs, were supplied by Mr. Martin A. Brower of the Irvine Company; and for the Browers' pleasant hospitality I would like to thank Mr. Brower's wife, Tamar. In Santa Ana, Dr. Horace Leecing, Mr. Jim Sleeper, and Mr. Bernardo Yorba were also helpful in supplying regional history and information. I owe a special word of thanks to Miss Leslie Berkman of the Los Angeles *Time*'s Orange County Bureau.

In the East, I am grateful to Dr. Edward Lahniers of Cincinnati for psychological insights as well as special sleuthing into the mysterious circumstances of Myford Irvine's death. I must also thank my editor, Michael Korda, for inspiration and guidance, and my literary agent, Mrs. Carol Brandt, for her customary efficiency, level-headedness, and support.

While all these people have contributed greatly to the book, I hold myself accountable for its errors and shortcomings.

S.B.

For Carol Brandt

THE GILDED MAN

*Californians are a race of
people; they are not merely
inhabitants of a State.*

O. HENRY

FOR YEARS Texas has laid proprietary—and quite undeserved—claim to everything American that pertains to bigness. Compared with California, however, Texas can boast only the larger acreage. Everything else about California is much, much bigger. And what is astonishing about California's bigness is that it all came about in a little over three generations' time. Never in history have so few men, who started out with so little, made so much out of a place that seemed to offer so little to begin with.

Consider California as recently as 1850, when the fledgling state had a population slightly larger than the nontransient population of present-day Bermuda—about ninety thousand. By 1880 the state's population was nearly a million, and thirty years later the figure was approaching two and a half million. Today, with a population of over twenty-two million, our most populous state contains more people than modern Afghanistan, and the city of Los Angeles alone is bigger than Dallas, Fort Worth, and Houston combined. And the end is not in sight.

At the same time, one of the difficulties of coming to grips with California, with its wealth, what it is and what it means, is that one is dealing with an ancient, romantic dream, along with a generally accepted fact of modern life, which is that dreams and reality almost never mesh. In reality, the success of California was based on plunder, thievery, bloodshed, and other familiar forms of physical, emotional, and economic violence. In the process the tinker's son became a great landowner, the preacher's son an oil tycoon, the butcher's son a cattle baron, and the glove salesman became Samuel Goldwyn of Hollywood.

The dream was all quite different, and much prettier, and much older than any of California's great fortunes, which, by comparison, sprang up only yesterday. It was a dream of El Dorado—literally, in Spanish, "The Gilded Man." Few people realize that El Dorado was originally a person, not a place. He was said to be the king, or the highest of the high priests, of a South American tribe of Indians, whose city-kingdom was thought to exist somewhere along the Pacific Coast—not far, so the legend went, from Santa Fe de Bogatá. No one knows exactly how the tales of El Dorado started, but stories about him spread and flourished throughout the Middle Ages. The kingdom that El Dorado ruled was said to be rich beyond mankind's wildest dreams; it had to be, because once a year, at his principal religious festival, El Dorado covered his naked body completely with a shower of gold dust.

Gradually El Dorado began to be interpreted as a city, whose name was variously given as Manoa and Omoa. But about the exact location of this city of gold there was much dispute. Finally it began to be assumed that El Dorado was much more than a city, that it was, in fact, an entire country where gold and precious jewels could be found in great abundance. By the time of the sixteenth-century Spanish explorers and conquistadors, the existence of El Dorado was taken very seriously, and a number of men received substantial financial backing to set out to find it. The only thing that anyone seemed certain of was that El Dorado lay in some tropical or semitropical climate—pleasant weather seemed an appropriate requisite for such a dream—and South America continued to seem the likely region.

One of the most celebrated searches for El Dorado was led by Diego de Ordaz. And in 1531 one of his lieutenants, Martínez, reported success. As he told the story, he had been rescued from a shipwreck by a band of tall, powerful, and richly dressed Indian warriors, who had led him inland to the city of Omoa. There, Señor Martínez related, he had been lavishly housed and entertained by none other than El Dorado himself. He had witnessed the rite in which El Dorado showered himself with gold dust—of which there was a vast abundance in Omoa—and he had seen and touched the diamonds, emeralds, rubies, sapphires, and pearls with which El Dorado's coffers overflowed.

Of course Martínez was lying through his teeth, but there was no one to challenge his assertions, and so others set off to try to find the wondrous place where he had been. Their object was to accomplish what Martínez had failed to do—to conquer El Dorado.

There were the various journeys, for example, in 1540 and 1541, of Orellana, who searched for El Dorado along the Rio Napo and into the valley of the Amazon, and from 1541 to 1545 of the German explorer Philipp von Hutten, who led a party from Coro to the coast of Caracas. Neither of these men was successful, nor was Gonzalo Jiménez de Quesada, in 1569, who started in the place where the legend appeared to have started, in Santa Fe de Bogotá.

In 1595 the English adventurer Sir Walter Raleigh, backed by Queen Elizabeth, took up the search and soon demonstrated that, despite his reputation for chivalry, he was no more truthful than Martínez. He too claimed to have found the fabled city. However, he pointed out, it was called Manoa, not Omoa, and he located it exactly on the shores of Lake Parimá, in Guiana. So seriously was Raleigh's discovery taken that the city and the lake were dutifully marked on English and other maps of South America for the next two hundred years. It was not until the nineteenth century that an explorer named Von Humboldt proved that there was no such city in Guiana, and, furthermore, no such lake.

In the meantime El Dorado had become a synonym for any distant, elusive place where great riches could be accumulated very quickly. Because the legend of The Gilded Man persisted, it was supposed that he had also discovered the secret of immortality, and the search for El Dorado became confused with the search for the Fountain of Youth and for other impossible places, such as the lost city of Atlantis. El Dorado began to symbolize one of mankind's oldest grails: a life of riches and pleasures, without work and without care, in a land of perpetual youth and sunshine.

One can imagine the excitement, therefore, when as recently as the mid-nineteenth century great veins of gold were discovered in a place no one had paid much attention to—California, where the peaceful, agricultural, basket-making native Indians were not dangerous or even particularly interesting. It seemed as if El Dorado had at last been found. In the Sierra foothills, east of Sacramento, where some of the first placer mines were dug, a county was triumphantly named El Dorado, and its county seat was christened Placerville. Glorious futures for Placerville and El Dorado County were envisioned.

Placerville today is not much of a place; it has a bawdy house or two, popular with the military personnel stationed in the area. And, indeed, El Dorado County does not have much to offer except mountain scenery. Because California was no more an El Dorado than any other of the mythical places where it was claimed to be. And yet the myth of California as El Dorado is special in that is has continued, no matter how many times it has been disproved. The gold rush came, and went, and still more people came. In the years since, millions have come to California in search of easy riches, youth, an easy life. And, to be sure, a number have found at least some of these treasures. So they continue to come, as the dream of El Dorado goes on exerting its golden lure.

Perhaps it always will, in spite of the fact that the California dream is always being rudely shattered by the reality that great riches do not solve all life's problems, that, in fact, El Dorado's rewards are also bitterness, hatred, murder, despoliation, and disillusion. For every fortune made in El Dorado, it seems, there is also a heavy price.

But that reality has been unable to kill the dream; the California dream goes on. After all, California put the fabulous El Dorado on a legitimate map, and so California keeps getting bigger. Los Angeles, a sleepy backwater as recently as 1920, now threatens to eclipse Chicago and New York in size and become the nation's largest city. Already it is difficult to tell where Los Angeles ends and the next big city, Long Beach, begins. They come in jet planes and in vans and pickup trucks, all absolutely convinced that there are riches here, that there is a pot of gold at the end of the long California rainbow.

And perhaps there is.

PART ONE

THE
SEED
MONEY

CHAPTER ONE
Liquid Gold

CALIFORNIA, IT has been pointed out, has never, for all its riches, produced a fortune to equal the riches amassed in the East by such men as John D. Rockefeller, Jay Gould, and E. H. Harriman. Perhaps this is because in the 1850s and 1860s, when Rockefeller was putting together the Standard Oil Company, California was still too new and inexperienced a place to contain more than one get-rich enthusiasm at a time, and the enthusiasm of the moment, of course, was gold. The California gold fortunes had a way of being lost rather quickly, though the men who followed the prospectors—the speculators and con men, the supply merchants, the gamblers, the saloon-keepers and madams—did somewhat better. In the 1850s some quarter of a million Americans thronged across the valleys and mountains of California in search of gold-rush wealth, ignoring the black viscous substance that squished beneath their feet, the substance that was making Rockefeller rich.

It lay all about, in pools and open pits and puddles. It oozed from canyonsides. The coastal Indians had been making use of the sticky stuff for generations. They used it to waterproof their woven baskets, to caulk the bottoms of their canoes, and as a sealant to make containers of food both air- and watertight. They had also learned that when swallowed, it made an excellent if not very tasty purgative, that rubbed on the skin it made a soothing balm for cuts and burns, and that it could itself be burned for heat and light. The coastal tribes traded their *brea*, or tar, with tribes of the interior for spearheads and furs. The first Spanish settlers were puzzled by the tar pits. Arriving in Upper California from Mexico in 1769 with Don Gaspar de Portolá and Fra Junípero Serra—whose orders from Carlos III were to oust the Jesuits from the missions and replace them with Franciscans—the Spaniards concluded that the tar pits perhaps caused the earthquakes and were somehow connected with volcanoes in the distant mountains. Though the black substance was cool to the touch, it was assumed to be some form of molten rock.

In 1855, taking their cue from the Indians, the Mexican General Andrés Pico and his nephew, Rómulo, had begun in a modest way to market the crude oil they scooped up from pits in a canyon north of the San Fernando Mission. General Pico was the brother of Pio Pico, the last Mexican governor of California, and was a fallen hero of the Mexican War—he had defeated the American General Stephen Kearney in 1847, but had later been forced to surrender to General John C. Frémont. The Picos peddled their "coal oil" as a medicine, as a lubricant for squeaky oxcart axles, and as a cheaper— and much smokier and smellier—substitute for whale oil in lamps. (Whale oil could then only be afforded by the well-to-do; the very poor went to bed when the sun went down.) To the gold and silver prospectors, meanwhile, the oil was simply a nuisance. It seeped into streams and rivers and polluted their drinking water.

In 1857 a former New York sperm-oil dealer named George S. Gilbert built a primitive oil refinery near the Ventura Mission. In order to reduce his oil to axle grease, which he hoped to market, he boiled the oil, and, in the process, the vaporous fumes of what would one day fuel the automobile industry escaped into the blue California sky. One of Mr. Gilbert's first sales that year was a consignment of a hundred kegs of grease to one Mr. A. C. Ferris of Brooklyn, New York. Alas, the heavy burden of Gilbert's oil was too much for the mule teams assigned to carry it across the Isthmus of Panama. The hundred kegs were jettisoned somewhere in the jungle. If Mr. Gilbert's oil had reached its intended destination, the birthplace of the oil industry might have been southern California instead of Titusville, Pennsylvania, where, that same year, a blacksmith named Uncle Billy Smith dug a hole in the ground that became America's first oil well. Within two years the great Pennsylvania oil stampede had begun and the desolate little farm community of Titusville had become a boomtown. And down from Cleveland, less than a hundred and fifty miles away, young John D. Rockefeller was already on hand.

It was not until April 1892 that the California oil industry was ready for a man named Edward L. Doheny. Ed Doheny was a most unlikely character to signal such a momentous event. He had been born in 1856 in Fond du Lac, Wisconsin, the son of a poor Irish immigrant who had fled from the great potato famine of the 1840s and had headed westward lured by the siren song of riches. The senior Doheny, however, had never found them, and at age sixteen his son had run away from home. Ed Doheny had worked variously as a booking agent, a fruit packer, a mule driver, and as a singing waiter at the Occidental Hotel in Wichita, Kansas, where he also picked up bits of change acting as a procurer of young ladies for the traveling drummers who passed through town. At the age of eighteen he embarked on what was to be his lifelong occupation—searching for wealth underground—and become a gold prospector.

For the next few years Ed Doheny was a man without a permanent address, and the chronology of his wanderings is unclear. He is known to have spent time in Texas, Arizona, New Mexico, and Mexico, sometimes making a small strike, sometimes going broke. During these years he acquired a reputation in prospecting circles that was unsavory, not to say dangerous. The sheriff of Laredo in 1878 described the passage through that town of one "E. Dohenny

[sic] a rough character." Doheny had early learned to use a gun and was quick to reach for his holster in tough situations. It was rumored that he had once killed a man—or possibly several. He seems to have been a man able to adapt himself easily to one side of the law or the other as he moved through the one-street towns of the Southwest, and in New Mexico, Doheny was known as the man who had cleared the little town of Kingston of local cattle thieves and bad men. One of these was said to have fired sixteen bullets at Doheny before Doheny was able to overpower and disarm him. As a prospector, however, he employed more mystical methods, and for a long time his principal mining tool was a divining rod. When the rod quivered and dipped in his hand, Doheny stopped on the spot and began digging for gold, occasionally finding some but usually not.

He was thirty-six years old in 1892 when he arrived in the still-raw California town that had been dedicated to Nuestra Señora de Los Angeles, and his prospects for discovering a real bonanza had begun to look exceptionally dim. He was still rawboned and fast on the draw, but youth was slipping away. His mining adventures in Arizona and New Mexico had all been failures and he was virtually penniless. But then one of those queer strokes of incredible luck that have marked the beginnings of so many American fortunes came to Ed Doheny. Passing in the street one day he noticed a black man driving a horse and wagonload of black, steaming, tarry stuff. Doheny asked the man what the substance was, and was told that it was *brea*, and that it bubbled from a pit on the edge of town, and that the poorer families of Los Angeles collected it without charge and used it for fuel.

From his diggings around the West, Doheny knew even without his divining rod that the *brea* was crude oil, and set off to investigate the bubbling pit. He located it in Hancock Park, decided that it looked promising, and with a small amount of hastily borrowed cash, leased the land. Because he could not afford to buy or lease a drill, Doheny dug by hand with a pick and shovel, arduously extending a four-by-six-foot shaft into the ground. At a depth of 460 feet he was able to dip up four barrels a day. The deeper he went the more oil came up, and within a few months he had brought in the first real gusher in California.

All at once, as news of Doheny's hand-dug discovery spread, it was Titusville all over again. Anyone who could scrape a few hundred dollars together began leasing land west of downtown Los Angeles to dig or drill for oil. The wells were shallow and cheap to dig; the average cost was $1,500, including tanks and pumps, and by 1899 there were more than three thousand wells pumping oil, all from a narrow tract of land varying from 800 to 1500 feet wide and about four and a half miles long. The silhouettes of oil rigs dominated the skyline, and the drilling became so frenzied that the city fathers of Los Angeles declared that oil wells were a civic nuisance, and a moratorium was pronounced on further drilling within city limits. The moratorium did no good whatever. Everyone in Los Angeles, it now seemed, needed to drill a well for water. The city council could not deny its citizens the right to do that, and so the drilling continued. If the water wells spouted oil instead—well, that could be dismissed as just a lucky accident.

There were, as it turned out, economic reasons more pressing than esthetic ones for trying to bring oil exploration under some sort of control. Within five years of Ed Doheny's find so much oil had been pumped out of the Los Angeles basin that the market was glutted. It cost less to buy oil by the barrel than it did to drill for it, and boom was followed by panic. By the end of 1899 oil leases were going begging, and it was in this panic that Edward Doheny made his next important move. Quietly, systematically, he began buying up leases at bargain-basement prices. The market for oil, he reasoned, did not have to be limited to southern California. Los Angeles, after all, offered something that western Pennsylvania did not. Titusville was an inland city and oil could only be shipped out expensively overland by rail or by pipeline. Los Angeles was a port city. To be sure, no canal yet existed across the Isthmus of Panama, and various schemes and projects to build one had languished over the years since the French construction had been undertaken in 1879 and abandoned ten years later. But the Spanish-American War of 1898 had given tremendous new impetus to the idea of a canal, and in the minds of most of the American public it had become almost an article of faith that such a canal had to be built and would be built, and would be built soon, and would be built and controlled by the United States. A canal through the isthmus would greatly enlarge the market for California oil. With this thought in mind, Edward Doheny set about seeing to it that within ten years of his first bonanza in Hancock Park he would own or control nearly the entire oil production of California.

MEANWHILE ANOTHER character had arrived on the turbulent California oil scene. He was Lyman Stewart, and his future would one day be entwined with Ed Doheny's. In character and background Lyman Stewart was totally unlike Doheny. For one thing, Stewart was an easterner, and whereas Doheny's rich strike had been a matter of luck, Stewart brought to the business a certain amount of experience. He had been "born to oil," barely ten miles from Titusville, and had already made and lost—and partially recouped, to the extent of about $75,000—a fortune in oil before he set out for California in 1882. Where Doheny was rash, impetuous, and headstrong, Stewart was cautious and precise. Doheny was rough-spoken and hard-drinking, and Stewart was abstemious and pious almost to the point of prudishness. He had descended from a long line of strict, Bible-quoting Scottish Presbyterians.

In his oil-exploration activities in California, Stewart had avoided the Los Angeles basin, primarily because the cost of Los Angeles city land—as much as $1500 for a twenty-five-foot lot—went against his Scotch grain. He had begun drilling farther north, in the Central Valley, and though he had one or two good strikes, a discouraging share of Stewart's wells were dusters. Stewart's early efforts were handicapped by a variety of factors. For one thing, South America had begun exporting oil to the United States, and each time a freighter full of oil sailed into San Francisco Bay the price of California oil plummeted. There was also the matter of Stewart's hard-line religiosity. If, for example, a choice option on a piece of promising oil property became available on a Sunday, Stewart refused to consider it because he would not conduct business on the Sabbath. His stubborn refusal to work on the Lord's Day often cost him money, because for some reason a number of his better wells had had the perverse habit of coming in on a Saturday night, and by the time Stewart permitted his crews to go back to work on Monday morning, much of the black gold had spilled away.

He was equally strict in dictating the moral code for his employees. Once, inspecting the progress of one of his wells, Lyman Stewart noticed a frail young boy drenched with perspiration from his labors at the rig and commented to the youth that his was pretty heavy work for a man of his tender years. "Mister," replied the boy, "she is a son-of-a-bitch, and you can tell the whole Goddamn world I said so!" Horrified at such language, Stewart quickly withdrew from earshot, and immediately decided to establish, with his meager profits, a chapel in Torrey Canyon, and hired one Reverend Mr. Johnson to conduct services in it. Not long afterward Stewart set aside funds to erect a "temperance rendezvous" for the neighborhood. This establishment would contain "a temperance bar, a library, a reading room, a gymnasium and so forth for the purpose of giving men and boys a place to spend their evenings and keeping them out of saloons." The temperance rendezvous, which was indeed built, was something less than a popular success with members of the drilling crews.

Fortunately, perhaps, for Lyman Stewart, his son William, who had come with his father from Pennsylvania and worked as his father's field superintendent, was much more liberal in his views. At one point in his California career the senior Mr. Stewart received a report that one man on his drilling crew was a perpetual drunkard, that the fellow arrived at work in the morning sober and left half drunk at the end of the day. Mr. Stewart ordered the man immediately dismissed. But William Stewart interceded on the man's behalf and argued with his father that regardless of the man's condition he was a superior worker and more than worth his wages. "Actually," William Stewart said later, "what my father heard about the man was completely untrue. He didn't come to work in the morning sober and go home drunk. He came to work in the morning drunk, and he stayed drunk all day long."

Despite Mr. Stewart's problems, however, he was able—on a shoestring, and a borrowed shoestring at that—to put together, in 1890, the Union Oil Company. Three years later, in the wake of Doheny's bonanza in Hancock Park, the Stewarts made their first moves into the Los Angeles area, but, unfortunately, they did not have Doheny's immediate good luck. No sooner had the Stewarts got three producing wells dug in Los Angeles than oil prices took one of their periodic nose dives. Discouraged, the Stewarts moved northward again, into the San Joaquin, Lompoc, and Santa Maria valleys. Ed Doheny meanwhile had also lost interest in the Los Angeles area—though not in his lands and leases—and was expanding his exploration southward into Mexico.

Ironically, what none of the restless explorers in the Great California Oil Scramble yet realized was that beneath the Los Angeles basin, and stretching out under the ocean beyond, lay one of the widest and deepest oil lakes in the world. It was 46 miles across and 22 miles long, and from it in time would come three and a half billion barrels of oil. In the 1890s a visiting professor of geology at Yale named Benjamin Silliman had speculated that there was more oil beneath the soil of California "than in all the whales in the Pacific Ocean." Professor Silliman's projection was considered a naïve easterner's wild-eyed exaggeration. His estimate would turn out to be very much on the conservative side.

The California oil rush, of course, would always be overshadowed by the gold rush. The gold rush, after all, had more glamour. Gold is mankind's most ancient symbol of wealth, the basis for his most valuable coins. And yet, for all practical purposes, gold is an almost useless metal. Unlike other precious substances, including diamonds, there is little industrial use for gold, unless one counts dental inlays. (Recently, computer technology has found a few new uses for gold.) Gold is pretty, yes, but the beauty of gold is a matter of opinion, its value a matter of faith. It serves no practical, but only an emotional need, a religious need, and has decorated history's greatest altars and temples. And yet, for all the impracticality of gold, explorers and conquistadors throughout history have set forth in search of gold, of King Solomon's Mines. The quest of the Argonauts has always been a bit like the search for the Fountain of Youth, because once one finds gold, it doesn't quite work. Perhaps the ephemeral, spiritual context of gold, and the fact that the use of gold is essentially ornamental, explains why all the gold that was mined in the California gold rush—some three billion dollars' worth—made no man permanently rich. It slipped like dross through its finders' fingers and made its way underground again, to Fort Knox, the temple of United States currency.

With oil, on the other hand, the explorers were seeking a product that would have many practical uses and would reign as the most potent source of energy until the splitting of the atom. In the single year of 1950, for example, the output of California oil wells surpassed in dollar value the entire output of all the state's gold mines since the discovery of gold at Mr. Sutter's mill in Sacramento, which set off the gold rush. And oil made a number of California men permanently rich.

Meanwhile, throughout both rushes—the gold and the oil—the explorers and pioneers displayed a spirit and a character that would become typically Californian. The California élan involved a special doughtiness, a certain daring, a refusal to be fazed or put off by bad luck or circumstances, an unwillingness to give up. To the California pioneer, after all, California was more than the end of the rainbow; it was the last stop for the Conestoga wagon. The California pioneer had reached the edge of the continent, the last frontier, the last horizon. He could go no farther, and he would not turn back. To have made it to California was to have made it *all the way*, and those who did not make it were by definition failures. To those who made it to California success was the only possibility. The place had to be made to work. In the winterbound Sierras the Donner party would turn to cannibalism in order to make it over the hills to California.

In the early days of the California pioneers the region was not particularly hospitable. Northern California was damp and foggy most of the year, while the south was hot and waterless. The state was cut off from the rest of the country by an implacable backbone of rugged mountains, and most of its wide central valley was barren desert. And yet the Californians would change all that. They would change the landscape and, in the process, the climate. They would make the desert bloom with everything from cotton to peaches, lettuce, tomatoes, strawberries, artichokes, and alligator pears. In the process they would become rich.

They would remain daunted by nothing and they would retain the gambler's heart. They would build houses on mountainsides that were slipping into the sea, on the rims of canyons where in dry weather a single match would ignite a hillside and make it burn like kerosene and where when it rained the hills would be deluged by mud slides. They would confidently build houses with swimming pools along the notorious San Andreas Fault and facing beaches that were periodically swept away by high seas. Had there been any live volcanoes, Californians would have built houses beside their craters.

In the aftermath of the great earthquake of June 29, 1925—a shock that registered 6.3 on the Richter scale and virtually leveled the city of Santa Barbara—it was rumored that a huge tidal wave, miles high, was headed across the Pacific toward the southern California coast. It is rather typical of the California spirit that, when this news was heard, thousands of citizens of Los Angeles hurried eagerly to the beaches to see it come. They were actually disappointed when it didn't arrive.

But there is still more to the California spirit than a willingness to gamble and accept dares. Having arrived at the rim of the continent, the California pioneers, with no farther to go, became almost obsessive about the need to fight for a share of whatever it was they had found. From their faraway perch, the Californians promptly acquired rather large chips on their shoulders, and, in addition to a certain hauteur, the California character became notably disputatious and competitive. And, besides the amount of skulduggery, larceny, and blackmail that might be considered routine in the making of all great American fortunes, California's money was made by men who were ready, literally, to shoot it out with one another and would stop at nothing—not even murder—to get what they wanted.

Spanish explorer Sebastián Vizcaíno and his exploring party landing at Monterey in 1601. The Spanish were hoping to reach the East, but soon became excited by the prospect of riches from Californian gold and silver. *Collection of the Architect of the Capitol / Library of Congress*

When Mexico refused to sell the United States its vast western landholdings, America seized them by force. Pictured is the last battle (1847) in what is now the Los Angeles suburb of Vernon. *Library of Congress*

This cartoon, first published in 1849, makes fun of those rushing off to California to find gold. *Library of Congress*

The California gold diggers sought gold with religious fervor, but the gold found during the Gold Rush—some $3 billion worth—made no man permanently rich. *Bancroft Library/University of California, Berkeley*
Society of California Pioneers

Society of California Pioneers

The Belcher Mine, just one in the Comstock Lode, produced over $26 million worth of gold and silver by 1916. *Mackay School of Mines/University of Nevada*

Drawing ore from a mine shaft. *Globe Photos*

Ulysses S. Grant (fourth from right) and his wife (third from right) visit the Comstock Lode, 1879. Extreme left: John William Mackay. Extreme right: James Graham Fair. *California State Library*

Pioneers bedding down for the night. "California was more than the end of the rainbow; it was the last stop for the Conestoga wagon." *Corcoran Gallery of Art*

A pioneer's drawing. "The California pioneer had reached the end of the continent, the last frontier, the last horizon." *Henry E. Huntington Library and Art Gallery*

Families such as this one, pictured in 1886, packed all their possessions onto horse-drawn wagons and trekked out West. When they got to California they discovered that the huge landholdings of the California rich made their dreams of owning a small farm impossible, and many of them became tenant farmers. *Library of Congress*

The interior of a covered wagon that traveled from Cincinnati, Ohio, to Yolo County, California, in 1849. *Library of Congress*

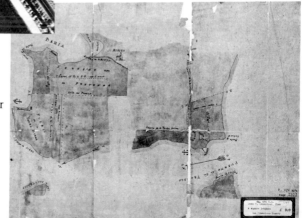

California pioneers still pouring into the last frontier with the hope of establishing their fortunes. *UPI*

An original California land grant for four square leagues of San Francisco County. *Bancroft Library/University of California, Berkeley*

San Francisco in 1849. *Wells Fargo Bank, History Room*

San Franciso today. *UPI*

Because the corrupt city police could not be trusted to apprehend criminals, citizens formed vigilante groups to protect their rights. Here, a parade of armed vigilantes held in San Francisco in 1856. *New-York Historical Society*

Michael DeYoung, cofounder and publisher of the *San Francisco Chronicle*, sometimes used his paper as an instrument of blackmail, which made him one of the most feared and hated—and powerful—men in the city in the 1880's. *UPI*

Flood's palatial house in suburban Menlo Park, which became known locally as "Flood's Wedding Cake." *California State Library*

James C. Flood, another of the Silver Kings. "Perhaps no other individual in the history of American capitalism catapulted himself from grim squalor to glittering splendor in so short a time as the ex-bartender and his wife, a former chambermaid." *Culver Pictures*

Ralston's mansion. *Culver Pictures*

William Ralston, founder of the Bank of California, made a number of other San Franciscans rich through his banking, but left no fortune as a result of one of the most stunning cases of business treachery in California history. *Culver Pictures*

The spectacular Palace Hotel, built by William Ralston, in 1900. *Culver Pictures*

William Sharon, the man Ralston made richest of all, became a Senator from Nevada before betraying his benefactor. *Culver Pictures*

The Palace Hotel today. *UPI*

Southern Pacific

Stanford University Libraries/Special Collections

Southern Pacific

Bancroft Library/University of California, Berkeley

Southern Pacific

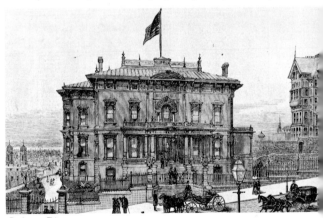

Culver Pictures

UPI

Charles Crocker, Mark Hopkins, Leland Stanford, Collis Potter Huntington: a quadrumvirate unusual in railroading because they seemed to get along with one another, reaping a fortune from the coast-to-coast Central Pacific Railroad. Also shown are the Crocker, Hopkins and Stanford residences.

President and Mrs. Rutherford Hayes at the house of Senator Leland Stanford (hat in hand), Menlo Park, California. *Culver Pictures*

Oriental interiors were fashionable in nineteenth-century California mansions. *Culver Pictures*

Born virtually penniless in Dublin, John W. Mackay became a multimillionaire through his part ownership of the Bonanza Mines of the Comstock Lode. *Culver Pictures*

Mrs. John W. Mackay, transformed from a destitute young widow to the heights of wealth and society by her marriage to a millionaire miner. *Culver Pictures*

Mackay's daughter and heiress married Prince Colonna of France. *Culver Pictures*

Maude ("Emerald") Burke failed socially in San Francisco and New York, but became one of London's most popular and powerful hostesses after she married Sir Bache Cunard. *Culver Pictures*

After the devastating San Francisco earthquake of 1906. *Author's Collection*

Amadeo Peter Giannini, whose little Bank of Italy became the largest commercial bank in the world, the giant Bank of America. *Culver Pictures*

The Bank of Italy on Montgomery Street in San Francisco, back in business shortly after the 1906 earthquake and fire. (Owner Giannini had escaped the disaster with his entire supply of gold tucked into produce wagons.) *Culver Pictures*

This emergency branch of the Bank of America in Southern California's Engineering Exposition building served customers during the aftermath of the 1933 earthquake. *UPI*

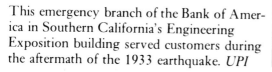

In 1862, an Act of Congress was passed by which some $25 million in 6-percent government bonds, along with 4½ million acres of public lands, were placed at the disposal of the founders of the Central Pacific Railroad. *Southern Pacific*

A magazine cartoon reflecting the pride Americans felt in the supreme technical feat of joining the entire nation by railroad. *Southern Pacific*

The Golden Spike Ceremony took place in 1869 in Promontory, Utah. The golden spike was 18 ounces of pure California gold. *Dept. of Parks and Recreation/State of California*

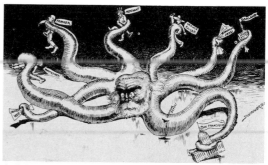

A jab at railroad baron Collis P. Huntington, head of the Central Pacific-Southern Pacific "octopus." The monopoly wielded power over the legislature, the courts, and the business people of California. *California State Library*

When the arbitrary rates of the Southern Pacific Railroad soared too high, sugar manufacturer Claus Spreckels built a railroad of his own. *San Diego Historical Society/Title Insurance & Trust Collection*

California's reputation as a Garden of Eden was established only after ways were found to redistribute the state's water supply. This watercolor shows a farmer opening a sluice gate to irrigate his crops. *The Oakland Museum, Gift of Dr. and Mrs. Frederick G. Novy*

This 1907 advertisement caricatures Californians' pride in their superior fruits and vegetables. *California Historical Society*

The opening of the 225-mile Los Angeles-Owens River Aqueduct in 1913 helped turn the city from an arid cow town into a metropolis. *California Historical Society*

Huge crowds came to see the first cascade of Owens River water sluicing down into the San Fernando Valley on its way to Los Angeles. *California Historical Society*

William Mulholland was the self-taught "Wizard of Water" who planned the Los Angeles Aqueduct. But his miscalculations in building St. Francis Dam, just north of the city, caused one of the area's worst floods. *California Historical Society*

Jaw Bone Canyon Siphon in the San Fernando Valley—just a fragment of the hundreds of miles of water pipeline that "made the desert bloom." *California Historical Society*

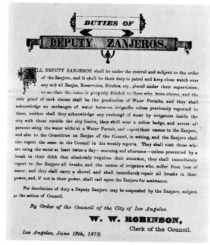

DUTIES OF DEPUTY ZANJEROS.

ALL DEPUTY ZANJEROS shall be under the control and subject to the order of the Zanjero, and it shall be their duty to patrol and keep close watch over any and all Zanjas, Reservoirs, Ditches, etc, placed under their supervision; to see that the water is properly divided to those who have claims, and the only proof of such claims shall be the production of Water Permits, and they shall acknowledge no exchanges of water between irrigators unless previously reported to them, neither shall they acknowledge any exchange of water by irrigators inside the city with those outside the city limits; they shall wear a police badge, and arrest all persons using the water without a Water Permit, and report their names to the Zanjero, and also to the Committee on Zanjas of the Council, in writing, and the Zanjero shall also report the same to the Council in his weekly reports. They shall visit those who are using the water at least twice a day—morning and afternoon—unless prevented by a break in their ditch that absolutely requires their attention; they shall immediately report to the Zanjero all breaks, and the names of irrigators who suffer from loss of water; and they shall carry a shovel, and shall immediately repair all breaks in their power, and, if not in their power, shall call upon the Zanjero for assistance.

For dereliction of duty a Deputy Zanjero may be suspended by the Zanjero, subject to the action of Council.

By Order of the Council of the City of Los Angeles.

W. W. ROBINSON,
Clerk of the Council.

Los Angeles, June 13th, 1879.

Water was so precious to California settlers that they set up special patrols to oversee its disbursement. This document details their duties. *California Historical Society*

The St. Francis Dam after its collapse in 1926. The flood destroyed three towns, claimed 420 lives, and covered much of Ventura County with a blanket of mud. *UPI*

Chief Engineer Mulholland at the coroner's inquest following the St. Francis catastrophe. He took complete responsibility for the disaster, saying, "If there was an error of human judgment, I was the human." *UPI*

CHAPTER TWO

Grants and Grabs

ACTUALLY, THE success of California has depended on a far more basic liquid than petroleum, and any California story becomes in the end a story of water.

There has always been plenty of water in California, but the trouble was that nature didn't distribute it very evenly. The Sierra Nevada mountains were dotted with lakes and streams and rivers and in winter collected huge amounts of water in the form of snow. Below, the Central Valley is actually a pair of valleys placed end to end, created by two rivers—the Sacramento, which flows southward out of the northern Sierras, and the San Joaquin, which rises in the southern Sierras and flows northward. The two rivers merge in a fan-shaped delta east of San Francisco and then empty to form San Francisco Bay. At the end of their journeys the converged rivers spill out through the Golden Gate. The topography of the double valley—

which on a relief map looks as though a great scoop had been drawn down through the center of the state, cutting it to just above sea level—is responsible for the state's special climate. Cool, moist air from the Pacific is turned back by the coastal range of mountains, and on the Central Valley's eastern flank the towering Sierras collect westward-moving weather in the form of rain or snow. Thus, when the first white settlers came to California they found a central valley that remained hot and parched throughout most of the year, where it "never" rained from April through October. The northern seaport, furthermore—San Francisco—was blessed with the infusion of not one but two important rivers, while southern California and Los Angeles had hardly been given a single tiny streamlet.

The unfairness of this arrangement has long been the cause of bitterness between southern and northern Californians. The legendary rivalry between the cities of Los Angeles and San Francisco has, as its basis, nothing to do with San Francisco's alleged superiority in culture, architecture, and views of hills and bridges. It is about the unequal distribution of water. If the San Joaquin River had done what most American rivers do, which is to flow southward, there would have been no problem. But the San Joaquin perversely headed the wrong way and cheated Los Angeles. There are still some conservative souls in California today who feel so strongly on this issue that they would like the state to be divided into two states, with a cutoff line between the two somewhere around Tehachapi.

From the earliest days of California settlement men struggled with the problems, and the promises, which this peculiar climate offered. During the long, hot summers the rivers of the Central Valley shrank to trickles or dried up altogether, and the Valley became a desert of cracked earth more forlorn than the craters of the moon. In spring, when the snows on the mountains melted, the Valley waited like a huge catch basin and became an inland swamp for weeks. Early settlers in the Valley had to build their houses on high pilings, like lake dwellers in Peru and Mexico, because of the annual threat of floods. Obviously what the Central Valley needed was a way to catch and store the vast amounts of water from the spring thaws and to distribute this water during the dry summer growing season. From the first sandbagged levees along the Sacramento River and the digging of the first canals, ditches, and sloughs, the battle for water and the control of it have engaged California's major efforts.

One of the first to recognize the Central Valley's potential in a large way was a man called Henry Miller (no kin to the writer of the same name, who also made his home in California). For all his importance to history, Henry Miller remains in some ways a figure of mystery. His real name was not Henry Miller. He was born Heinrich Alfred Kreiser, the son of a German (or perhaps Austrian) butcher, and came to the United States in 1847 at the age of nineteen, with just six dollars as his entire capital. He found work as a butcher. When news of the discovery of gold in the tailrace of Mr. Sutter's mill reached him, he headed for California. But when he went to pick up his steamer ticket to Panama he noticed that for some reason the ticket had been made out in the name of Henry Miller. This, at least, was what he always claimed. Had he come upon the ticket dishonestly? Had he stolen it? In any case, the ticket was stamped "Non-transferable," and so the young man, who spoke little English, decided that the most prudent thing to do was to pretend to be Henry Miller rather than risk losing his ticket. He kept the new name for the rest of his life.

Once in California, he did not involve himself in gold exploration. Indeed, he seemed to have lost interest in it. He worked for a while as a dishwasher and then as a sausage peddler. It was as a sausage man that he first entered the Central Valley and was struck with its possibilities. He was a quiet, reclusive young man, and as far as is known, he had no formal engineering training or experience. And yet in his spare time he began designing levees, dams, reservoirs, and intricate irrigation systems. He also began to buy land that was considered worthless and that he could buy dirt-cheap. Henry Miller—who in his later years developed grandiose ideas about himself and his capacities and took to comparing himself with King Solomon—may have been a genius. But more than anything, he was a clever salesman, and he was probably a scoundrel. In the days of feverish railroad-

building—and the speculation in land that was central to railroads—
Miller was able to do such a thing as persuading fledgling railroad
companies to lay their tracks along certain routes. Then, when tracks
were ready to be laid, Miller would discover "better" routes. The
first routes would then be abandoned, and their elevated roadbeds
would become, by default, ready-made levees for Miller's expanding
irrigation system. He also acquired land from the early Spanish settlers by fair means and foul. Once, buying a parcel of land from a
Spanish owner, Miller agreed to accept "as much land as a boat can
circle in a day" in return for the price he offered. He then strapped
a canoe to his wagon, set off at a fast clip across the countryside,
and by nightfall had claimed a considerably larger portion than if
his journey had been made by water.

From stories such as this one it is possible to conclude that the
early Spanish land-grant families were foolish, gullible, or at best
naïve. But this was hardly the case. The relatively small handful of
men who had come up, by way of Mexico, with Portolá and had
established families in Alta California—the Sepulvedas, the Figueroas,
the Yorbas, the Picos—had been granted vast tracts of land and had
been enormously successful as cattle rancheros. The great adobe
hacienda of Don Bernardo Yorba, one of the sons of José Antonio
Yorba, who had come with Portolá's party, contained over a hundred
rooms and was operated, as southern plantations were, as a ducal
city-state, with its own carpenters, millwrights, cobblers, and iron-
mongers. The daughter of Thomas Yorba, who owned 60,000 acres
of the Rancho Santa Ana, was an early nineteenth-century fashion
plate. She owned outfits costing over a thousand dollars each, including more than 150 dresses "made of the finest satin and silk, each a
distinct pattern, and low shoes with silver buckles, bright sashes,
belts of brilliant colors, and a rebozo which was worn over the head
and shoulders, with elaborate jewelry to match." The Spaniards
brought horses with them, animals the native Indians had never seen
before, and the Indians at first assumed that the horses were human
women in disguise and that the men on their backs were their children, since this was the way that Indian women carried their chil-

dren. The Spaniards also demonstrated the superiority of their guns over the Indians' bows and arrows by hanging a bearskin from the branch of a tree and showing how an arrow, fired at the bearskin, merely bounced off, while a bullet tore through it. The Indians were suitably impressed.

On the great ranchos, cattle roamed freely without fences. Indeed, the history of California might have been quite different—and the entire state might still be owned by the descendants of roughly a dozen Spanish families—if it had not been for a series of not entirely unrelated events. The first, of course, was California's independence from Mexico in 1846 and subsequent admission to the Union in 1850. Immediately the federal government began challenging the validity of the Spanish grants. According to the treaty with Mexico that was concluded in February 1848, the United States promised that the property rights of owners of California land would not be disturbed and that Spanish land-grant owners would be protected just as if they were citizens of the United States. But this stipulation covered only property that could be proved to have been acquired in California prior to July 7, 1846. Fortunately for the heirs of Bernardo Yorba—who had no less than twenty-three children—the Yorbas were able to prove that their large rancho had been granted in July 1834. But other Spanish families were less successful in defending the challenges from Washington, which, despite the treaty, clearly tended to view the Spanish families as Mexicans—as indeed they had become—and therefore as outsiders, aliens, enemies.

Simultaneously, the great rush of gold-seekers and squatters that began pouring into California in 1849 and 1850 created a new and very serious problem for the Spanish landowners. According to a contemporary report, the newcomer did not hesitate to set up a small tent or rough cabin on any piece of land. In the mining regions the miner was free to stake a claim, but this was not true of fertile land in the agricultural valleys and with the land on which were started many of the early towns. Some of these lands were grants made to individuals by the Spanish or Mexican government and were, therefore, private property. These private grants often covered many square miles. The new immigrants to California refused to accept or believe that any single person could own so much land. By 1856 not even half of the land claims studied by the Federal Land Commission had been satisfactorily settled.

Adding to the problem of who owned what was the fact that there were no fences and that the boundaries claimed in the various land grants were often very loosely and imprecisely designated. A typical parcel of land, for example, was described as bounded by "the old road," extending to "the prickly pear patch," and from there to "the steer's skull" and "the tumbleweed," or "the small stone." Invariably, each of the descriptions of these parcels ended with the phrase *"mas o menos"*—"more or less"—and, needless to say, the tumbleweed over the years might have tumbled elsewhere, and the steer's skull and the small stone might have been buried in the drifting sand. In trying to settle the many claims, the Land Commission occasionally ruled that a claimant owned quite a bit more land than he thought he did—particularly if he happened to be an Anglo, or gringo. But more often, particularly in the case of a Spanish Mexican, it determined that he owned much less.

Finally, adding to all these vicissitudes, complications, prejudices, and bureaucratic red tape from the federal government, there occurred an event that virtually spelled the doom of all but the doughtiest of the great rancheros of California. In the end they would be destroyed by something they could not possibly fight in a court of law or otherwise: the weather. The Great Drought began in 1860, and it continued through 1861 and 1862. In 1863 and 1864 it was even worse. Streams diminished into trickles and then into troughs of dust. Even the most sophisticated irrigation systems were useless without a source. The cattle, which had made the rancheros rich, began to die. Soon the corpses of thousands of head of beef lay strewn across the thousands of acres of brown hillsides like so many moldering gunnysacks. The hot air reeked of decaying flesh. If skinned in time, hides could be sold for a small sum and the carcasses could be shipped to a glue works, but the physical process of dealing with so many dead animals was overwhelming.

Quickly on the heels of the Great Drought came a band of avid moneylenders, as the once rich rancheros found themselves suddenly unable to pay their taxes. What the moneylenders offered, in return for cash, were mortgages, and in the space of a few short years huge amounts of land that had once belonged to the Spanish passed through foreclosures into the hands of gringo bankers in San Francisco. At least, the descendants of the Spanish land-grant families today tend to blame the gringo bankers for their massive losses of land.

Of course, in later generations the descendants of the gringo bankers would defend the actions of their forebears, saying that the Mexicans had lost their land at least partly through their own faults—their fondness for gambling, for betting on their own horses (which the Anglos didn't do) in their rodeos and races, their participation in what was general corruption, and their habit of producing large, unwieldy families that had trouble controlling the land. The Mexicans, the Californians like to say, were their own undoing.

Indeed, there were also cases in which rancheros were betrayed by members of their own aristocratic class, and even by members of their own families. One of the most notorious moneylending companies of the day was the nongringo firm of Pioche & Bayerque in San Francisco, which charged an interest rate of 5 percent per month, compounded monthly, and this quickly became the going rate. So desperate were the rancheros for ready cash that even a man with only a few hundred dollars to lend could find himself in a few months' time the forecloser on a great tract of land.

In southern California, Abel Stearns—a Yankee from Massachusetts and, when he arrived in 1829, one of the first American-born men in the region—had married a fourteen-year-old Spanish girl named Doña Arcadia Bandini of a proud ranchero family. Stearns became a naturalized Mexican citizen, adopted the ennobling "Don," and during the drought became a moneylender to the rancheros, including his wife's relatives. The land that Don Abel Stearns accumulated in the process became the basis of the Stearns Rancho Corporation, which has been a principal developer of the western side of Orange County down to the present time. Similarly, Don Juan (born John) Forster was an Englishman who came to California and married Ysidora Pico, a sister of Pio and Andrés Pico. Like Stearns, Forster became a naturalized Mexican citizen; in 1873 he sued his brother-in-law, Pio Pico, claiming that during the drought period he had loaned Pico money that Pico insisted he had never received. In the now Anglo-dominated courts of California it was again a case of English-speaking versus Spanish-speaking people, and Forster won his case. It was appealed in the State Supreme Court by Pico, but once more Forster was declared the victor. His prize was the Rancho Santa Margarita y Las Flores, and title to some 133,440 acres in San Diego County.

WHETHER Henry Miller ever indulged in this sort of unlovely activity has never been clear, but it is perhaps more than a coincidence that some of his largest landholdings were acquired during the early 1860s, the years of the Great Drought. And as more of Miller's land became arable, he began stocking it with beef and sheep, and from the livestock the money really began to roll in. With California a part of the Union, it was now possible to obtain even more land through simple bribery and fraud. Some of Miller's most valuable business associates promptly became the employees of the Land Commission's office, the California government executive departments, and both houses of Congress in Washington. Of course Miller was no longer alone. The land-grabbers of California were all using Miller's methods, and perjury, fraudulent surveys and entries, and collusion with local, state, and United States officials were all part of the technique.

Miller's methods were no different from those that had been commonplace in California for several years, nor were acts of chicanery confined to the Anglos. The Mexican government in California was overthrown by the American forces officially on July 7, 1846, but it had been apparent for some months prior to this that the Mexicans' cause was lost. That his days as governor were numbered was quite clear to Pio Pico, and in May of that year Señor Pico began routinely handing out enormous grants of land in return for bribes, in anticipation of his imminent retirement from public life. Seeing what was going on, a number of other Mexican officials, as well as private citizens, embarked on a lively business of selling land grants over Governor Pico's forged signature. Some of these forged and fraudulent land grants were crude and primitive, but others were clever, sophisticated, and almost convincing. When American capitalists such as Henry Miller moved into California and started buying up these grants, it fell to the courts to decide which were legitimate and which were not.

Millions of acres of the richest agricultural, grazing, mining, and timber land were involved—not only in California, but in New Mexico, Arizona, and Colorado as well. In some cases the Mexican land grants were for entire California towns and cities. And so it is perhaps not surprising that the local courts throughout California and the West tended to be sympathetic to the land-grabbers' claims and to uphold them. Moreover, many western judges were in collusion with the claimants, while others were engaged in land-grabbing operations of their own. The sweet smell of money to be made in California was on all sides and was just too heady to resist.

One Californian, for example, Henry Cambuston, claimed that eleven square leagues (about thirty-three square miles) of pasture land on the Sacramento River had been granted to him by Governor Pico on May 23, 1846. The California courts decided in his favor. The government, however, pressed its case to the United States Supreme Court, charging that the alleged grant was fraudulent and forged. In 1857 the Supreme Court handed down a decision expressing doubts about the genuineness of the grant and reversing the decision of the California court. Another claimant, named Fuentes, carried his claim for eleven square leagues to the Supreme Court, where it was denounced by Attorney General Black as "fraudulent and spurious, a base and impudent forgery . . . It is in the handwriting of Manuel Castro, a part of whose business consisted in forging land grants." The Fuentes grant, Black stated, was dated Monterey, June 12, 1843, but had actually been forged in Mexico City in 1850. The court agreed with Black and disallowed the claim. James R.

Bolton turned up with a claim to ten thousand acres outside San Francisco—a claim worth, at a conservative estimate in 1851, more than $2,000,000. Bolton produced documents to show that Governor Pico had granted the land to one Santillan, a priest, in 1846. Bolton had bought it from Santillan in 1850 for $200,000. The Supreme Court rejected all Mr. Bolton's evidence and dismissed the claim. Even Governor Pico's brother, Andrés, was deemed in the eyes of the Supreme Court to be in fraudulent possession of a forged grant for *his* eleven square leagues of California (eleven square leagues was a popular size for a parcel) and had his claim thrown out.

By 1869, thirty-six private California land claims had been rejected by the Supreme Court. Some had been almost successful, such as that of José Limantour, who was very nearly able to steal—with the help of state officials—over a half million acres of California land with a forged grant from Governor Pico. And at the same time, nearly an equal number of claims—thirty-three in all—were confirmed by the court. Most of these were probably just as fraudulent as the ones rejected, but during these years Washington was thronged with lobbyists for the land-grabbers. A number of important congressmen also had financial interests in the success of the false claims. And it was widely rumored—though never proved—that at least one Supreme Court justice who had been appointed during the Civil War, a jurist whose vote often decided the fate of the claims, had more than a passing interest—either financial, political, or friendly—in the success or failure of certain land grants. Still, though it was quite clear that the Americans involved in the great California land grab were just as unscrupulous as the Mexicans, the popular attitude was to place all blame for malfeasance and skulduggery on the Mexicans. In 1869, for example, in an investigation into the California land scandals, the House Committee on Claims referred piously and scathingly to "a bagful of affidavits of drunken and venal Mexicans who can be hired for five dollars apiece to swear to anything."

THE MEXICAN land-grant scheme of acquiring California land—since it often involved lengthy court battles—frequently turned out to be both complicated and costly. Other methods, in the meantime, were almost childishly simple. There was the "swampland" ruse, for example. If land could be declared swampland, it was deemed officially worthless and could be bought for next to nothing. All one had to do was to get one's surveyor to pronounce the land a swamp—which, for a price, most surveyors were willing to do even if the land was not a swamp. Or one could get one's surveyor to appraise the land during the spring melt, when it was indeed a swamp. The swampland laws were wonderfully loose and flexible. In the 1870s it was possible to file a "claim" for real or alleged swampland. A claim cost nothing and could remain inactive for an indefinite number of years. All one had to do was wait until a buyer came along who wanted to buy the land in good faith, and then one could sell one's "rights"— rights to land for which one had never paid a cent and never intended to pay a cent.

In 1873 the Swamp Land Investigating Committee of the California Assembly was formed to look into the activities of the land-grabbers, which had been going on for years. Among its findings, the committee sonorously announced, was a "mighty mass of evidence . . . that through the connivance of parties, surveyors were appointed who segregated lands as 'swamp,' which were not so in fact. The corruption existing in the land department of the General Government has aided this system of fraud." A quick stop, the committee implied, would be put to this shameful business. But as often happens with the findings of investigative committees, it was too late for the findings to do much good. By then more than 17,000,000 acres of the lush Sacramento Valley were owned by about a hundred men. In the San Joaquin Valley, which was harder to irrigate, the average landholder had 100,000 acres. Henry Miller and his partner, Charles Lux, another ex-butcher, by then owned 14,539,000 acres of the richest land in California and southern Oregon. The Miller-Lux empire embraced more than 22,500 square miles, a territory three times as large as the state of New Jersey and twice the size of Belgium. On this land more than two million head of cattle grazed.

Miller and Lux were America's first cattle kings, and Henry Miller liked to boast that he could ride from Mexico to the Oregon border on horseback and never need to sleep on land that was not his own. He had also been responsible for pushing through the California Assembly its Law of Riparian Rights, which provided that anyone owning land along a river could use that river's water to whatever extent he wished. This gave Miller virtually complete control of all the water in the San Joaquin Valley—a considerable resource.

A joke of the era had it that "whatever land in California Henry Miller doesn't own the Southern Pacific Railroad does." This was of course an exaggeration, but not a flagrant one. Miller had 14,500,000 acres, and the Southern Pacific had 16,387,000—clearly somewhat more land than would be required for laying down tracks and building switchyards. Of California's 101,563,523 acres, Miller and the railroad owned close to 31,000,000, leaving a little over 70,000,000 acres for other people. The railroad had acquired its land much the way Henry Miller had, but in the case of the railroad, its greed for land had begun to have an unexpected, and unpleasant, side effect: it was discouraging further immigration to California, and the small farmer who wanted to farm a hundred acres or so was being driven out. The railroads had been willing to sell land—at exorbitant prices, of course—to small farmers, and to those with insufficient capital the railroads cheerfully offered mortgages. When small farmers could not make their mortgage payments the railroads just as cheerfully foreclosed. But a railroad, unlike a Henry Miller, had to count on an expanding population to make it pay—an increase in people, produce, livestock, and other goods to transport. The railroads had counted on cities growing out of the California wilderness. But now, with so much land in the hands of so few people, where would the cities go? The huge landholdings had made much of California seem a very empty place. The small landholder in California found himself surrounded by boundless acres of a rich man's land, friendless, neighborless.

By 1875 the Great Gold Rush was over and the greatest land grabs were completed. In their wake came another psychological reason why the lure of California seemed to fade in the minds of Americans, why California seemed to lose its appeal as a goal for the ambitious immigrant, and why the Southern Pacific had begun to worry that it might become a railroad with nowhere to go and nothing to carry. As Bailey Millard, a reporter who had investigated the California land frauds extensively, wrote in *Everybody's Magazine* in 1905: "This grabbing of large tracts has discouraged immigration to California more than any other single factor. A family living on a small holding in a vast plain, with hardly a house in sight, will in time become a very lonely family indeed, and will in a few years be glad to sell out to the land king whose domain is adjacent. Thousands of small farms have in this way been acquired by the large holders at nominal prices."

Still, despite these wistful observations, there was no mass exodus from California during the 1880s and 1890s. The allure of California as Shangri La was still powerful, and the state's population grew at a steady clip—the rural population growing at a somewhat faster rate than the urban. Small farmers had seen what a man like Henry Miller could do with irrigation, how the desolation of the Central Valley could with the addition of a summer water supply be turned into extraordinarily rich farmland, and they arrived in droves. In time this land would yield more than two hundred varieties of produce—which would become 10 percent of what America ate—as well as year-round grazing pasture for all manner of livestock. But the disproportionate share of land that the big landholders owned did have one profound effect. Many of the new settlers were forced to become tenant farmers. In 1890, 28 percent of the farms in California were tenant-operated. By 1910 the figure had jumped to 37 percent, an increase of 32 percent in twenty years' time. By 1925, tenant farmers accounted for almost half the agricultural operations in the state.

Obviously this was a situation that did not displease either the large individual owners such as Miller and Lux or the railroad giants such as Southern Pacific and Union Pacific. Their holdings had become so unwieldy that they were happy to rent or lease their land for income. And an odd economic fact was that tenant farming increased steadily throughout both good times and bad. In times of prosperity, tenancy increased, because as property prices went up, it was less expensive to lease land than to buy it. In periods of depression, tenancy again increased, because owners, unable to meet their obligations, lost their ownership status and became tenants. And through good times and bad, California men were making money. Today the average California farm consists of 617 acres and is worth $500,000. The national average is 389 acres, worth only $100,000. And it is all due to the blessing of irrigation.

EVER SINCE the operations of Henry Miller, water has been at the heart of every Valley triumph and every controversy. Feelings about water can be joyful. Several years ago, at the opening of a canal carrying water from the Shasta Dam in the north into previously unirrigated southern areas, a bright indigo dye was thrown into the water at the source, and as the purple water made its way into each Valley settlement along the course of the new canal the populace turned out and there were civic celebrations, speeches, parades, cheering, and all-night dancing in the streets. Children were let out of school and given seedlings of shade trees to plant in village parks and squares up and down the thoroughfares of little towns that would soon be big towns.

Feelings about water can also be grim, stirring up bitterness and resentment. In the northern part of the Central Valley many people were angered about a plan to lift water out of the Sacramento Delta and carry it through a mountain tunnel into Los Angeles, where it has long been badly needed because of that city's rapid growth. What right does Los Angeles have to "our" water? the northerners ask. A bit of graffiti in a Valley men's room at the height of the controversy read, "Please flush after using. Los Angeles needs this water."

In the years since the pioneering Henry Miller, water has been chained behind a series of high dams and directed through hundreds of miles of canals and pumping stations, tunnels, reservoirs, and power systems. The Operations Control Center of this system, in Sacramento, resembles the interior of a futuristic space ship, complete with wall-sized maps, flashing lights, computerized controls, all coordinating the release and flow of water throughout the Central Valley Project. The control center not only regulates the amounts of water that flow out, and where these gallonages go, but also the kinds of water—for drinking, for irrigation, or for industrial use—that are needed in any given part of the state at any given time. From here the levels of rivers are controlled to keep barges afloat, to keep salt water from encroaching on peach orchards, to keep water temperatures at the proper levels to promote the spawning and growth of fish. The center is an operation of stupendous proportions, and it is getting bigger all the time. New dams are being built "that make Aswan look just like another Pacific Gas and Electric project," according to one Valley engineer. The Folsom Dam, west of Sacramento, already dwarfs the Aswan.

The drawing boards teem with other plans to harness water, because, after all, California keeps right on growing. So does the importance of the state's agricultural output. For the most part, too, the quantity of available water in California depends not so much on rainfall as on the amount of winter snow that annually collects in the Sierras, so California farmers still look nervous when the Sierra snowpack is reported to be less than normal. One of the most ambitious schemes to collect water involves throwing a dam across the Golden Gate. If San Francisco Bay, which is now a tidal basin, were dammed, it would gradually fill with fresh river water and become a huge reservoir. San Franciscans of course are not happy with this idea—not for esthetic reasons but because the destination of much of this water would be Los Angeles.

The economic rule of the Central Valley is: the cheaper the water, the more valuable the land. This means that in the northern part of the Valley, where water is much more plentiful and therefore cheaper, a farmer can operate quite profitably on a smaller acreage. The northern Valley is blessed with a larger river, the Sacramento, has more rainfall, and has the added boon of a huge underground lake, called Lake Lassen, which makes irrigation possible through the use of wells. In the southern Valley, where water must travel a greater distance and is therefore more expensive, larger acreages are required for a farm to make money. The amount—and cost—of water also determines which crops can be grown most profitably. Bakersfield, in the south, for example, which was once almost entirely owned by Henry Miller, is ideally suited for cotton. Further north, in the irrigated land around Fresno, a great variety of crops is grown, and Fresno County, in the geographical center of the state, has become the richest agricultural county in the United States, a fact of which very few inhabitants of Fresno will neglect to remind the visitor. Modesto concentrates on peach orchards and vineyards. Stockton, Sacramento, and nearby Delta towns concentrate on tomatoes. Still farther north, in Colusa and Chico, there is an emphasis on almonds and walnuts, whose larger and deeper root systems require a larger water supply.

Entering the Central Valley today, one senses a special smell, which changes with the seasons, from that of loamy earth to the perfume of blossoms and unfolding leaves, to the drying of eucalyptus bark at the end of summer. Each harvest has its smell—sweet and winy grapes, dusty tomatoes. And through it all is the smell of money being made—in Modesto by the Gallo Brothers, largest wine producers in the world, and in Fresno by such hugely wealthy families as the Giffens. From an office furnished with eighteenth-century antiques Russell Giffen directs a ranching operation with acreage in the hundreds of thousands (so many hundreds of thousands that he himself is not sure just how much land he owns), raising cotton, barley, wheat, safflower, alfalfa seed, melons, tomatoes, and a good deal more. Central California farmers today live in air-conditioned houses with heated swimming pools, drive air-conditioned Cadillacs and Rolls-Royces. The men who drive the big harvesters for one farmer who, among other things, harvests twelve hundred acres of rice outside Colusa, sit in comfort in air-conditioned cabs. Another Valley farmer has a fleet of custom-built Cadillac pickup trucks, also air-conditioned, said to be the only vehicles of their sort in the world. In Stockton the Weber family, founders of the city, own vast ranches of peaches and tomatoes. In Rio Vista, in the Sacramento Delta, Peter Cook is said to be "so rich that he doesn't lease out his gas wells—he drills them himself." Nearby there are people such as the Alex Browns, so rich that they found it more practical to open their own private bank than bother with ordinary commercial accounts.

Of course there is a certain amount of nervousness; farming is always a gamble. And water has wrought such great changes on the face of central California that there are worries about unpleasant side effects. The exact nature of earthquakes, for example, is still far from fully understood. There is fear that adding so much water to a terrain that was once waterless may have some dark, profound effect on what is going on in the bowels of the earth (just as there is concern that pumping so much oil out of California may have some effect on the earth's substructure and make it more earthquake-prone). The number of dams that have been built along and about the San Andreas Fault has made some people wonder what would become of the Central Valley if there were a serious earthquake and all California's dams broke at once. (It would become a very wet place.) But such fears are easy to lay aside when one is making so much money.

The plentitude of water meanwhile has had its effect on matters environmental as well as economic. Californians now in their forties can remember when, as children, they could stand in the center of the Valley and address a horizon peaked with the stern, implacable snowcaps of the Sierras. The mountains once stood out with dazzling clarity, but no more. Today they are blanketed behind a perpetual sunny haze. The internal-combustion engine of course is part of the reason that the Central California Valley has lost its vistas of the mountains, but the Valley haze also consists of water particles in the air evaporating from irrigated fields, canals, and reservoirs. Making the Valley green has also changed its climate. Summer rains, once a rarity, are now much less so—in fact, they are a hazard to some of the crops that water was brought into the Valley to nourish: such tender-skinned fruits as peaches, pears, and nectarines. As short a time as twenty years ago, Valley residents used to remind visitors that despite the scorching summer heat—daytime temperatures rising into the hundreds—theirs was a *dry* heat; one didn't notice it so much, and, besides, the nights were cool. One doesn't hear such boasts so often now; with so much water vapor in the air, summer days are often smotheringly humid, and the humidity doesn't go away at nightfall. Air-conditioned cars and houses are no longer a luxury but a necessity. By the same token, with so much moisture in the air, winters can be bone-chillingly damp. Still, it is all considered worth it—for the sake of water.

HENRY MILLER, one of the first to see what water could do for the Central Valley, died in 1916. No sooner was he buried than, like cormorants descending, claimants to shares of his estate appeared from everywhere, and the court battles began. Both the state and federal governments tried to seize the Miller ranches for inheritance taxes, and it took Miller's daughter eleven years before she finally prevailed in that legal struggle. Then the trustees of Miller's estate were charged by the heirs with fraud and conspiracy, and another ten years—and the services of fifty-three lawyers—were consumed before that case was settled. In the process a number of the lawyers involved became millionaires. It was not until 1965—forty-nine years after Henry Miller's death—that any of his descendants received any of his money, and at that point hardly a member of Miller's family was speaking to another. A San Francisco judge ruled that the estate be divided equally between two branches of the family, the Nickels and the Bowleses.

The Nickels were outraged. There were many more of them, they protested, than there were Bowleses, and their branch demanded a proportionately larger share of the money. But the judge, who had studied the crudely written will for a month—Miller was not a master of the English language—ruled that Miller had wanted his heirs to share the inheritance "according to their roots, and not in equal shares." One disappointed Nickel was Mrs. William Wallace Mein, Jr., the former Sarah Miller Nickel, a Henry Miller granddaughter, who received only $5,000,000 instead of the $6,000,000 her lawyers had been fighting for, less than her cousin Henry Miller Bowles was awarded.

In the years since the 1965 distribution of his estate the holdings of Henry Miller have been further broken up and subdivided. His far from egalitarian riparian-rights law has been modified beyond recognition; it is no longer possible for one large landholder to control the water in an area, and the division of water among Central Valley farmers is carefully regulated.

Despite their quarrels, all Henry Miller's heirs were made comfortably wealthy by their enterprising patriarch. And, removed by a couple of generations from the great land grabs, frauds, and scandals of the past, the Miller heirs went sailing into American high society—on the water of California, as it were. Still, the history of the Miller fortune would seem typical of a great many tales of California riches. Money that was made by pioneers through a combination of muscle and brains, innocence and guile, and no small amount of luck has had a way in California of being passed along to further generations through great thunderheads of acrimony, bitterness, litigation, and even bloodshed.

The founders of some of the great California fortunes might wonder, if they were around today, whether it was really worth the trouble.

CHAPTER THREE
The Big Four

THE EARLIEST known mention of California in literature occurred in a romantic Spanish novel called *Las Sergas de Esplandian*, printed in the year 1510, which portrayed the majestic "Isle of California," described as being located at the "right hand of the Indies and very near to the Terrestrial Paradise." The island was ruled, according to this book, by an Amazon woman, Queen Calafia. Early maps of the New World continued to show California as an island, and it was not until the late seventeenth century that it was recognized as part of the continent.

Even as late as the 1850s—despite the wealth that was pouring out of California during the years preceding the Civil War—Californians suffered from acute feelings of isolation, of insularity, of being cut off from the mainland. Geographically the state was remote—at the farthest rim of the continent—and access to California was difficult. To reach California from the East required a slow, laborious, and dangerous journey by stage or wagon across arid plains and daunting mountains, or by ship around the Horn, or by muleback across the malarial Isthmus of Panama. When President Zachary Taylor died in 1850, California did not learn of it for weeks. By the mid-1850s the most popular topic of conversation on the West Coast involved the dream that one day California might be linked to the rest of the country, and the world, by means of a railroad.

The principal dreamer had been a young engineer named Theodore Judah. Judah had prepared charts and maps and surveyors' reports demonstrating how, indeed, a railroad could be constructed through the rocky passes of the Sierras, and had actually laid twenty-one miles of track, which he called the Sacramento Valley Railroad. But Judah had been unable to get any real support for what at the time was considered the most ambitious and difficult railroad project in human history until his notions came to the attention of four men —Collis P. Huntington, Leland Stanford, Charles Crocker, and Mark Hopkins.

Huntington, Stanford, Crocker, and Hopkins were a quadrumvirate that would become unusual in railroading by virtue of the odd fact that the men actually seemed to get along with one another, even to *like* one another, at least in the beginning of their association. In the East the great railroad barons—Commodore Vanderbilt, Jay Gould, Russell Sage—had all been at one another's throats, each man cheerfully determined to destroy all the others. Not so the California foursome, who decided to pool their talents. Their talents of course had nothing to do with railroading. All four had come to California in the years following the gold rush. Huntington had opened a hardware and mining-supply store in Sacramento and Hopkins had become his partner. Crocker was also a hardware and dry-goods merchant, and Stanford was a lawyer. All four men, however, possessed a common skill as salesmen and promoters. Mark Hopkins, for example, discovered a shipload of heavy blankets on a dock in San Francisco. The city was going through a sultry summer and no one wanted blankets. Hopkins bought the lot and stored them until winter, when the demand for blankets—and the price—skyrocketed.

Physically they were quite unlike. Hopkins was lean and gaunt, a teetotaler, a vegetarian, and a nonsmoker. Charles Crocker was a huge, burly man with a great fiery red beard. Stanford was also heavy, beetle-browed, and bearded, a picture of lawyerly uprightness. Huntington was handsome, but with a shifty look and a taste for both ladies and whiskey. None of the four was much intrigued by Mr. Judah's romantic notion of building a railroad through impenetrable mountains to provide an umbilical cord to the eastern seaboard, but all four agreed that the owners of such a railroad, if it were built, could expect to make a goodly sum of money, particularly if someone else could be made to pay for it. In fact, they argued, the only people who might stand to make more money than the owners of such a railroad would be the contractors whom the owners hired to build it.

The Civil War years were ideally suited for the sort of scheme Huntington, Crocker, Hopkins, and Stanford had in mind. The entire country was caught up in the emotional and financial upheavals of those convulsive times, and everyone—including the United States Congress—was looking the other way. At the very beginning of the war the four organized the Central Pacific Railroad Company with a capital stock of $8,500,000. This figure was almost entirely a fiction. Actually the four had pooled only about $7000, but legislators in both Sacramento and Washington were too busy with other, more pressing matters to ask for a look at the books. Huntington was dispatched to Washington to lobby for congressional funds and support. Stanford, whose sober demeanor and pompous manner had been used to provide an aura of respectability for the group, now had another, more important function. He had been elected the first Republican governor of California, and from this post he was quickly able to work wonders for his business partners in the state. The city of Sacramento, for example, offered to donate $400,000 to the Central Pacific's cause. Placer County offered to lend the railroad $550,000, and the state of California generously handed over $2,100,000 to Governor Stanford's favorite cause. (The California legislature had often been charged with graft and corruption, and whenever these charges seemed a bit too threatening, the legislature would piously investigate itself for a week or so and then announce that the investigation had proved the legislative body to have been beyond reproach.)

Collis Huntington meanwhile was doing excellent missionary work for the Central Pacific in Washington. In 1862 an act of Congress was passed by which some $25,000,000 in 6 percent government bonds, along with four and a half million acres of public lands, were placed at the disposal of the San Francisco foursome. Here and there a few mild voices were heard in protest over the government's generosity, but the complaints were quickly dismissed. After all, the San Francisco group pointed out, the government was fully protected; its loans to the Central Pacific were covered by a first mortgage, and should the company default, the government could always step in and recover its money. It all sounded logical enough, and two years later Huntington succeeded in influencing Congress again, and the Central Pacific's land grant was doubled.

Other interesting perquisites for the railroad were worked out with Congress. The government offered to pay the Central Pacific $16,000 a mile for track laid over flatland and $32,000 a mile for track across foothills and mountains. Huntington accepted this but apparently felt that it was not quite generous enough, even though, with the cheap Chinese labor he planned to use, the actual cost of laying track was estimated at only half these figures. Huntington remedied this by drawing up a new map of California. In the Huntington version of the California topography the Sierra Nevada mountains were placed some twenty-five miles west of where they actually started. By coincidence, this was the exact point at which the Central Pacific planned to start laying track. For twenty-five miles of imaginary mountains the San Francisco quartet accepted an additional fee of $400,000 from the United States government.

Now it was time to select the contractors to build the road. Theodore Judah, who had done the extensive original groundwork of making surveys, plans, and estimates—and who, in fact, had had the original idea for the line—quite naturally assumed that the plum would be given to him. He was mistaken. When the board of directors of the contracting company were announced, their names were Collis P. Huntington, Leland Stanford, Charles Crocker, and Mark

Hopkins. Furious, Judah sailed off to Washington to protest this arrangement. Crossing the Isthmus, he contracted yellow fever and died. On January 8, 1863, amid much fanfare, celebrating, band music, and speechmaking, Governor Leland Stanford, president of the Central Pacific Railroad, lifted the first shovelful of earth from the bank of the Sacramento River and deposited it into a wagon draped with red, white, and blue bunting. Construction of the quartet's railroad was under way.

The four men divided their chores carefully. Huntington was in charge of finances and of dealing with Washington and the Congress. Stanford was in charge of political dealing and lawmaking in the California capitol. Crocker supervised the actual building of the railroad, and when criticized for employing 16,000 Chinese laborers instead of native whites, he airily replied, "They built the Great Wall of China, didn't they?" As the line pushed eastward he followed it in his private railroad car, dismounting by day to take to his horse; from his mount he bellowed to his workers in the roadbeds and supply camps to dig harder and faster. Mark Hopkins' bailiwick was office detail, and, a great string-saver, he saw to it that the partners' money was spent as frugally as possible. He inspected office wastebaskets for bits of paper that might be reusable, and when he rode out to inspect the tracks he kept his eye out for stray nuts and bolts. It was Mr. Hopkins' suggestion that the Chinese laborers be paid in cash, in gold and silver coins. Thus there would never be a clear record of just how much the Central Pacific had cost to build.

Once the initial government loans and gifts had been collected, the foursome abandoned all pretense of honesty and set out to defraud any and all in sight—not only the state and federal governments but also the other states, cities, and counties through which the Central Pacific was to pass. At one point a gift of $50,000,000 was received from the state of Nevada. In addition the partners issued themselves $33,722,000 in bonds and $49,005,000 worth of stock. In the meantime work progressed with astonishing speed under the driving whip hand of Mr. Crocker. On good days, where the terrain was relatively flat, as much as a mile of track a day was laid, and depending on whether the territory appeared on Mr. Huntington's new map as flatland or mountain, the company received another $16,000 or $32,000 from the United States government. A feverish race had begun between the Union Pacific Railroad, in the East, which was building westward, and the Central Pacific, moving eastward, each line determined to outdo the other in the number of miles of track laid. Finally, on May 10, 1869, six years after construction had started, the two railroads met at Promontory, Utah. Two locomotives draped in flags moved slowly toward each other, one from the East and one from the West, and pulled to a stop a few feet apart. There was tumultuous cheering, and Governor Stanford made a long, windy speech promising vast riches to every town and hamlet through which the transcontinental railroad passed. The last polished tie was ceremoniously laid in place. A final golden spike was set into place, and the portly governor solemnly raised a silver mallet, aimed at the golden spike, swung, and missed. The miss was symbolic of the chaotic state of American railroads at the time, but no one caught the symbolism.

When the news reached San Francisco by telegraph that the east and west coasts were now linked by a ribbon of steel, there was great public celebration. Church bells rang and fire and police whistles blew. From the bars of the steamy Tenderloin to the mansions of Nob Hill there was more singing, shouting, and cheering. Across the coast-to-coast railroad, Californians were assured, would come even greater riches to the West.

And indeed the riches did come—for a while, at least. But by far the greatest riches from the Central Pacific had already accrued to Messrs. Stanford, Crocker, Hopkins, and Huntington. Just how much they had made has never become quite clear, but according to one estimate it had cost $27,217,000 to build the 1171 miles of Central Pacific track, while the foursome had collected more than three times that sum. After the completion of their line they loaded it down with a capitalization of $139,000,000, which was only the beginning of still more stock inflation. The money that the four men made, furthermore, was based on not a dollar of their own investment.

The first to die was Mr. Hopkins, in 1876. The size of his estate was "nominally" estimated at $50,000,000, an indication that he may have been worth a good deal more. His widow, Mary, inherited it all. The Hopkinses had already built a palatial house in San Francisco, and Mary Hopkins now embarked on a career of building castles. She built a huge place called Kellogg Terrace in Great Barrington, Massachusetts. It cost $2,000,000. She built a townhouse in New York, another summer place on Block Island, and yet another house in Massachusetts. In 1887, when she was quite an old lady, she married a man named Edward F. Searles, who was twenty-two years her junior. Mr. Searles had been Mrs. Hopkins' interior decorator, and she could not, she said, live without his constant advice on matters of decor, despite the fact that when Mr. Searles moved into her house he brought with him a male friend named Arthur T. Walker. Mrs. Hopkins' adopted son, Timothy, became alarmed at the situation, and four years later his alarm was justified when his mother died, leaving her entire fortune to Mr. Searles.

A familiar battle began for the Hopkins millions, and Timothy Hopkins sued the estate. A settlement was eventually made, and Timothy was given some $8,000,000. The rest went to Mr. Searles, who, with Mr. Walker still at his side, lived as a recluse behind high walls on his estate in Methuen, Massachusetts. When Mr. Searles died in 1920 the bulk of his estate went to Mr. Walker. One Searles nephew, dissatisfied with a bequest of only $250,000, sued the Searles estate. Again a settlement was made; the nephew received $4,000,000. Now Mr. Walker had the rest of the Hopkins fortune. When a reporter called on Walker about a year before his death—which occurred in 1927—to see how the new multimillionaire was spending his money, the reporter was disappointed. Walker, with the lion's share of the penny-pinching Mark Hopkins' fortune, was living in a tiny two-room walk-up flat on Pierrepont Street in Brooklyn. With him lived seventeen cats. In the six years he had spent as a very rich man Arthur Walker had not even purchased a single stick of furniture.

In the meantime the remaining three directors of the Central Pacific had not been exactly idle. No sooner had the golden spike been driven home in Promontory than Stanford, Huntington, and Crocker leased their own lines to themselves for $3,400,000 a year, to be paid to them out of freight and passenger revenues. Then, as they had done earlier, they hired themselves as contractors to build a hundred-and-three-mile extension to the Central Pacific, and to finance this they issued $8,000,000 worth of stock plus $4,500,000 worth of bonds. Both the stock and the bond issues sold out, despite the fact —which didn't seem worth commenting upon at the time—that the total market value of the stock and bonds was then only $8,340,000. The cost of building the extra hundred and three miles was $3,505,000, and so the personal profits of the three men from that transaction alone came to about $4,834,000.

In 1871, Congress had chartered the Texas & Pacific Railroad to run from Marshall, Texas, to San Diego. At the same time a charter was granted to the Southern Pacific Railroad to run from El Paso to San Francisco. With the charter of the Texas & Pacific went 18,000,000 acres of public lands, and with that of the Southern Pacific, 5,000,000 acres. At the head of the Texas & Pacific group was an eastern capitalist named Thomas A. Scott, of the Pennsylvania Railroad; the right to build the Southern Pacific was given to Collis P. Huntington et al. A glance at a map would have revealed that at some point the two lines would, if built, be on a collision course, and that throughout much of New Mexico and most of Arizona they would be running roughly parallel to each other and competing for the same markets. Naturally each group quickly introduced bills in Congress designed to destroy the other, and, understandably, it became a contest to see which railroad could bribe congressmen more effectively.

On the surface it seemed that Mr. Scott's forces had certain advantages. During the Civil War, Scott had been placed in charge of government supervision of railroad transportation, and he had made quite a nice thing out of charging excessive fees for transporting troops, equipment, and supplies. This fortune had been the basis for Scott's acquisition of the Pennsylvania Railroad. The Pennsylvania, furthermore, served Washington, D.C., which enabled Scott to serve congressmen and senators from, as it were, their home bases. Congress found itself showered with free Pennsylvania Railroad passes.

"Scott," Huntington wrote in 1876, "is making a terrible effort to pass his bill. . . . It has cost money to fix things, so I know his bill would not pass. I believe with $200,000 we can pass our bill." A few months later, however, it appeared that Huntington had underestimated this cost, and he was writing to his West Coast partners to say, "I am glad to learn that you will send to this office $2,000,000 by the first of January."* It had come to Huntington's attention that Scott had offered at least one member of Congress $1,000 in cash outright if he would vote for Scott's bill, plus an additional $5,000 when the bill was passed, along with $10,000 worth of bonds in the Texas & Pacific, when issued. Still, despite these inducements, the victory went to Huntington and in a later Congressional investigation of Huntington's machinations it was estimated by the investigating committee "that a large portion of $4,818,535 was used for the purpose of influencing legislation."

As far as Huntington was concerned, it was money well spent. He and his partners then proceeded to force the eastern group out of the Texas & Pacific and, quite illegally, to absorb that line into their own, claiming with it the Texas & Pacific's eighteen-million-acre land grant.

In 1882, when the committee on the Judiciary finally got around to looking into what was going on with western railroads, it was noted that Thomas Scott's charter, along with the eighteen million acres, had been granted only on condition that the line be completed within ten years' time. More than ten years had gone by and not a single foot of track had been laid between Marshall and San Diego. The committee declared that the Southern Pacific should be forced to forfeit this swath of territory across Texas, New Mexico, Arizona, and California, and it righteously drafted a bill of forfeiture and urged its passage by Congress by joint resolution. This bill was presented to Congress. It did not pass.

* Huntington's revealing letters to his partners came to light in a lawsuit between the two adversaries. They were later published in full in *Driven from Sea to Sea* by C. C. Post.

CHAPTER FOUR
How to Buy a King

STILL ANOTHER newly arrived Californian had begun to concern himself with the possibilities of profits that could be turned as a result of the vagaries of western transportation. He was Claus Spreckels, who had been born in Germany in 1828. Many years later the Spreckels family would enjoy claiming that the name had originally been Von Spreckelsen, which would indicate membership in the German nobility, but this was a charming fiction and there is no indication that the family was entitled to the ennobling "von." Claus, a tall, heavy, muscular youth with a distinctly Hanoverian mien, was the oldest of six children of John Diedrich Spreckels and Geseina Spreckels, poor German peasants, and in 1848, at the age of twenty—faced with revolutionary upheavals in Germany and with the threat of conscription into the German military —Spreckels did what many young Germans were doing. He scraped enough money together—about forty dollars—to book steerage passage to "the land of limitless opportunity" and crossed the Atlantic, taking nine weeks.

Claus Spreckels arrived in New York penniless and was able to find work as a grocery delivery boy. Within two years he was promoted to clerk and permitted to handle money. He was apparently frugal. Though he had met and married a young German-born girl named Anna Mangles, who promptly began bearing his children—thirteen in all, eight of whom died in infancy—by 1856 he had been able to put aside the imposing sum of eight hundred dollars. With this, though the gold rush was virtually over, Spreckels decided to move his family to San Francisco, where he opened a small grocery store of his own.

One of the first things Spreckels noticed, now that he was a food merchant on his own, was the high California price of that important household staple sugar. Sugar was largely derived from cane grown in Hawaii, and it was expensively shipped to refineries on the East Coast of the United States, particularly to those owned and operated by Mr. Henry O. Havemeyer's American Sugar Refining Company in Philadelphia. From there refined sugar made its way back to California. Surely, Spreckels reasoned, there had to be a cheaper and more economical way to do it. In his native Germany, for example, the entire population was supplied with sugar derived from German-grown beets. After a quick trip back to Germany to study German beet-sugar refining methods, Claus Spreckels in 1863 built a small beet-sugar refinery of his own in San Francisco, using beets grown in the rich adobe soil around Salinas. Now Mr. Spreckels' sugar was the least expensive that could be found in the state. To be sure, beet sugar—as table sugar—was not of the same quality as cane sugar, but, he was able to demonstrate, it was excellent when it came to fattening beef cattle for the slaughterhouse. Led by such men as Henry Miller, California's beef-cattle industry was flourishing. Soon Mr. Spreckels' Western Sugar Refining Company was also prospering, though, compared with Havemeyer's East Coast operation, Spreckels' was still very much small potatoes.

All went well for Claus Spreckels' beet-sugar business until 1876, when there was terrible news. That year the United States government entered into a treaty with the kingdom of Hawaii that provided for Hawaiian cane to be brought into the country duty-free. This was to the decided advantage of cane refiners such as Mr. Havemeyer, but it threatened to be the ruination of beet-sugar refiners such as Spreckels. Spreckels bitterly opposed the new treaty, and to see what could be done to salvage the situation he journeyed to Hawaii. Here he soon managed to get on friendly terms with King Kalakua, the islands' easygoing monarch. The two men became poker-playing cronies, and at the end of one evening's playing, Claus Spreckels found himself the winner of a large part of the island of Maui.

According to a persistent (though seemingly improbable) family story, Claus won the Maui property through the following ploy. He declared that his poker hand contained four kings. When he laid down the hand, however, he had only three. Kalakua asked where the fourth king was and Claus Spreckels replied, "The fourth king, sir, is yourself." The king supposedly thought this a wonderful joke. In any case, the youthful monarch accepted his loss in good spirits, and the two men remained lifelong friends. Later Kalakua knighted Claus's eldest son, John, and presented to him a handsome medal.

With the Maui real estate went hundreds of acres of sugarcane. Now Claus Spreckels was a plantation owner and the beneficiary of the new American tariff laws. With plantations of his own in the islands and beet-sugar refineries in California, he had the best of both worlds, and as he put it later, "If we lost in one direction, we could make it up somewhere else." On top of all this, King Kalakua, whose interest in the sugar business was desultory, decided to put Claus Spreckels in charge of Hawaii's sugar output. When Spreckels returned to the United States he had the Hawaiian cane business in his pocket—an overnight tycoon, "The man," as the newspaper headlines declared, "who bought the King." The king was certainly an important acquisition. Between 1876, the year of the

treaty, and 1911 (when the huge scale of the Spreckels sugar operations at last came under investigation in Congress) production
of Hawaiian cane climbed from 16,000 to 600,000 tons a year. On
Maui, hard by such romantically named towns as Wailuku, Ulu-
maiu, and Kahakuloa, there was soon the town of Spreckelsville.
The beet-sugar business was also doing well on the other side of the
Pacific, and near Salinas there arose the town of Spreckels, California.

The only other important crisis in Spreckels' sugar business occurred in 1890 in what was called the Great Sugar War, when
Spreckels and Havemeyer finally locked horns. After months of
furious price-cutting on both sides of the United States, Spreckels
finally determined to fight Havemeyer on the latter's home ground.
He took himself to Philadelphia, where he proved to be as persuasive
with Havemeyer as he had been with the Hawaiian king. Spreckels
pointed out that both men were losing money in their price war,
and Havemeyer conceded this. Then Spreckels drafted an elaborate
plan under which both men would pool their resources and become
partners. In effect, each man bought the other out, and then each
sold part of his shares back to the other. In the West, Spreckels and
Havemeyer leased plants to each other. The Havemeyer plants were
closed down, leaving the West Coast to Spreckels. The result of this
combine was the largest sugar-producing company in the world. As
the newspapers commented at the time, "Sugar Kings Share Their
Candy."

Claus Spreckels had by now adopted the grandiose style of living
that was so popular with wealthy Californians. He built an enormous stone mansion on Van Ness Avenue, and traveled about the
country in a series of private railway cars. As they moved about the
West, Mr. and Mrs. Spreckels customarily had their private car
drawn off on a siding for the night. There, in the dining room of the
car, they were served dinner on heavy silver plates by a butler and
two footmen in livery. And, as the curtains in the car were never
drawn, humbler folk in the little towns through which they passed
invariably gathered in little knots along the track to watch the rich
people consume their sumptuous repast. However, life was not with-

out its vicissitudes. At the time of the 1906 earthquake and subsequent great fire, the city of San Francisco decided that the only way to contain the blaze was to stop it at Van Ness Avenue. To do this, every building along the street would have to be dynamited, including the Spreckels mansion. There was not time even to remove any of its furnishings. Among the last to evacuate the house was Mrs. Spreckels' personal maid, Emma Kretschmar, and the Irish scullery maid. As they were leaving, the Irish maid pointed to a porcelain horse on a hallway table and said, "Do you think Mrs. Spreckels would mind if I took that?" "No," said the righteous Emma. "That would be stealing." The two women departed empty-handed and moments later the house and its contents were reduced to dust.

Though no longer locked in combat with Henry Havemeyer, Claus Spreckels now found himself in a series of terrible battles with members of his own family. (A Spreckels family tendency toward intramural bickering would become noticeable in future generations.) By 1890, Claus Spreckels' four sons—John Diedrich, Adolph, Claus Augustus, and Rudolph—were grown men and were ready to fight for control of the business. The two older boys, John and Adolph, allied themselves with their father against Claus's two younger sons. At issue was money and power. The senior Spreckels had by now become something of an autocrat and was accustomed not only to getting what he wanted but also to striding roughshod through anything that smacked of interference with his wishes. When the arbitrary rates of the monopolistic Southern Pacific Railroad seemed too high, Spreckels had built a railroad of his own to ship his cane and beets to his refineries—a move that did not endear him to the reigning railroad kings. To combat the established public utility firms of San Francisco, Spreckels organized independent gas, light, and power companies. He built a street railway in the city to compete with the existing line. Meanwhile, in an attempt to outdo their father, his two younger sons financed rival gas and electric companies of their own. Rudolph Spreckels even had the temerity to establish a sugar business in competition with his father's.

As a result of all this, Claus Spreckels attempted to disown his younger sons, and the family squabbling erupted in a series of acrimonious lawsuits—a pattern that would become drearily familiar throughout the histories of so many California fortunes. For a while, however, Rudolph Spreckels prospered from his defection from his father. He made an independent fortune in sugar and from his gas company, and then turned to politics. He became an ardent progressive reformer and advocate of good city government. Still later he invested in a radio manufacturing business, but lost his entire fortune in the crash of 1929. He died virtually penniless in 1958. Claus Augustus, who had sided with his brother Rudolph in most of the family fights, also prospered from sugar. But he had little interest in either business or politics, and eventually he expatriated himself to France.

In 1905 there had been an attempt at a reconciliation between the battling Spreckelses, but it had been short-lived. In 1908, Claus Spreckels senior died, and immediately John and Adolph contested their father's will, which, in addition to establishing large bequests for them, had also made provision for their younger brothers. Referring to their brothers as "the enemy," John and Adolph claimed that their father had been kept "prisoner" in his house for the last years of his life, that their father had been mentally and physically incompetent, and that he had been forced by Rudolph and Claus Augustus to sign over bequests to them. Apparently there was sufficient evidence of enmity between the father and the younger sons to convince the courts, because the will was eventually broken and the bulk of their father's estate was ordered divided between John and Adolph. It amounted to some forty million dollars.

Adolph Spreckels took over management of the established family businesses and John D. Spreckels set out to expand them. John Spreckels was a yachtsman, and on his 84-foot schooner, the *Lurline*, he had "discovered" San Diego when, on a summer cruise in 1887, he had put into the sleepy southern California port for provisions. San Diego at the time might not have seemed to have much to commend it. Throughout much of the year the town was without a water supply, and water was peddled to the populace in cans, like milk. Except for the rich—who could afford private storage cisterns—baths were unheard-of luxuries. But San Diego did possess a deep harbor, which, though smaller, was not unlike San Francisco's, and San Diego's white beaches and benign sub-tropical climate were already attracting winter tourists from the chillier north. When San Diego's city fathers learned of the wealthy San Franciscan's presence in their midst, they immediately offered John Spreckels, free of charge, a "wharf franchise" with which to build a then nonexistent wharf to attract then nonexistent shipping.

This struck Mr. Spreckels as an attractive deal, and the Spreckels Wharf became the first of a number of wharves and coal depots where coal ships could unload their cargoes to fuel San Diego's growing industries—which included, naturally, more sugar refineries. Spreckels also financed the building of outlying dams and reservoirs to give the city a dependable water supply, and otherwise took on the task of building a modern city from scratch. He bought the city streetcar line, the newspaper—the San Diego *Union*—built the San Diego ferry, and, to capitalize on the growing tourist business, developed the nearby resort of Coronado and built its famous beachside Hotel del Coronado, where, before long, United States Presidents would vacation. For lesser folk Spreckels built Mission Beach, a public amusement park, and for good measure he acquired something called the Savage Tire Company, which manufactured bicycle tires. The age of the automobile, he suspected, was on its way. Because of all his industrial enterprises in San Diego, John D. was given the nickname Smokestack Spreckels. He made sure, however, that San Diego should not lose its tourist appeal because of an overabundance of smokestacks. If San Diego today is considered one of the most beautiful of American cities, it is due to Spreckels' insistence that the city council include a landscape gardener, who laid out boulevards with parklike malls filled with John Spreckels' favorite flowers, geraniums.

But by 1900 it was clear that San Diego would never achieve true city status unless a railroad connected it with the rest of the continent. In 1907, Spreckels invited Mr. E. H. Harriman (who by then had acquired the Southern Pacific from the San Francisco four-some) to spend a week at the Spreckels mansion in Coronado and made Harriman a proposal. If Harriman and the Southern Pacific would supply the financing, Spreckels would oversee the construc-tion of a line between San Diego and Yuma, Arizona, the Southern Pacific's southwesternmost terminus. Harriman agreed, and the building of the San Diego & Arizona Railway began. Then, in 1909, Harriman died, and the Southern Pacific immediately reneged on its commitment to Spreckels and even instituted a lawsuit against him to try to recover the money that he had already spent. It was a dark moment for Spreckels. The most difficult miles of track had still to be laid, across the San Bernardino mountain range. But Spreckels, determined that the city he had begun to think of as his own should have a railroad, decided to continue construction of the line on his own. While fighting his lawsuit (which was eventually thrown out of court) he turned to his brother Adolph in San Fran-cisco for financial support, and work went on. The cost of the line exceeded all estimates. At one point John Spreckels was required to buy two entire mountains in order to assure his right-of-way. With the outbreak of World War I all construction of railroads in the United States was ordered to cease, but John Spreckels had in-fluential friends in Washington. All railroad construction ceased— except for the San Diego & Arizona.

On November 15, 1919, at the summit of the huge Carriso Gorge, John Spreckels drove his own golden spike into the last tie of the S.D. & A., which meant that the line was finally completed. His aim was better than Leland Stanford's, and two weeks later, at 4:40 P.M. on December 1, the first train chugged into San Diego. The town went wild. Thousands of people lined the streets to watch the night-long parades and celebrations. At the head of every parade, waving to the cheering citizenry, rode Smokestack Spreckels. The San Diego & Arizona, among other things, opened up what would become one of the richest agricultural regions in the state, the great Imperial Valley.

It is interesting to note how quickly the second generation of California rich acquired the trappings and veneer of Old Money—the mansions, the yachts, the stables of horses, the valets and footmen and chauffeurs—and how desperately these new-rich Californians tried to emulate the ways and manners of firmly established easterners. As more and more California towns and cities became connected to the East Coast via the railroads, more and more Californians began to think of themselves as the spiritual cousins of well-placed residents of such cities as New York, Philadelphia, and Boston. In 1910, for example, John D. Spreckels was able to replace his schooner, the *Lurline*, with an even more imposing steam yacht, the *Venetia*, which rivaled anything that had been owned by J. P. Morgan. With an over-all length of 226 feet and a displacement of 1000 tons, the *Venetia* was powered by an engine capable of developing 1000 horsepower. In it John Spreckels would cruise through the Straits of Magellan around the Horn to the West Indies, as well as through the Panama Canal to New York.* In San Francisco his brother Adolph built for himself the imposing white "Sugar Palace" overlooking the Bay in Pacific Heights, while John Spreckels' huge house in Coronado was an Italianate villa with rooftop pergolas and gardens, which reminded many people of August Belmont's earlier villa in Newport. John Spreckels also built an even larger home in San Francisco, at 2080 Pacific Street.

And yet, for all the Old Money—and Old World—accouterments that the second-generation Californians gathered around them, somehow an unmistakable spirit of the western frontier remained. Behind the elegant façades of these men there lurked a brawling, roughneck, hard-drinking quality that London tailoring barely concealed. John Spreckels was no exception. Tall, handsome, and silver-haired, with a handlebar mustache, he favored high-

---

* In World War I the *Venetia* was turned over to the United States Navy and was one of the vessels that helped sink the German U-boat that allegedly had sunk the *Lusitania*. This feat was immortalized in a windy volume, *Venetia—Avenger of the Lusitania*.

collared shirts, tweed vests, Norfolk jackets, a gold stickpin, watch chain and fob. But his Man of Distinction appearance did not quite hide the man himself, who could be tough-talking and bawdy and was possessed of a cowhand, not to say barnyard sense of humor. In the early 1900s, John Spreckels was famous throughout southern California as a prankster, practical joker, and wag, and the examples of the Spreckels wit suggest the somewhat primitive state of West Coast humor at the time. For instance, according to his affectionate biographer Austin Adams, Mr. Spreckels derived no end of "innocent amusement out of the facts of nature, from which the prudish and the Puritanical avert their eyes." Once, Mr. Adams tells us, Mr. Spreckels playfully served a tableful of guests at a dinner party in Coronado a dish containing "pretty little articles . . . which proved to be . . . scarcely edible, let alone toothsome." Just what the little articles were Mr. Adams refrains from mentioning, leading the reader to imagine the worst of what could be derived from the "facts of nature."

John Spreckels' friends were jokesters too. Once, for a bit of sport, a friend surreptitiously placed a mongrel puppy on Mr. Spreckels' doorstep. The puppy was taken in, and Spreckels then tried by a process of elimination to discover which of his friends had played this joke on him. It took him two years—at the end of which time the dog had grown into an enormous canine of no discernible lineage—before he had narrowed down the possible donors of the dog to one man. At this point the dog died. Spreckels had the dog packed in excelsior, crated in a large wooden box, and shipped to his friend's house. "I'm returning the dog you let me borrow," Spreckels said. "I always repay my debts." Everyone roared. The dead-dog story circulated for years. It was considered one of the funniest things that had ever happened in San Diego.

John Spreckels' love of practical jokes was so famous that on the occasion of his sixty-fifth birthday, in 1918, it was decided that the ultimate practical joke should be played on him. A gala dinner was announced in honor of San Diego's preeminent citizen and all the local worthies were invited to attend. Further, it was revealed that Arthur Cahill, a prominent young portraitist of the period, had been commissioned to undertake a life-size portrait of Mr. Spreckels, and the capstone of the evening's festivities was to be the unveiling of the portrait.

On the night of the banquet some seven hundred guests filled the ballroom of the Hotel del Coronado. John D. Spreckels was seated at the head of the speakers' table and on a tall easel just behind him stood the heavily veiled painting. There were many ceremonious toasts and speeches, all attesting to the personal and civic virtues of the city's great benefactor until, at last, the moment came for the unveiling. Performance of this honor fell to George Brobeck, chairman of the executive committee of the J. D. & A. B. Spreckels Company, who rose and said, "And now, Mr. Spreckels, on behalf of my associates and myself I have the honor and pleasure to present to you, and beg you to accept, this lifelike portrait of him whom we admire and esteem above all other men—yourself." Mr. Brobeck then drew aside the veil and the hushed room filled with wild applause.

Then, just as quickly, the applause subsided and a ghastly silence fell as the assembled company began to take in some of the details of the portrait. John D. had been depicted standing in front of a dinner table in white tie and tails. He had been made to appear some forty pounds heavier than he actually was. His black vest strained at its buttons, and below it a considerable paunch emerged. His famous gold watch fob dangled awkwardly below his waist, and his white tie was askew. On one lapel was pinned an upside-down American flag. The expression on the face was fiercely choleric, the eyes strangely glazed. The right hand—adorned with what appeared to be an enormous diamond ring—clutched a large soiled dinner napkin. The left hand held a large smoking cigar, its long ash threatening to fall into the plate beneath it, which held the carcass of a chicken. Beside the plate were strewn various pieces of silverware and an empty wine glass. Of the shocked faces in the room none was more frightful to behold than that of the honored subject. Mr. Brobeck collapsed in his chair. Then, as a climax, tiny electric lights in the diamond ring and shirt studs began to wink.

When the hoax had had sufficient time to ripen, accompanied by gasps of nervous laughter, the real Cahill portrait was unveiled. It portrayed Mr. Spreckels properly slim, in his familiar English tweeds and high collar, looking dignified and kindly. The room broke up in thunderous laughter and applause. Even Mr. Spreckels looked, at last, amused.

IT IS perhaps significant that the ultimate joke played on John D. Spreckels—and the ultimate tribute to him—should have been an oil painting by a locally acclaimed master. By the second generation, wealthy Californians had become painfully aware that, though they had supplied themselves with mansions, yachts, servants, and English tailors, their lives lacked something that more solidly established easterners appeared to have in plenty. Something was required to smooth out the rough ranch-hand edges and to supply Californians with the true patina of ladies and gentlemen. That necessary something of course was culture.

CHAPTER FIVE

Chronicle of Power

IN HER new book on etiquette that was sweeping the country Emily Post, an easterner through and through, had begun referring to Californians as "the new-rich Westerns." The new-rich westerners, she implied disdainfully, might be long on money but were short on taste and cultivation. In California this judgment rankled, because, as in everything else the new-rich Californians undertook, their rush to culture was as headlong and haphazard as their rush to gold. Culture was embraced with a reckless abandon, with the result that its early monuments seemed either pathetically insignificant or ridiculously larger than life. It was to establish himself as a man of culture that John D. Spreckels decreed that the music room of his Coronado mansion be the biggest room in the house, occupying an entire wing. (Even his yacht, *Venetia*, had a music room.) Conceived as a true temple of art, the Spreckels music room was designed to resemble a cathedral choir. Carved mahogany pillars supported its high vaulted ceiling, painted blue and gold, and a gigantic organ and choir filled the apse. The organ's pipes were sunk in the floor of the basement below and continued upward, so that music emerged through flues concealed in the gilt grillwork that ran about the ceiling twenty feet above. With such an organ it seemed beside the point that neither Mr. Spreckels nor his wife could play. (Years later John D. Spreckels' granddaughters would argue over whether he played the organ with his hands or used rolls. The answer was rolls.)

Nor had Mr. Spreckels been remiss when it came to bestowing cultural gifts on the general public. He donated the Coronado Public Library, which for many years was notable for containing far more shelf space than books. He also built the huge Spreckels Theatre in San Diego, designed for stage, symphony, and operatic productions, which, at first, were in short supply. But his most spectacular gift to the city was the $100,000 Spreckels Organ in Balboa Park. Placed at the center of a vast colonnaded amphitheater, open to the air and surmounted by an archway somewhat resembling London's Marble Arch, the pipes of the Spreckels Organ were as tall as forty feet. The organ was dedicated at the opening of the Panama-California Exposition of 1914, of which Mr. Spreckels had been a principal sponsor, and was billed as "the only out-door organ in America, probably in the world." Sixty thousand people attended the opening performance, and thereafter one Dr. Humphrey Stewart was engaged to give daily recitals, the sounds of which carried to the distant hills.

San Francisco meanwhile was not about to be outdone by an upstart city in the south and had early set out to establish itself as the Athens of the West. In 1869, William Ralston—a clerk on a Mississippi steamboat before striking it rich in the Comstock Lode—had opened the California Theatre in San Francisco, and seven years later George S. Baldwin opened a rival theater in his new hotel. The emphasis, however, of both theaters was more on interior decor than on performing art. Mr. Baldwin advertised that when it came to acres of red plush, satin, gilt, and crystal ornamentation, his theater "had no rival, even in art-loving Europe."

By the late 1870s the rage of theatergoing England had become Gilbert and Sullivan, and theatergoing San Francisco was determined to have a Gilbert and Sullivan production. Unfortunately, according to San Francisco social historian Frances Moffat, Messrs. Gilbert and Sullivan were unwilling to sell the rights to their works in the United States. Faced with this slight problem, American theatrical entrepreneurs decided simply to pirate Gilbert and Sullivan. On the night that *H.M.S. Pinafore* opened in London, stenographers were stationed in the audience to take down the dialogue. Other agents were able to bribe musicians in the orchestra pit for a copy of the score. Thus, within days of the London opening, a purloined version of *Pinafore* was able to open in New York, and on Christmas Eve of 1878 in San Francisco to a packed house. In *Pinafore*'s journey from East Coast to West, however, someone had forgotten to note that it was a comic operetta, and in San Francisco it was advertised and performed as a high drama of the sea. "A real ship mounted with real sailors!" exclaimed the program. "Real cannon! A realistic production!" Where some of the music had seemed too light and frolicsome, the producers had changed it and inserted new, heavy warlike themes and sea chanteys. San Francisco audiences found the production thoroughly gripping.

The San Francisco success of Gilbert and Sullivan was not topped until 1887, when the "Divine" Sarah Bernhardt made her California debut at the Baldwin Theatre. The vehicle Bernhardt chose— a baroque melodrama called *Fedora*—was performed entirely in French, a language few San Franciscans understood, but when the opening-night curtain rang down, the entire audience rose to its feet and began shouting whatever French it knew—"Magnifique!" "Bonjour!" "Au revoir!" "Comment allez-vous!" Frances Moffat, who has had the distinction of reporting society doings for both the *Chronicle* and the *Examiner*, tells us that in his review of the performance "The *Examiner* critic reported that Michael de Young of the *Chronicle* was madly looking through a French dictionary" for something appropriately French to shout. Hundreds of red roses were tossed on the stage, and the standing ovation continued through seven curtain calls.

In San Francisco, culture created a kind of umbrella under which the dissident factions of the city's rich could bury their hatchets and meet to present the appearance of a polite society. Culture called not only for the best clothes and jewels but also for the best manners, and at the theater the warring heirs of Henry Miller, the Nickels and the Bowleses, could briefly forget their bitter legal battles and smile distantly at one another. Culture performed still another interesting function in San Francisco. In a number of American cities culture has been supported—even spawned—by the power of newspapers. But in San Francisco the reverse had happened and a newspaper actually had been created by culture.

Michael de Young and his brother Charles had been born in St. Louis, the sons of a Dutch Jewish immigrant. In Holland the name had been De Jong, and Michael had been born Meichel. In America the name had become de Young, with determined emphasis on the lower-case *d*. The de Young brothers had been brought to San Francisco as young boys by their parents in 1850 at the height of the gold rush. The boys' father had not prospered. Then, in 1865, noticing the enormous popularity of the theater in San Francisco, the de Young brothers decided to publish the *Daily Dramatic Chronicle*, with theater news and reviews of current plays. The first press run of the *Daily Dramatic Chronicle* was seven thousand copies, which were distributed free. These were snapped up so quickly that the brothers decided to *sell* the paper, and editorials and bits of local news were added. Soon the words "Daily" and "Dramatic" were dropped, and the San Francisco *Chronicle* was on its way to becoming the city's leading paper.

The function of the San Francisco *Chronicle* was to entertain its readers, primarily with local scandals, and its wide circulation was a testament to how well it did its job. When a good scandal could not be turned up locally the *Chronicle* merely imported one from elsewhere and presented it as though it had happened in San

Francisco. Thus a front-page headline that screamed GIRL'S NUDE TORSO FOUND IN VALLEY might reveal, further in the grisly story, that the valley had actually been in New Hampshire. Michael de Young was in charge of the paper's business end, and Charles de Young was the *Chronicle*'s principal reporter and editorial writer. Charles's editorials, in which he attacked political, clerical, and other public figures to the right and to the left, became noted for their vitriol and for the amount of mud that could be slung in the space of a few short paragraphs. "Thief," "liar," "scoundrel," and "rogue" were his favorite epithets, and he flung them about with abandon, to the delight of his readers.

And, to be sure, there were usually plenty of local San Francisco scandals to keep the pages of the *Chronicle* filled—quite a number of them within the very offices of the *Chronicle*. In 1880, for example, Charles de Young chose as the object of one of his verbal attacks a Baptist minister named Isaac Kalloch, who was running for mayor of San Francisco. Kalloch retaliated from the pulpit with an even more fiery attack on de Young. De Young, incensed, strapped on his pistol, drove to the Reverend Kalloch's church, cornered him in the baptistry, and shot him in the leg. De Young spent the night in jail and received a small fine for this misdemeanor. But that was not the end of the affair. Kalloch's son took matters into his own hands, charged into the office of the *Chronicle*, took aim at Charles de Young and shot the editor dead. For this murder the younger Kalloch received no punishment. It was considered an act of manly revenge. Even with the onslaught of culture, the spirit of the Wild West died hard in San Francisco.

Following his brother's death, Michael de Young took over the editorship of the *Chronicle*, and his editorials were only slightly less vicious than Charles's. Michael de Young, however, discovered an even more interesting purpose for his newspaper. It could, he realized, be used as an occasional instrument of blackmail—a use employed very profitably in New York a few years later by "Colonel" William d'Alton Mann in his notorious *Town Topics* column. If the editor of the *Chronicle* happened on a juicy bit of news involving a wealthy San Franciscan—a tiny violation of marital fidelity, for example—de Young would offer to print the story—or, for a price, refrain from printing it. In the 1880s William Crocker was building a superlative mansion for himself on Nob Hill at 1919 California Street. The Crockers moved in, and then, barely a month later, moved out in a suspicious hurry. Overnight the Crocker mansion became the de Young mansion, and at the time it was widely assumed that de Young "had something" on Crocker and the house was the price for silence. Such occurrences soon had the effect of making Mike de Young one of the most feared and hated—and powerful— men in the city.

Not long after the Crocker mansion episode, de Young elected to take on John D. Spreckels' younger brother, Adolph, and in a series of editorials the *Chronicle* asserted that Adolph Spreckels was cheating the stockholders of his sugar companies. Furious, Mr. Spreckels decided to emulate the younger Kalloch and marched down to the offices of the *Chronicle,* where he announced, "Mr. Spreckels is here to shoot Mr. de Young," and a frightened secretary ushered him in. What happened next is unclear, but by all accounts Mr. Spreckels was a poor shot. According to one story, Spreckels was able to fire one shot, which de Young managed to escape by ducking under his desk. According to another, Spreckels fired bullets all over the room—into the draperies, desk, woodwork, windows, and lamps—before he was finally subdued and dragged away. A third version had de Young firing at least one shot of his own, wounding the attacking Spreckels in the elbow. But whatever the facts, a shooting incident did occur, and it became the basis of a bitter feud between the Spreckels and de Young families that would last for nearly a hundred years—until, in fact, there were no more heirs of Mike de Young or Adolph Spreckels bearing the names de Young or Spreckels.

Years later Adolph Spreckels' widow, Alma, by then a leading social power in San Francisco as well as one of the richest women in California, could not be expected to attend any functions that were also attended or sponsored by any de Young. By then, Monday lunch in the Mural Room of the St. Francis Hotel had become a standard society ritual (continued until fairly recent years, when the space occupied by the Mural Room was given over to a dress shop). Ernest , the longtime maître d'hôtel of the Mural Room, used coolly to seat "my ladies," as he called them, according to their social standing—the best ladies getting the prime tables on either side of the center aisle, and lesser luminaries being placed in Siberia, along the outer edges of the room. Mrs. Spreckels and the de Young sisters, who were no less social powers, were always a special problem for Ernest, who had to make sure that Alma Spreckels and the sisters were seated at some distance apart. The sisters were the four daughters of Michael de Young—Phyllis (Mrs. Nion Tucker), Helen (Mrs. George Cameron), Yvonne (Mrs. Charles Theriot), and Constance (Mrs. Joseph Tobin). All had gone sailing into the earliest editions of the San Francisco *Social Register*, had made impeccable marriages, and their Jewish heritage (their mother was not Jewish) had been carefully forgotten. Through their mother the sisters had acquired exquisite manners, poise, cultivation, and, though not great beauty, what was considered great charm. Mrs. Spreckels, their social rival, was an imposingly tall, no-nonsense woman who, had she not been so rich, might have been considered vulgar. One never knew what Alma Spreckels might say next, but one thing was certain: she always spoke her mind. Once, in the late 1950s, when leaving the Mural Room, Mrs. Spreckels was obliged to pass by the sisters' table. In the expectant hush that fell upon the room Mrs. Spreckels—who had a booming voice—was heard to remark to her companion, "You know, those de Young women are *nice*. But of course we've never been intimate since my husband shot their father."

FOR ALL the violence and bloodshed that spilled around Michael de Young's untidy life—he was eventually privileged to die a natural death—he seems not to have lost sight of his central mission, to promote culture in San Francisco. By the early 1880s, San Francisco had theater, an opera company, and a fledgling symphony orchestra.

Culturally, what did it lack? A museum, of course. In 1885, de Young was instrumental in organizing the San Francisco Mid-Winter Fair—Californians had hit upon the device of staging periodic civic expositions whenever their city's economy appeared to flag—and it was such a success that de Young suggested that the $75,000 profit from the fair be used to establish a permanent museum in the fair's Fine Arts Building. This proposal was quickly accepted by the city.

To be sure, none of de Young's own money initially went into the museum, but—helped by the *Chronicle*'s enthusiastic publicizing —the institution quickly became known as the de Young Museum. Nor did de Young do anything personally to dispel the public misconception that the museum was a de Young benefaction. Moreover, at the outset the museum was not a museum of fine art at all. Its collection consisted mostly of miners' picks, shovels, caps, boots, panning equipment, and other relics of the gold rush. Such pieces of art and bric-a-brac as the de Youngs accumulated were relegated to basement storage rooms. Still, the museum was an immediate success with the public, so much so that Michael de Young eventually was persuaded to donate a new building for it, where, at last, there would be room for the actual display of art.

The museum continued to be called the de Young Museum, even though it was operated by the City of San Francisco. After de Young's death the *Chronicle* began referring to it grandly as the M. H. de Young Memorial Museum, even though, as Frances Moffat points out, "it was not a memorial to Michael de Young, but to the Mid-Winter Fair. For years, by editorial order, daily attendance was dutifully reported in the *Chronicle*." In that way the story that the museum had been the singlehanded cultural creation and contribution of Michael de Young became official and a matter of public record. And to assure that the record remained unchanged, the de Young family and other "friends of the San Francisco *Chronicle*" placed a large statue of Michael de Young at the museum's entrance in Golden Gate Park.

Needless to say, among those San Franciscans watching the creation of the myth of M. H. de Young, philanthropist and art patron, were Alma and Adolph Spreckels. Mr. and Mrs. Spreckels observed the steady posthumous elevation of de Young's reputation from common blackmailer to leading citizen with grim amusement and no small amount of resentment, even jealousy. Gradually they began to conceive of a fine arts museum that they themselves would build and present to San Francisco. Naturally, the museum that Adolph Spreckels and his remarkable wife would build would be bigger, grander, finer, and artier than what they considered "that civic hoax," the despised de Young Museum. As we shall see, it was.

CHAPTER SIX
The Great Museum War

FOR ALL its interest in art and culture, San Francisco remained for many years somewhat parochial in its tastes and tended to lavish praise on the works of local artists at the expense of anything foreign or even from out of town. As late as 1936 the art critic of the San Francisco *News* would be saying that the frescoes on the Coit Tower on Telegraph Hill were better than anything that had been painted by Vincent Van Gogh. Van Gogh, according to this critic, was an "amateur" and his paintings "worthless daubs." Van Gogh's art, furthermore, was "imported," and his fame was the result of "paid ballyhoo." The conclusion: "If Van Gogh was a great artist, we have lots of great artists in the Bay Region." Of course anything from southern California was disparaged, though this same critic did once condescendingly admit that a painter from Los Angeles named Barse Miller was, of all things, "a good artist. . . .

That Miller may not always achieve what he strives for is beside the point. What artist does?"

Art, meanwhile, had become a valuable tool for social climbing— a pastime in which Mr. and Mrs. Adolph Spreckels had surprisingly little interest. In fact, the northern California branch of the Spreckels family, in addition to wanting to outdo Mr. de Young, genuinely appeared to want to give a resplendent museum to the city.

In their efforts, of course, they could not count on the support of the *Chronicle*, which continued to plague Adolph Spreckels. (Once de Young went so far as to hire a prostitute who was instructed to lure Mr. Spreckels to bed, where, if the plan had worked, the *Chronicle* intended to surprise and photograph him.) But they did receive support from another powerful San Francisco press figure, William Randolph Hearst.

Like Adolph Spreckels, Mr. Hearst cared little about San Francisco society—nor did San Francisco society care much for him. After marrying a New York woman named Millicent Willson, he had more or less abandoned her for a mistress, whom he kept in Sausalito. Later came his long involvement with the actress Marion Davies. All of this scandalized San Francisco society, and society was even more irked by the fact that Hearst didn't mind being ostracized. He flaunted his profligate life-style.

Hearst's feud with de Young was almost as long-standing as Spreckels'. His father, George Hearst, had come, like de Young's, from Missouri in 1850, but George Hearst had been much more successful. At a time when everyone was speculating in gold stocks George Hearst bought a good one, in the Homestake Mine in South Dakota. Soon he was worth several hundred million dollars. He then invested in silver and copper, and was lucky again, with the Anaconda Mine in Montana. His holdings expanded to include mines in Mexico, ranches in California and South America, and, almost by accident, an ailing San Francisco newspaper called the *Examiner*. George Hearst sent his only son, William, to Harvard, which promptly expelled him. Casting about for something to do, William Randolph Hearst asked his father for the *Examiner*. Reluctantly—

the senior Hearst had hoped for something more "respectable" than newspaper work for his son—the *Examiner* was turned over to William Randolph Hearst in 1887.

Immediately W. R. Hearst set about outdoing the *Chronicle* in the luridness of its stories. On the first day of young Hearst's stewardship the *Examiner*'s front-page headlines read:

DEAD BABIES:
BLOODY WORK:
MORE GHASTLY LIGHT ON THE SLAUGHTER OF
THE INNOCENTS:
THE DARK MYSTERIES OF A GREAT CITY

Like Michael de Young, Hearst was theater-struck. It was Hearst who had seen the news potential in Sarah Bernhardt's San Francisco debut in *Fedora* and had orchestrated her much publicized arrival. A Hearst reporter had escorted her through Chinatown, taken her to a Chinese theater where she had made good copy by walking onstage and chatting with the actors, and accompanied her to an opium den, where, at the sight of dazed bodies lying about in the gloom, La Divine had exclaimed, "C'est magnifique!"—making more good copy. Hearst had infuriated de Young when it turned out that Bernhardt had agreed to give interviews exclusively to the *Examiner*. While the *Chronicle* imported grueling tales to San Francisco from wherever it could find them, Hearst reporters were instructed that when no startling news was available they were to create some of their own. A reporter might fling himself into the Bay and wait to see how long it took for someone to rescue him; or feign a suicide attempt from the roof of a high building in order to report the reactions from the street below: PRIEST WEEPS, CRIES TO SUICIDE: "DON'T JUMP!"

Hearst's ambitions far outdistanced those of Michael de Young. De Young's fortune was based primarily on his one newspaper. Hearst's money, which was inherited, would carry him on to the ownership of some twenty newspapers across the United States, a stable of magazines, his own motion picture production company, a feature syndicate, a wire service, a newsreel company, and, at one point, more California real estate than any individual since Henry Miller. It would also carry him to the point, as a compulsive spender, at which he had very nearly spent it all. Hearst had no particular interest in building a new museum in San Francisco. He was, after all, busily building a private museum of his own at San Simeon—his hundred-and-fourteen-room Moorish castle, on a mountain overlooking the Pacific, composed of rooms and filled with furniture collected from all over the world—and his own private zoo. But he was interested in anything that would annoy Mike de Young, and so he happily lent the *Examiner*'s editorial support to Mrs. Spreckels and her museum.

It was, indeed, *Mrs.* Spreckels' project, supported financially by her husband's huge fortune. Of Mrs. Spreckels' origins rather little is known, and throughout her lifetime that was the way she preferred things to be. She was born March 24, 1881, probably in San Francisco—though she was a little vague about that too—as Alma Emma de Bretteville. Later she would enjoy saying that her full name was Alma Emma Charlotte Corday le Normand de Bretteville, to which she would add for good measure "von Spreckelsen." (She was somehow descended, or so she claimed, from Charlotte Corday, the mad French aristocrat who stabbed Marat in his bathtub, and in this connection, she would often open conversations with "Got anyone you want murdered?") The De Brettevilles had been forced to leave France at the time of the Edict of Nantes and had fled to Denmark, whence Alma's Danish-speaking parents had emigrated.

Alma Spreckels never liked to speak of her childhood, and it is assumed to have been mean and poor. But as a young woman her Junoesque figure and handsome if not beautiful face caused her to be much in demand as an artist's model. In the early 1900s she posed, in long flowing robes, for the tall "Winged Victory" sculpture that stands at the top of the Dewey Monument in the center of San Francisco's Union Square. And in various bay-front saloons there were said to be other poses of the well proportioned Miss de Bretteville without the robes. Her youth was apparently peripatetic, adventuresome. At one point in the 1890s she brought a lawsuit against a gold miner in the Klondike for "personal deflowering," and was able to collect ten thousand dollars in personal damages. For a while she worked as a nurse for a family in Woodside, California. For a while too she studied art and art history at San Francisco's Mark Hopkins Institute, and at the time of the great earthquake and fire of 1906 she helped salvage that institution's collection of paintings and sculpture from the flames. In the quake's aftermath she also showed her public-spirited side. San Franciscans were forbidden to build fires or to cook in their homes, and Alma de Bretteville organized communal cook kitchens in Golden Gate Park.

Just how this bohemian and free-spirited creature met Adolph B. Spreckels is unknown unless, as has been rumored, it was in one of the private rooms of the Old Poodle Dog, a San Francisco restaurant that also offered discreet accommodations to its patrons. But in 1908, in Philadelphia, Alma de Bretteville and Mr. Spreckels were married, not long after Adolph's father had died and left him roughly half of the vast sugar fortune. She was twenty-seven and he was fifty-one. Adolph's marriage fairly late in life would mean that his children would grow up as contemporaries of his brother John's grand-children.

The newlyweds spent their honeymoon making a grand tour of Europe, and returned to Mr. Spreckels' white sugar-cake mansion, with its indoor swimming pool and third-floor ceiling of Tiffany glass, in Pacific Heights. At the time, San Francisco's unquestioned Queen of Diamonds was Mrs. Leland Stanford, who was said to own more jewels than any crowned head in the world, with the exceptions of Queen Victoria and the Czarina of Russia. Her collection included four matching sets of diamond pieces, part of a million-dollar cache of stones that had belonged to Isabella of Spain. Each set consisted of a necklace, spray, earrings, tiara, bracelets, and pins. One set "emitted violet rays by day," another was composed of yellow diamonds, the third of pink diamonds, and the fourth of pure white gems. Mrs. Stanford also owned a large pear-shaped black diamond and a necklace of varicolored diamonds said to be the finest necklace in the United States. She also owned sixty pairs of diamond earrings. Incredible though it seems, it was reported that she once wore her entire collection to a private dinner given by William E. Dodge, choosing a black dress with voluminous folds on which all her little ornaments could be pinned and clipped. Adolph Spreckels was eager to have his new wife enter into a competition for the title held by Jane Stanford. But Alma Spreckels cared little for jewelry, though she did accept several fine strands of pearls, two magnificent diamond clips, and several diamond-and-emerald pieces. Alma Spreckels was much more interested in art.

At the French pavilion of the 1915 Panama-Pacific Exposition in San Francisco, Mrs. Spreckels first became aware of and admired the works of Auguste Rodin. Soon she was off to France to visit Rodin in his studio, where the sculptor had recently completed "The Thinker." Alma Spreckels liked "The Thinker," and rather than pester her husband for the money, she simply pawned some jewelry and bought one of the eighteen castings of the sculpture for fourteen thousand dollars. (When her husband discovered what she had done, he was so embarrassed that he quickly retrieved the jewels from the pawnbroker.) She presented the statue to the city, and it was placed in Golden Gate Park. This was the germ of her idea to give San Francisco a museum that would concentrate on French art and culture. It would be called the California Palace of the Legion of Honor and would be designed as a replica of the Palais de la Légion d'Honneur in Paris. Before it was finished it would be declared also a memorial—not to Alma and Adolph Spreckels but to the California dead who had been killed in World War I. Originally Mrs. Spreckels had planned to build her museum directly across the street from her house. But with the help of her friend Loïe Fuller, she selected an even more dramatic site, on a high bluff in Lincoln Park overlooking the Pacific and the Golden Gate.

Though it was completely intuitive, Mrs. Spreckels' choice of the Rodin sculpture as the focus of her museum was a shrewd one. A number of important private art collections had already been assembled in the East—in New York, Philadelphia, and Boston. But for some reason, moneyed San Franciscans had been slow to turn to art collecting in any significant way. Perhaps it was because the West Coast had no great art dealers comparable to Nathan Wildenstein or Lord Duveen to encourage and guide the tastes of wealthy westerners. What San Francisco had instead was Solomon Gump and his sons, who started out supplying gilded cornices and mirrors for the mansions of the city's new-rich millionaires. Gump's store branched out into European and Oriental *objets d'art*, and he also sold paintings—primarily bosomy nudes—which decorated the walls of San Francisco's best bars and fanciest brothels. The rest of the art sold by Gump's consisted primarily of heavy and elaborate picture frames that housed large, dark, and undistinguished oil paintings; one had the impression that San Francisco paintings existed merely to show off their frames. In such a frame Gump's had sold Collis P. Huntington a nude painting of the Empress Josephine. Otherwise, according to Leon Harris in *Merchant Princes*, Gump's and San Francisco's tastes ran to "socially acceptable subjects such as praying peasants, frolicking tots, noble animals, and inspiring landscapes."

But there may have been another reason why San Franciscans had not collected great art. To San Francisco's male-dominated society there was something sissified about paintings. The Impressionists in particular seemed both effete and effeminate. A painting of a charging buffalo or the massacre of an Indian tribe, on the other hand, was something that a San Francisco businessman could relate to. As for Rodin's sculpture, it was both massive and monumental. Here was no "decadent" Degas or Corot or Manet. There was no question but that "The Thinker" was thoroughly muscular and masculine. Rodin was the perfect sculptor for San Francisco of the 1920s.

Still, though Alma Spreckels had the enthusiastic support of Mr. Hearst and the *Examiner* (while her endeavors were being virtually ignored by the *Chronicle*), and even though she had Rodin, she soon found that raising funds for her project would not be as easy as she had first supposed. Second-generation California rich, it seemed, were more interested in party-giving, opera-going, and being seen at the right tables in the Mural Room than in philanthropy. That was part of it. But part of it also had to do with Alma Spreckels' almost overpoweringly imperious personal style. Like Mr.

Hearst, she seemed to feel that she was *above* society, unaccountable to it, impervious to its little niceties and rules and regulations. She was chauffeured around town in a huge Rolls-Royce with basket-weave sides, her knees beneath a chinchilla lap-robe. She occasionally inspected the building site of her museum wearing one of her mountainous mink coats over nothing but a nightgown, her feet in bedroom slippers. She loved to shock. She liked to hold museum meetings in her bedroom, where she held court in a swan-shaped bed, and at one such gathering of distinguished civic leaders she opened the proceedings by announcing, "Guess what? I just found my cook in bed with the butler!" Once, during a lull in the conversation at a dinner party where the guests included impresario Sol Hurok, Mrs. Spreckels said suddenly in her loud voice, "Mr. Hurok, do you know why they won't let Diaghilev dance in Russia?" Mr. Hurok did not know, and was no doubt bemused by the question, since Diaghilev, like Hurok, was an impresario, not a performer. "Because he won't wear a jockstrap," said Mrs. Spreckels.

In addition to her booming voice she had a haughty, almost baleful stare which she would fix on anyone who displeased her. Considering Alma Spreckels' origins and somewhat questionable past, San Francisco society found her more than a little hard to take. But she could not be ignored. Once, on a gallery-going trip to New York with her curator, Thomas Carr Howe, she asked him if he would like to go to the theater that night and, if so, what he would like to see. Howe replied that the great Broadway hit of the moment was *Lady in the Dark*, starring a new-found comedian named Danny Kaye. Howe added that he doubted that they could get tickets. Fifteen minutes later a messenger delivered tickets for two seats in the third row on the center aisle to Mrs. Spreckels' suite. Mrs. Spreckels, however, was unimpressed by Danny Kaye. In the middle of the first act, in a hoarse stage whisper that could be heard through half the house as well as across the footlights, Mrs. Spreckels cupped her hand against Howe's ear and declared, "Mr. Howe, I think Danny Kaye is a *fairy!*"

She could, on the other hand, be gregarious and generous—if not to a fault, at least to a degree that was quite beyond the limits of San Francisco's right-fork-conscious new high society. She was fond of asking acquaintances of both sexes to come for a swim with her in her indoor pool, invariably adding, "Of course, pet, I swim in the raw. Hope you don't mind." Those who had the temerity to accept her swimming invitations reported that she did indeed swim in the raw. Also, from time to time she liked having her chauffeur drop her off at various wharf-side saloons, where she enjoyed bellying up to the bar with sailors and stevedores and chatting with them in language even saltier than their own. She might be outrageous, but she was certainly not a snob. One afternoon, at the Spreckels country place, a huge ranch in Sonoma called Sobre Vista, a salesman selling pins and needles rang the doorbell. "See who's there!" roared Mrs. Spreckels, and the salesman was ushered in. After a few moments of conversation Mrs. Spreckels asked, "Do you have a wife?" The salesman replied that he did. "Bring her over," said Mrs. Spreckels. The salesman did, and he and his wife remained as Mrs. Spreckels' houseguests for about a week.

She had a passion for bridge and a passion for very cold, very dry martinis; an icy pitcherful was never far from her reach. Bridge tables were set up in every room of her San Francisco house—even in the bathrooms, and there were twenty-five of these, all of them capacious—to be ready wherever and whenever a foursome showed up. Parties were called at the drop of a hat, or even sooner. Once, after a small electrical fire had broken out in the house and the fire department had been called, Mrs. Spreckels' family returned late at night to find the firemen sitting around and downing martinis with their hostess. But her martini consumption never prevented her from rising at dawn and tackling her day with the energy of a Southern Pacific freight locomotive. She once woke up Henry Ford at 6:30 in the morning to ask him to donate a Model T for a raffle she was having for her museum. She got her Model T.

Pomp and formality and pretension bored her. When the late Elsa Maxwell, who considered herself both a San Franciscan and a social arbiter, once asked Mrs. Spreckels how old she was, Mrs. Spreckels replied, "Old enough to remember when there was no such person as Elsa Maxwell." At a formal dinner that was followed by a long series of speeches—most of them extolling the civic virtues and cultural benefactions of Alma de Bretteville Spreckels—the honoree grew weary of the proceedings, and, turning to her companion, she asked in the familiar stage whisper, "Want to hear something dirty in Danish?" Her companion nodded, whereupon Mrs. Spreckels muttered a guttural, incomprehensible epithet. "But what does it mean?" her companion whispered. "Fire up your behind!" shouted Mrs. Spreckels. At one time she was required to have a cystoscopy, and afterward she asked a dinner companion if he had ever had such an experience. Wincing, he replied that he had and that it had been very painful. "Christ," said Mrs. Spreckels, "if they do that sort of thing to the rich, what do they do to the poor?" She also once said, "If I weren't rich, people would say I was crazy. As it is, I'm just eccentric."

And she always got what she wanted. A luncheon guest at Sobre Vista once commented that the view from the terrace would probably be improved if a certain large tree were removed. The party then repaired to the dining room. After lunch the group gathered on the terrace again for coffee. The large tree was gone. It was the same way with her museum. When outside contributions proved insufficient for its construction, Mrs. Spreckels simply came up with her own money—some two million dollars all told before it was finished. She wanted an important Rodin collection. "The Thinker" was moved from Golden Gate Park to the museum's courtyard, and Mrs. Spreckels also bought casts of such now famous Rodins as the "Prodigal Son" and the "Age of Bronze." She bought some thirty-two other Rodin pieces, and by the time she had finished, the Rodin collection of the Legion of Honor was the largest in the Western Hemisphere. Inside the museum went French paintings, tapestries, rugs, porcelains, and crystal, all bought by Alma Spreckels. Influential friends were also helpful, including King Frederick and Queen Ingrid of Denmark. ("I've got a picture of them hanging in my bathroom," she liked to say.) Queen Marie of Romania, on her famous tour of the United States, stopped to visit Mrs. Spreckels and presented to her a great deal of gold furniture, including the queen's golden throne. ("Very comfortable throne," said Mrs. Spreckels. "I kept some of the gold furniture out in my front hall for a while.") Eventually, of course, all this furniture went to her museum. ("Actually, pet," she once confided to a friend, "Queen Marie didn't exactly *give* that furniture to me. I bought it from her.")

When the Palace of the Legion of Honor opened its doors in November 1924, with a great ceremony attended by everyone of importance in the city (except the de Youngs), as well as by dignitaries and government officials representing both the United States and France, the occasion was such that not even the *Chronicle* could afford to ignore it. It was an international event. The great white marble Palace dominated Inspiration Point, a cultural capstone to a city that wished to create the illusion, at least, that it treasured culture above all other virtues (though, in fact, there were certain other obvious priorities). Throughout the dedication speeches and ceremonies there was only one sad note. Alma de Bretteville Spreckels was in widow's weeds. Adolph Spreckels had not lived to see the result of his wife's labors and his money. He had died in June of that year at the age of sixty-seven.

Though Spreckels and de Young were now both dead, the rivalry between the two museums went on for years, abetted by the partisanship of the *Chronicle* and the *Examiner*. Whenever a piece of art became available for acquisition, Mrs. Spreckels would cry, "Get it before the de Young!" In a sense the competitiveness of the two museums served them both well in that it made each try harder to obtain the best pieces and to display the best exhibits. But the tendency of each paper to run down the competition's product probably resulted in simply confusing the museum-going public and prompted at least one East Coast observer to comment, "If you put the two San Francisco museums together, you'd end up with one mediocre museum."

Early on, William Randolph Hearst had hired the brimstone-pen writer Ambrose Bierce as his art critic and had instructed him to write disparagingly of any exhibition presented at the de Young

Museum. Bierce complied and had written of a typical de Young show that the quality of the art, "while always detestable, has this year attained a shining pinnacle of badness. The pictures next year will necessarily be better than the pictures of this, but alas, there may be be more of them." Later *Examiner* art critics followed the Bierce example.

A great deal has been written about the demonic and despotic William Randolph Hearst, who treated kings and copyboys with the same disdain and impartiality. Yet those who knew him as a friend and host remember W.R., or "The Chief," as he was called, as a kindly, rather shy and self-effacing man, full of uncertainties, whose primary wish seemed to be to make his guests feel comfortable and happy. Once, after visiting Hearst at San Simeon, *The New Yorker* editor Harold Ross commented, "I went expecting to meet Dracula, and went away feeling that I'd met Mr. Chips." For years rumors circulated that Hearst had people killed who displeased him, and in particular that he poisoned (or shot, according to another version) movie producer Thomas Ince, who died shortly after dining on Hearst's yacht, for making a pass at Marion Davies. Miss Davies herself denied the stories. Mr. Hearst's guests and acquaintances, she explained, fell into four categories. "Either men worshiped W.R., or they worked for him, or they were our guests and *gentlemen*, or they hated W.R.'s guts but were scared of him," she explained. None of these categories of men would have dreamed of making a pass at her.

Hearst's one great character flaw—if, indeed, it was not a diagnosable neurosis—may have been that he was a compulsive spender. He acquired things wildly and erratically, buying priceless and worthless objects with the same reckless abandon. Like an alcoholic or a drug addict, he seemed to need a daily "fix" from spending huge sums of money. He bought rooms of castles, ceilings, frescoes, chandeliers, suits of armor, statues, paintings, tapestries, and enormous amounts of bric-a-brac that could only be described as junk. A psychologist would doubtless find in all this an expression of some deep and terrible insecurity. Over the years this ferocious habit escalated, and in the cavernous basement vaults of San Simeon, as well as in warehouses across the country, great crates of Hearst purchases piled up, many of them never opened. In the end his buying consumed him. The well of the Hearst fortune was not, as it had once seemed, bottomless. Though his publishing and motion picture empire yielded tens of millions of dollars a year in profits, they were eventually insufficient to support his habit, which, as it would turn out, would provide an ironic twist to San Francisco's great museum war.

When Hearst died in 1951 he was at Miss Davies' house in Beverly Hills. Miss Davies, according to her late account, had been up caring for him and reading to him much of the night and had taken a sleeping pill, so that when the end came she was in deep slumber. She may of course have been intoxicated. During his final illness Mr. Hearst had not been able to control Marion's drinking problem, as he had struggled to do for over twenty years. In fact, he disliked anyone who drank and tried to control the drinking of everyone with whom he came in contact. At San Simeon, beer was served with lunch, and before dinner a cocktail—or occasionally two—was offered, along with copious hors d'oeuvres, including huge bowls of caviar. Wine was served with dinner, and after dinner, following the inevitable screening of a Hearst motion picture, usually starring Miss Davies, a guest might be lucky enough to be offered a good-night highball. Aside from that, Hearst's evenings were nonalcoholic, and any guest who appeared to be intoxicated received an icy stare from the host and was told, "A car is waiting to take you to the night train." At dinner the Hearst butlers were instructed not to refill Miss Davies' wineglass. Once, when the butler had passed behind her chair without offering her more wine, she cried out, "Oh, please, W.R., let me have some more champagne! After all, I never get cross at you when you drink." "That is correct," replied the host. "You only get cross at me when *you* drink." To offset this situation Miss Davies kept a secret cache of liquor in the ladies' dressing room, where it was stored in perfume bottles. Women guests repaired there to freshen their drinks.

In any case, when the nurses at Hearst's bedside realized that he had died, Miss Davies could not be roused from sleep. A few days earlier, to try to prevent a financial debacle, she had lent him a million dollars. The first person notified of his death was Hearst's widow, and by the time Marion Davies awoke, Hearst executives had removed The Chief's body and every scrap of his possessions from her house. After thirty-two years as his mistress-companion-nurse, she was not permitted to bid him a final farewell. Nor was she allowed to attend his funeral in San Francisco. Millicent Hearst and her sons took charge of all arrangements. Though Marion had been specifically named in Hearst's will as the sole voting power in the Hearst Corporation, pressure from the family forced her to relinquish that right.

The family then set about trying to recoup as much of Hearst's exhausted fortune as it could by auctioning and selling off his vast accumulation of acquisitions. Because of Hearst's liaison with Miss Davies, the Hearsts had for years been denied a listing in the San Francisco *Social Register*, and the family now set about trying to redeem themselves and their tarnished image in the eyes of San Francisco society. This they decided to do by presenting a particularly impressive collection of tapestries to the city. To the astonishment of everyone who was aware of the long Hearst–de Young feud, the gift was made to the de Young Museum.

The choice of the de Young may have been capricious. Or it may have been perverse, a way of notifying such of Mr. Hearst's old friends as Mrs. Spreckels that they no longer wielded any power over his family. Of course the *Chronicle* fairly crowed with this news. Had Hearst himself been aware of it he would surely have been spinning furiously in his grave. The de Young Museum, on accepting the tapestries, announced that they would be displayed in an especially created new gallery to be called the Hearst Court. To the delighted de Young family it seemed as though the de Youngs had finally triumphed over William Randolph Hearst.

If Alma Spreckels was angry or even disappointed over these developments, she was wise enough to remain silent on the subject.

CHAPTER SEVEN
Silver Kings and Other Royalty

THOUGH THE families of the famous Big Four of the Southern Pacific and Union Pacific railroads—the Crockers, Huntingtons, Hopkinses, and Stanfords—had managed to glide more or less effortlessly into San Francisco's high society of culture and refinement, a second Big Four—the so-called Silver Kings—had more difficulty. It was a question of occupational status. Railroads, after all, were somehow a respectable endeavor. Railroads provided a comfortable and fashionable form of travel. Every really rich man had his private railway car. Everyone also invested in railroad stocks, which virtually had the endorsement of the United States government. Mining, on the other hand, was pick-and-shovel stuff, an occupation for roughnecks and gamblers. Most of the overnight gold and silver fortunes had been frittered or gambled away as rapidly as they had been made. Even John Sutter, on whose property California gold had first been discovered, setting off the gold rush, had died a poor man living in a boardinghouse on a meager pension.

The Silver Kings—or the Irish Big Four, as they were sometimes called—were James C. Flood, William S. O'Brien, James Gordon Fair, and John William Mackay. Jim Flood, described by Dixon Wecter as a "poor gamin of the New York streets," had, like so many of his contemporaries, gone west with the gold rush. But instead of heading for the hills as others did, Flood settled for the ramshackle village with rutted streets—whose hilltop mansions still looked incongruous and out of place on the frontier-town horizon—that was then downtown San Francisco. In San Francisco, Flood met another Irishman, Will O'Brien, and the two pooled their small resources to set themselves up in a storefront bar and grill called the Auction Lunch Rooms. It got its name from the Gold Exchange, near which it was located. Flood's job was to mix the drinks, which he did in generous proportions, and O'Brien worked behind the stove, where he soon received a certain neighborhood celebrity for his Irish fish chowder, thick with potatoes. The Auction Lunch Rooms soon became a popular gathering place for traders on the exchange, as well as for miners, who periodically came down from the hills to disport themselves in the city's fancy houses and to partake of hearty food and drink.

Inevitably, in addition to cooking and bartending, the two partners were able to eavesdrop on certain gold-related conversations, and, lubricated by whiskey, the miners and the traders occasionally revealed more about their business than they should have. It wasn't long before Flood and O'Brien, who had never set foot in a mining camp, had developed a fairly good feel for gold and silver mining. One particularly promising tip concerned the Comstock area outside Virginia City. And so, taking in two Irish friends, John Mackay and Jim Fair, as partners to provide further financial backing, the foursome set off for Virginia City to stake a claim. It was one of those rare occasions when a prospector's very first explorations yielded a bonanza, and the Comstock was even more than that. What the foursome discovered was the largest and most valuable single pocket of silver ever unearthed in the world—a huge vein of shiny metal some fifty feet wide. The initial estimates of the value of the Comstock Lode placed it at $300,000,000, but even that turned out to be on the low side. From its discovery in 1859 until its final depletion ten years later, the Comstock would yield, all told, over $500,000,000 worth of silver, making Flood, Fair, Mackey, and O'Brien four of the world's richest men.

William O'Brien took his share of the Comstock riches and retired to lead a quiet, unpublicized life. He had no use for society and was content simply to nurse his fortune. Not so Jim Flood. Perhaps no other individual in the history of American capitalism catapulted himself from squalor to glittering splendor in so short a time as the ex-bartender, who shared the glitter with his wife, a former chambermaid. Instant riches, to Flood, demanded instant luxury, and one of his first orders was for the construction of a massive brownstone mansion at the very top of Nob Hill, catercorner to the Mark Hopkins mansion. (Flood's house was so sturdily built that it was one of the few buildings in the city to survive the great earthquake and fire of 1906.) Flood also built another palatial house in suburban Menlo Park, which became known locally as "Flood's Wedding Cake" and was described by the late Lucius Beebe as "a miracle of turrets, gables, and gingerbread." It was seven stories high, surrounded by porches, painted white, and topped by a huge square tower supporting a pyramid that resembled the Eiffel Tower. So much carpeting was required to cover the floors of these two houses that John Sloane, the carpet dealer from New York who was brought in to handle the job, had to station representatives in California to supervise the carpet-laying, and soon found it simpler and more economical just to open a branch of his store in San Francisco.

Still, for all their display, the James Floods did not find it easy to break into San Francisco society. They were considered "uncultivated" and "lacking in refinement," as, to be sure, they were. Flood had to have his valet give him instructions on how to tie a necktie, though Mrs. Flood, who had waited on ladies of the gentlefolk, had learned some lessons in *comme il faut*. The Floods were fortunate, however, in that they had a beautiful daughter. Jennie Flood became an instant belle of San Francisco, famous for her fine dark hair, her wit, charm, and devastatingly large and flashing eyes. All the most eligible bachelors in the city were at Jennie's feet, and the Floods were certain that Jennie would marry well. In 1879, Jennie Flood was courted by no less than a United States President's son, Ulysses S. Grant, Jr., and the prospect of this match so pleased her father that he promised to build the pair an immense château in Newport as a wedding present. Alas, young Grant, it seemed, had an eye for all the ladies of the moment, and, returning from a trip east, he delayed so long in reaching Jennie Flood's house—"dallying along the way with Dora Miller and other adorables," as the *Chronicle*'s society writer put it   that Jennie angrily broke the engagement. Later she was admired and squired about by the British Lord Beaumont, and once more the Floods' hopes for a brilliant match were raised. But Lord Beaumont's courtship came to nothing, and in the end Jennie Flood never married anyone at all and died a spinster. She remained, however, a colorful and popular figure in San Francisco.

James Gordon Fair, meanwhile, earned the distinction of being the least likable of the Irish Four; he had managed to earn the nickname of "Slippery Jim" very early in his career. Born in Belfast in 1831, Jim Fair came first to Chicago at the age of twelve, and then moved westward at the age of eighteen. By the age of thirty, with his Comstock millions, he had a mill in Nevada, where he became chiefly responsible for driving San Franciscans out of Nevada development—making many enemies in the process—which he then managed to take over himself. He got the Nevada state legislature (which in those days elected U.S. senators) to appoint him to the Senate, where his career was undistinguished.

He had one particularly nasty habit. He enjoyed giving misleading tips on the stock market. Jim Fair's acquaintances soon learned that if Fair recommended a stock it was certain to go down, but before discovering this fact a number of people had been stung. In 1861, Fair married an Irish girl named Theresa Rooney, by whom he had four children—Theresa (Tessie), Virginia (Birdie), Charles, and James. At one point Mrs. Fair asked her husband to recommend a stock in which she could invest some money. Jim Fair then gave her a surefire tip, adding that she must promise not to tell any of her friends. Fair knew that his voluble wife could not keep a secret, and so Mrs. Fair and all her friends invested in the stock in question. It soon became worthless. "That," declared Fair, "will teach you a lesson." For this and other reasons Mrs. Fair divorced him and received custody of all the children except young James. Fair's namesake hated and dreaded his father, and soon after the divorce he committed suicide. Charles Fair made a youthful marriage that so displeased his father that he disinherited him, and shortly afterward young Charles and his bride were killed in an automobile accident. Both Birdie and Tessie made "brilliant" society marriages: Birdie married William K. Vanderbilt and Tessie married Hermann Oelrichs. Both girls specified that their father not be invited to their weddings, and as it came about, both marriages turned out unhappily. Birdie and Vanderbilt's ended in divorce. Tessie's marriage lasted, and Tessie went on to become one of the reigning dowagers of Newport, but she had always shown signs of mental instability. She had great manic rages, followed by black depressions. In her manic periods she would try to set fire to the curtains of her house. In her depressions she would remain in her bed for days. In the end she was declared insane.

Slippery Jim Fair became an alcoholic and, in the process, a bigamist. On various drunken sprees he took a series of women to the altar, promising each of them a share of his fortune. Following these marriages, he would disappear and his various wives would attempt to find him. In his last years Fair lived alone in a San Francisco hotel, solitary, bitter, completely without friends and estranged from his entire family. When he died in 1894 at the age of sixty-three his personal and financial affairs were in such a hopeless tangle that his will offered fifty dollars apiece "to any widows or children" of his who might be able to prove themselves such.

In the second generation the Flood family also had financial problems brought on by romance. In the 1930s a young woman sued Jim Flood's son, James L. Flood, claiming she was his illegitimate daughter. And it turned out that she was. Witnesses appeared to testify that they had seen James Flood wheeling the child up and down the street in a baby carriage. She was awarded seven and a half million dollars.

By far the most attractive, and probably the most talented, of the Irish quartet was John William Mackay. Mackay was a tall, slender, handsome man with deep-set eyes, a gentle nature, and a generous heart. After his first important strike in the mother lode, in which he made two hundred thousand dollars, he announced that this was enough money for any man and that "the man who wanted more than that was a fool." He had gone into the Comstock venture with more capital than his other partners and as a result had a two-fifths share of that bonanza—a fact that doubtless caused him to raise his estimate of how much money a prudent man needed. He had been born in Dublin in 1831 into a virtually penniless family, and at the age of nine, at the onset of the great potato famine, had emigrated to America. He first worked in New York as an apprentice shipbuilder, but when tales of western gold began to circulate, he headed for California. There he worked as a pick-and-shovel man for four dollars a day, but he shrewdly insisted on receiving only part of his pay in cash. The rest he asked for in stock in the mining company.

Thus when the mother lode came in he found himself a moderately rich man. In 1867, after the Comstock had made him a hugely rich man, he heard a sad tale of a poor widow in Virginia City, Louise Hungerford Bryant. Mrs. Bryant, the daughter of a New York barber, had married and gone west with her husband, and had been left with a small daughter and younger sister and virtually without resources. Mackay organized a collection for her, and, having gone to her house to give her the money, promptly fell in love with the young woman. When he asked her to marry him, he warned her to judge him for his qualities as a man, not on the basis of his money. As he reminded her, "Circumstances in the mining business change quickly." But even if he lost everything he had, he promised her,

"I can always dig a living with my bare hands." And he swore to protect her—"with my fists, if need be."

Mackay not only did not lose all his money but went on to make a great deal more. In 1874 he and his wife moved from Virginia City to San Francisco, and two years later they came east to New York. Though neither of the Mackays had any formal education to speak of, or any "breeding" in the social sense, they were both endowed with a gentle and soft-spoken Irish attractiveness and charm. Being rich didn't hurt them either, and they made friends easily. Nevertheless they were snubbed by New York society, which was then ruled by Mrs. William Astor and run by her social arbiter, Ward McAllister. But when the Mackays moved on to Europe they were welcomed everywhere. With their good looks and manners they charmed everyone, including the Prince of Wales, who called John Mackay "the most unassuming American I have ever met."

In 1883, back in New York, John Mackay formed the Commercial Cable Company and went to battle against Wall Street titan Jay Gould's Western Union telegraph monopoly. The financial community was certain that Gould, known as an unscrupulous, crafty fighter, would destroy the "Irish upstart," as Mackay was labeled, and was filled with awe for Mackay when Mackay won. He was twice nominated to the United States Senate and both times modestly refused to run. But he was still a fighter, and in 1891, when he was sixty years old, he had a chance to make good his early promise to his wife. A series of articles about Louise Mackay had been appearing in newspapers in both the United States and England stating that she had once been a washerwoman and later had sunk "even lower than that," having sent her tiny daughters into the streets of Virginia City begging with tin cups. Mackay set out to find the instigator of these stories, a man named Bonynge, and one day spotted him through a window of the Bank of Nevada. Mackay let himself into the bank through the back door and headed straight for Mr. Bonynge, who was taken completely by surprise. Whereas Adolph Spreckels had used a revolver to exact his revenge on an offending newspaperman, Mr. Mackay chose manlier means according to Oscar Lewis in *Silver Kings.* "I struck out with my right," Mackay said, "and hit him in the left eye. Then I hit him again. . . . I'm not so handy with my fists as I used to be twenty-five years ago on the Comstock, but I have a little fight in me yet, and will allow no one to malign me or mine."

Of the Irish Big Four, Mackay was also by far the most philanthropic, and a complete tally of his gifts will probably never be made, because when he gave to a charity that interested him he nearly always insisted on anonymity. He lent and gave away millions of dollars to friends and business associates, and these transactions were always unrecorded. Two of his biggest gifts, however, could not be hidden—the Mackay School of Mines in Reno and the building of the Church of St. Mary's in the Mountains in Virginia City. Throughout his life he refused to discuss his money, and when he died in 1902 his business manager told reporters, "I don't suppose he knew within twenty millions what he was worth."

WHILE THE fortunes of Flood, Mackay, Fair, and O'Brien were giving the city of San Francisco an "Irishtocracy," as it was called, other ethnic groups were emerging as economic forces to be reckoned with. In addition to the de Youngs (who never really advertised themselves as Jewish), a number of German Jewish families were achieving prominence in banking and retailing, among them the Haases, the Hellmans, the Zellerbachs, the Dinkelspiels, the Schwabachers, the Koshlands, the Fleischhackers and the specialty-store Magnins. "We are particularly fortunate here," as San Franciscans are proud of saying, "in having such a lovely class of Jewish people." Once, when old Mrs. Daniel Koshland explained to Phyllis de Young Tucker that she would not be able to attend a certain civic function because she was observing the festival of Succoth, Mrs. Tucker said, "Oh, how I envy you your traditions!" Somewhat tartly Mrs. Koshland replied, "You have a few of your own if you'd care to invoke them."

A number of Italian families were also becoming important in San Francisco, including the Ghirardellis (with a chocolate factory), the Aliotos (in the fishing industry), and the Baldocchis (in the retail flower business). The most spectacular Italian American success story, however, belongs to Amadeo Peter Giannini, whose little Bank of Italy, originally designed to serve the banking needs of his "own kind," became the giant Bank of America, the largest commercial bank in the world. Giannini, the stepson of a Genoese produce merchant, first got into the moneylending business by making loans to immigrant small farmers who brought their produce into San Francisco from the outlying valleys. His first important break occurred at the time of the 1906 fire, when he was able to load his entire supply of gold—some eighty thousand dollars' worth —into a pair of produce wagons and escape with it to San Mateo, where, lacking a safe, he hid the gold in the ash pit of his fireplace. After the fire, when other San Francisco bankers were urging a bank holiday, a six-month moratorium on loans, and the issuance of scrip instead of cash to withdrawing depositors, A. P. Giannini was able to open up shop behind a plank set on two barrels beside the Washington Street Wharf, where he conducted business as usual.

Giannini was an innovative banker in several ways. For one thing, he devised a then very novel floor plan for his bank. Instead of placing his officers behind the scenes or separated from the public by cages, Giannini scattered them at desks about the central banking lobby. The effect was good psychologically—it made the officers of the bank seem accessible to the customers—and this design eventually was copied by commercial banks throughout the country. He was also a pioneer, in California, of branch banking, and opened his first branch bank in San Francisco's Mission District in 1907, and his second in San Jose. Soon small branches of the Bank of America were opening in rural communities—which had never had banking services before—throughout the state. His favorite customers were businessmen with small-capital, high risk enterprises, such as farmers. He distrusted the oil business and—unwisely, perhaps—invested little in real estate. But he did see a future in southern California's fledgling motion picture business, and all the major movie studios, along with the great movie czars of their day, were built up with the help of loans from Mr. Giannini's bank at a time when more established banks were dismissing Hollywood as a cottage industry.

Long before these upstart twentieth-century fortunes were made, familiar rifts had begun appearing between members of California's older moneyed families. A crack had even appeared in the façade of the railroading Big Four. By the late 1880s only two of the four remained active. Hopkins had died, and Crocker had been incapacitated in 1886—ironically, for a railroad man, because of a fall from a horse-drawn carriage—and would die two years later. Collis Huntington and Leland Stanford now fell to bickering.

It had all started in 1885 when former Governor Stanford shouldered aside Huntington's best friend, A. A. Sargent, in order to run for the Senate. Huntington began saying that Stanford's sole contribution to the Southern Pacific after lifting the first shovelful of dirt was hammering home the golden spike, which he had accomplished only with difficulty after several clumsy misses. Stanford retaliated by calling Huntington "an old fool" and saying that he would trust him only as far as he could "throw Trinity Church up the side of Mount Shasta." Huntington spoke mockingly of the imperial way Stanford, as president of the Southern Pacific, ran his railroad. Whenever Leland Stanford's private car passed through, all railroad crews in the vicinity were required to stand at rigid attention, and all passing locomotives were ordered to blow their whistles in salute.

Leland Stanford was indeed a curious man. He weighed more than three hundred pounds—in the history of American politics he was perhaps outweighed only by William Howard Taft—but aside from his size and solidity he was most noteworthy for his silences. The Mount Shasta remark is possibly the only known example of the Stanford "wit." For the most part he was a mountain of muteness, often sitting for hours at a time staring straight into space, saying nothing. At times like these his associates often worried that Mr. Stanford might have died. When asked a question—even such a simple one as "How are you?"—he would pause for long minutes before forming an answer. It is possible that he was not very bright, and it is ironic that the Stanford name should now be associated with a great institution of higher learning. In social situations Stanford was without conversation. A visitor from England, invited to dine alone with the great rail magnate at his house, recalled the horror of spending an evening with a completely uncommunicative host. Desperately the dinner guest went from subject to subject, to none of which Stanford responded with as much as a word or a nod. At first the guest was sure that he was boring Stanford. Then he decided that Stanford might be sleepy, though the host's eyes stayed glassily open. Finally the guest concluded that Stanford must be gravely ill, though when the long evening was eventually over, Stanford rose, saw his guest to the door, shook his hand and said, "Thanks for the chat."

As a politician Stanford gave long, windy speeches—always written for him by underlings—that were full of rhetoric but, on analysis, short on content. It was impossible for him to speak extemporaneously or without a prepared text. Once at an outdoor gathering where he was speaking a sudden gust of wind blew the manuscript pages of his long speech off the lectern and scattered them in all directions. Stanford simply stopped speaking and stood gazing dully at his audience for the ten minutes or so it took to gather up the pages and reassemble them in their proper order. Actually, Leland Stanford's inarticulateness became one of his greatest assets as a politician. Watching this large man painstakingly read his boring speeches, the average voter found it impossible to believe that a man of such towering dullness was not a man of complete honesty and probity. When interviewed by the press, Stanford was without opinions and therefore completely uncontroversial. It hardly seemed likely that behind his impassive façade was a man who purchased laws and legislators with cheerful abandon when it was to the benefit of his railroad.

There were occasional brief though misleading hints that Stanford might have had a sense of humor. After eighteen childless years of marriage Mrs. Stanford, in 1868, had finally produced an only son, Leland Stanford, Jr. When the baby was only a few weeks old the

Stanfords invited a large group of friends for dinner. When the guests were seated, a butler entered carrying a large covered silver serving tray and placed it in the center of the table. "My friends, I wish to introduce my son to you," said Mr. Stanford. The lid was then lifted, and there lay the baby on a bed of fresh flowers. The tray and the baby were then passed around the table for the guests to admire. A few might have been tempted to laugh, but a look at the host's solemn face assured the assemblage that this was no joking matter.

The feud between Huntington and Stanford simmered for several years, until Huntington at last saw a chance to make his move. Confronting Stanford, Huntington claimed to have gained access to "certain papers" and "documents" in "the Sargent matter" which would conclusively prove that Stanford had purchased his Senate seat at the expense of Mr. Sargent. Huntington's price for silence on the Sargent matter was the presidency of the Southern Pacific, and he asked Stanford to step down. Apparently this blackmail threat sufficiently frightened Stanford. He resigned the presidency, and the new president became Collis P. Huntington. But Huntington was still not through with Stanford. The railroad's new president immediately went back on his word and announced to the press not only that Stanford had bought his election but that he had bought it with funds purloined from the railroad's treasury.

Needless to say, the two men never spoke to each other again—nor, thereafter, did their wives, who had been friends. Both Stanford and Huntington—each man convinced that the other had plans to assassinate him—took to traveling with heavily armed guards at their sides. It was a feud that would only end with Leland Stanford's death, of natural causes, in 1893.

CHAPTER EIGHT
Disasters, Natural and Unnatural

IN THE year 1843 there were exactly forty Americans living in Los Angeles. Even by the 1850s, after California had been admitted to the Union, it remained a sluggish, dispirited place and also a reasonably violent one. Lynch law prevailed instead of justice, and at one point the mayor of Los Angeles resigned to join a lynching party. After the lynching he was promptly reelected. A local newspaper, the *Southern Californian*, commented in the early 1850s on the Los Angeles murder scene with as much interest as might be given to a weather report: "The week has been comparatively quiet; four persons have been killed it is true, but it has been considered a poor week for killing; a head or two has been split open, and an occasional cutting has occurred, but these are minor matters and create but little feeling."

It was not until after World War I that anyone in California thought much about the southern city. By then most of the rest of the state had got into the habit—so infuriating to Angelenos—of referring to San Francisco simply as "the city." After all, San Francisco was the only California community of city size and importance, and so when one said, "I'm going up to the city tomorrow," it could only mean that one was going to San Francisco.

As late as 1915 most of the streets of Los Angeles were still unpaved. The streets ran up to the edge of the foothills, where they ended, and from the foothills onward there was nothing but sagebrush and wild mountains filled with coyotes and rattlesnakes and little wild deer that came down into the town at night. There were a few automobiles, but not many, and a couple of streetcars—with signs at the back saying *"Don't Shoot Rabbits from the Rear Platform!"*—and the "red trains" that ran from the center of town out to the beaches, from Pasadena to Newport and from Huntington Beach up toward Santa Ana. Otherwise transportation was primitive, and the most sensible way to get around was on horseback. Children rode their horses to school. Sunset Boulevard, which wound through the hills following the course of an old cattle trail, ended long before it reached the coast, and down the center of much of its length ran a bridle path.

What first put Los Angeles on the map of course was the motion picture business. A few fledgling movie companies had straggled out to California prior to the First World War—an outfit called Nestor, which represented Centaur Films in Bayonne, New Jersey, followed in 1909 by the New York Motion Picture Company, which opened a small "studio" (a former roadhouse) which was taken over by Mack Sennett in 1912. Vitagraph Films had opened a western branch in Santa Monica in 1911. But no one had paid much attention to the movie people and their storefront businesses because no one thought that movies would last. It was not until World War I that, faced with wartime fuel shortages and the escalating cost of heat, movie men began migrating to California from the East in large numbers. Here there was hardly ever any need for heat, and the fruit-growing Cahuenga Valley—later known as Hollywood—was known as the

Frostless Belt. The abundance of sunshine was another important economic factor—moviemaking required lots of light—along with the varied landscape and the fact that in nonunion Los Angeles labor was cheap. Quite often movie extras would work for nothing, just for the fun of being photographed for the silver screen.

But other things had been happening in Los Angeles to help spur its rapid growth from an arid cow town to a sprawling—well, "metropolis" might not be the best word to describe Los Angeles, the second-largest city in the United States. What hindered the growth of Los Angeles was lack of water, and it was not until the early 1900s that a man named William Mulholland began devising ways of bringing water into the dry Los Angeles plain and the parched San Fernando Valley. In California history William Mulholland is either a hero or a villain, depending on who tells the tale. He may have been the father of the Los Angeles water system and the man who made the desert bloom, but he accomplished all this at the cost of a great deal of money and not a few human lives.

Prior to the advent of William Mulholland the Los Angeles water-supply system had consisted of a primitive series of ditches and open canals, dug by the town's Spanish founders, which were fed by the Los Angeles River—an unreliable stream that in the long dry season diminished to barely a trickle. Arriving in California from his native Ireland in 1877 at the age of twenty-two, Mulholland went to work as a ditchdigger for the water company, which was then privately owned. By 1902, when the city took over the facility, Mulholland had been promoted to superintendent, and he was named chief engineer and general manager of the new municipal department. Mulholland's first ambitious notion was to tap the Owens River, which ran through Mono and Inyo counties north of Los Angeles, and to carry this water across the Sierras and down into the Los Angeles Basin by means of what would amount to a giant syphon system. To this end he laid out the Los Angeles–Owens River aqueduct—225 miles of canal, with 52 miles of tunnels.

Needless to say, the benefits from this project which would be felt at the Los Angeles end would be offset by severe disadvantages to the two counties whose water would be sucked up to supply Los Angeles. The reactions to the plan in rural Inyo and Mono were violent as farmers saw what would happen: their green oasis turned into a desert simply to create the opposite effect in a city several hundred miles away. But the priorities of California's cities over farming communities were now becoming established, and Mulholland's scheme was approved by the legislature. This did not mean that building the aqueduct would be easy. Throughout the ten years it took to construct it, crews were attacked and beaten and kidnapped by masked vigilantes from the Owens River valley towns. Head gates were captured and dynamited, and sections of the canal were repeatedly sabotaged and bombed. When the aqueduct opened in 1913, huge crowds turned out to see the man-made cascade of Owens River water sluicing down into the San Fernando Valley on its way to Los Angeles.

There would be less cheering, however, for Mulholland's next project, which was to build a dam and reservoir at the head of the Santa Clara River valley, just north of the city. The purpose of this was to provide a year's reserve supply of water for Los Angeles. Placed well below the San Andreas Fault line, this reservoir could quickly be tapped in case supplies from the aqueduct were disrupted by earthquakes. By now William Mulholland was being hailed as southern California's "Wizard of Water," and his plans were quickly approved. In 1924 construction of the St. Francis Dam began. Early on, several engineers warned Mulholland that a vein of schist running through the sandstone at the damsite made the site an unreliable foundation. But Mulholland dismissed the warnings and announced that he had complete confidence in the project. The dam was completed in the late fall of 1927 and the new reservoir began to fill. It had not filled far before water began to seep through the dam's base. Mulholland dismissed the leak as inconsequential, and the reservoir continued to fill until a high-water mark of 1832 feet was reached, when Mulholland ordered that storage be stopped.

In the early spring of 1928 a second leak in the St. Francis Dam was reported. Once again Mulholland assured the city that the dam was sound. On March 12 the dam keeper of the St. Francis anxiously telephoned Mulholland to report that a third leak had appeared and he did not like the looks of things at all. Mulholland hurried up to the dam and inspected it personally. And again he declared that the St. Francis Dam was secure.

It was a warm and hazy evening—already the plentiful new water supply had begun to work subtle changes on the city's climate, turning the dry air moist—and citizens of Los Angeles and neighboring Ventura County were sitting on their porches listening to their radios, comforted to hear the Wizard of Water's assurances, making nervous jokes about the big leaky dam not far away. Just before midnight the lights of the city flickered as the voltage dropped. Then to the north there was a distant rumble, like summer thunder, and many people assumed that the lights were dimming because of an electrical storm. The rumble grew, and the next thought was *earthquake*—and the ground was indeed now trembling. A wall of water as high as a ten-story building came plunging into the valley, sweeping up in its wake houses, automobiles, trees, livestock, people. Some were lucky and managed to make it to high ground. Others were not. Meanwhile fruit orchards were uprooted, citrus groves flattened. Huge sections of the dam—some weighing ten thousand tons—descended like bits of cork on the lip of the wave and shattered entire towns. When it was over, three towns—Castaic Junction, Santa Paula, and Fillmore—were wiped from the face of the earth, and much of Ventura County lay under a blanket of mud.

Considering the scope of the disaster, it seems incredible that more people were not killed. The county coroner counted 420 bodies.

Los Angeles was now ready to lynch its Wizard of Water, and might indeed have done so if, in the general disarray of everything, it had had the slightest idea of where to find him. Signs declaring "*Murder Mulholland!*" appeared on the walls of public buildings, and, overnight, William Mulholland became one of the most hated men in southern California, even though his aqueduct had been a pivotal factor in the growth and prosperity of Los Angeles.

Several explanations can be offered for what were Mulholland's obviously gross miscalculations in the building of the St. Francis Dam. He may have begun to believe in his own Wizard of Water myth and to think of himself as infallible. He also was a pioneer, and pioneers have often been known to make mistakes. It should be remembered too that Mulholland had had absolutely no formal engineering training and was completely self-taught in his field. But California had by now a long history of placing great faith in self-taught men, and some of its most stunning success stories had involved the ill-trained and self-educated men who had made it to the top through a combination of unscrupulousness, stamina, and luck. Fortunes had been made in California by men foolish enough to believe that they were lucky, and by 1928, William Mulholland's luck had just run out. By 1928 too Mulholland was seventy-three years old, and perhaps, past his prime, he had lost his touch.

In the St. Francis Dam catastrophe the possibility of sabotage cannot be ruled out—Mulholland had had to deal with the problem of sabotage before—but it seems unlikely. To his credit, Mulholland never tried to shift the blame for the disaster to saboteurs. He shouldered it himself, which caused Los Angeles at least partially to forgive him. At the Los Angeles coroner's inquest that followed he said, "Don't blame anybody else; you just fasten it on me. If there was an error of human judgment, I was the human." But 1928 nevertheless was the year of William Mulholland's retirement as Chief Engineer and General Manager of the Los Angeles Department of Water and Power.

OTHER UPHEAVALS had been taking place in southern California. By 1908, Lyman Stewart's Union Oil Company, whose 1884 production had amounted to only 2661 barrels, was producing almost 5,500,000 barrels a year, but the growing company was having problems. Most of these centered on its abstemious founder and president, Mr. Stewart. For several years Mr. Rockefeller's Standard Oil had been attempting to swallow up Union, and though some of his directors favored the merger, Mr. Stewart resisted—once replying to Standard that he would "consider" their offer if Standard would contract to buy 40,000,000 barrels of crude oil from Union. This condition seemed so outrageous that Standard abruptly terminated all negotiations. To help him keep Standard Oil at bay, Mr. Stewart invited the other great oil tycoon of the day, Edward Doheny, to sit on Union's board of directors—a move Stewart would later regret—and Doheny accepted. "We all want the benefit of Mr. Doheny's counsel," Lyman Stewart explained.

Doheny and Stewart first crossed swords over the matter of Mr. Stewart's salary. Though Stewart now controlled a multimillion-dollar company, he took pride in the fact that he accepted only a nominal wage for doing so. For years he had paid himself only five dollars a day, which was less than his oil drillers got. In 1903 he had asked his board to give him a raise—to three thousand dollars a year —so that he "wouldn't have to keep a daily expense account." Doheny considered the request ridiculous and an embarrassment to the company. He therefore proposed that the president's salary be increased to at least $1,000 a month, whereupon Stewart adamantly refused the increase.

Lyman Stewart, in fact, was becoming peculiar, and no one knew it better than his son, Will, with whom the senior Stewart increasingly disagreed—an upshot more often than not of the old man's religious fervor. In 1908, to meet certain financial requirements of his company, Lyman Stewart underwrote $375,000 worth of stock that was being sold on the market. The issue was oversubscribed, and so Stewart bought none of the stock for himself. But under the terms of the subscription Stewart was entitled to an underwriter's commission of $2\frac{1}{2}$ percent. This commission also he refused to accept, directing his treasurer to turn the money over to "a fund for the purpose of promoting temperance and morality among the men through the advancement of their general welfare."

He had begun promoting the Scriptures as enthusiastically as he had once searched for oil, and his religious crusade was getting mixed up with his business. In 1909 he appointed a man named Robert Watchorn to the strategic position of treasurer of Union Oil. Watchorn had been a commissioner of immigration and had had no experience in either finance or oil. When asked to explain this curious appointment Mr. Stewart said, "Mr. Watchorn is a very popular man. Every time he appears at a Presbyterian Convention he is greeted with a Chautauqua salute."* Stewart's board of directors accepted their president's choice of a treasurer, but with heavy misgivings. To many, Mr. Watchorn seemed completely incompetent.

Together, Messrs. Stewart and Watchorn plunged the Union Oil Company into a period of heady high finance and frenzied borrowing, not only for the company itself but for the various religious institutions and endeavors that Mr. Stewart was funding. Money was needed now not just to expand oil-exploration programs but also to found the Bible Institute of Los Angeles, to recruit and support Christian missionaries in China, and to "provide a Bible for every Chinaman." By 1910, Stewart had persuaded his stockholders to approve a bonded indebtedness of $20,000,000 for the Union Oil Company, and California banks were beginning to view the Union situation with alarm. The Crocker Bank had turned Watchorn down when he had approached them for money, and A. P. Giannini—who distrusted oil companies to begin with—had refused to meet with either of the two zealots. Watchorn then turned to New York banks and Wall Street, where, ironically, he found the Jewish investment-banking firm of Hallgarten & Company willing to help finance the spread of the Christian doctrine throughout the world. Hallgarten agreed to underwrite a $5,000,000 bond issue for Union Oil, but its price was high. Hallgarten demanded that Union agree not to sell more than $1,500,000 worth of new stock during the next thirty years without Hallgarten's consent. Mr. Watchorn signed this agreement.

The problem of Watchorn and his adventures in the money markets was now aggravated by the fact that Lyman Stewart was suddenly taken gravely ill. His life hung in the balance; he was not expected to live. This had the effect of giving Watchorn much more freedom to manipulate Union Oil's affairs than he might have had if Stewart had been up and about. By 1913 things were in a terrible tangle. The cost of supplying Bibles to the Chinese had risen to the

* Nineteenth-century revivalist tent shows were known as Chautauquas.

point where George H. Burr & Company of New York, to which the company owed $1,500,000, was pressing for payment and threatening to throw Union Oil into receivership if its obligations were not met immediately. Another note, for a million dollars, was due in May, and still another, also for a million, was due in August, when a fourth note for $700,000 would fall due as well. These were merely the Union Oil Company's obligations. In addition, Mr. Stewart's precious Bible Institute had overspent its budget in proselytizing and Bible distribution and was a million dollars in debt itself.

Typically, the company's pious treasurer put the needs of the Bible Institute ahead of those of the company. Mr. Watchorn approached Mr. Stewart on his sickbed and presented him with a blank piece of paper which he asked Stewart to sign. Watchorn would, he assured Stewart, fill in the necessary details later. What Watchorn filled in above Stewart's signature was a bizarre document tantamount to an option giving the bearer the right to buy all the Stewart family holdings for $150 a share. Watchorn then sold the option, for $1,000,000, to another oil man, Eugene de Salba, of the General Petroleum Company, and the proceeds, in the form of various checks and stock certificates, were turned over to the Bible Institute.

When Will Stewart discovered what his father had done he was appalled. So were the other members of Union's board. Not only had a million dollars slipped from the hands of the company into the hands of God but the entire future of the company was at stake. Should Mr. De Salba be able to obtain the financing to exercise his option—the option gave him a year in which to do so—the company would be his.

Also appalled, when he came to his senses, was Lyman Stewart. He had been delirious when he signed Watchorn's blank sheet and had had no idea of the stipulations Watchorn would later write in. Everyone had assumed that Stewart was at death's door, but, far from it, he was back on his feet and perkier than before. Angrily, he confronted Watchorn and informed him that his career with Union Oil was over.

But Lyman Stewart's troubles were not. There was an anxious year to face while the company waited to see whether Mr. De Salba would be able to exercise Watchorn's option. (As it turned out, De Salba would not.) In the meantime there was a more pressing and present problem. The $1,500,000 note to George H. Burr & Company was now due; Union Oil was without the funds to pay it, and the New York firm had dispatched an agent, John H. Garrigues, to collect it. Garrigues was not at all a bankerly Wall Street type. He believed, he said, in occult powers, and saw himself as a kind of Moses figure who had been sent west to "save" California and to accomplish four other things in the process: acquire control of the lumber industry of the Pacific Coast, acquire control of the oil industry, dominate and control California finance, and change and direct West Coast politics. It was a large order, but Garrigues flamboyantly announced, "Nothing can prevent me from accomplishing my purpose, not even Standard Oil, and you can get on my band wagon and ride through to the goal, or you can get in the road and get run over!"

Lyman Stewart decided to get on the Garrigues bandwagon, particularly as Garrigues offered a palliative of sorts. He could, he said, get Union Oil an additional $1,100,000 from Burr & Company, but on two conditions: that he be made the new treasurer of Union Oil, at $25,000 a year, and that he be given a free hand in the company's finances. Stewart agreed, explaining to his board that Garrigues offered the company "insurance—as cheap insurance as we could get."

Garrigues' first move as treasurer was to suspend all Union Oil Company dividends indefinitely, a decision that infuriated the company's stockholders. Lyman Stewart was forced to write a letter to Union stockholders explaining that despite the fact that "the volume of the company's business has doubled in the last four years . . . growing by leaps and bounds year after year from 10 million dollars gross sales . . . to 20 million dollars on a capital of 32 million dollars . . . the entire outstanding indebtedness . . . of the Union Oil Company of California . . . totals $12,653,000." This indebtedness, Stewart continued somewhat glibly, had "been brought about chiefly by too much prosperity."*

---

* *Black Bonanza* by Frank J. Taylor and Earl M. Welty.

Then, in 1914, more bad news came from New York. Hallgarten & Company reported that it could not carry out the terms of its original agreement and the final million dollars of its underwriting operation would not be forthcoming. By reneging on its part of the bargain, Hallgarten of course released Union Oil from the crippling promise it had made to let Hallgarten supervise its stock-selling operations for thirty years. But the need for cash was now desperate, and at this point Will Stewart took matters into his own hands. He rounded up a syndicate of financiers in Los Angeles who agreed to lend the company the million dollars it had counted on from Hallgarten, but on one condition: Lyman Stewart must step aside as president. "We feel," said John Jardine, the head of the new syndicate, "that on account of the option which Lyman Stewart had given Watchorn, the investing public had to a certain extent lost confidence in the Union Oil Company." This was putting it very politely. On April 14, 1914, Lyman Stewart submitted his resignation. It was immediately accepted by the board, and Will Stewart was elected president. His father was pushed upstairs and given the honorary title of Chairman of the Board. Thus, for lack of a million dollars, Lyman Stewart lost control of his thirty million-dollar company.

He was understandably bitter, and the rift between father and son widened. Lyman Stewart complained that his son was "too conservative," and Will Stewart replied that he wouldn't be so conservative if his father hadn't driven the company into debt by trying to buy up all the oil land in California and simultaneously give away Bibles to the entire population of China. Will Stewart had more urgent problems on his hands than his aging father. He had now to deal with the obstreperous Garrigues and his grandiose schemes and to regain the financial control of the company that his father had granted to the easterner. He also had a rebel in his midst in the person of Ed Doheny, one of his own directors, who now wanted to take over the company as part of a grand plan to combine a group of independent California companies and form the Pan American Oil and Transportation Company. Doheny's ambition was to create a company big enough to compete on equal terms with the Big Two of the oil world—Standard Oil and Royal Dutch Shell.

But Lyman Stewart was not at all ready to be put out to pasture. He had been recently widowed, and in August 1916 he married his young secretary, Lulu Crowell. Lulu had been one of Stewart's evangelical assistants. The bridegroom was seventy-six years old. The break between father and son was now complete.

THE ASSOCIATED Oil Company, one of Union Oil's chief rivals, had in the meantime acquired a new stockholder. He was James Irvine, Jr., who was already consolidating one of the great fortunes of California.

Irvine's father, also James, had, like Lyman Stewart, descended from Scotch-Irish Presbyterian stock (there is a town of Irvine in Scotland), had emigrated from Belfast in 1846 at age nineteen, and in 1849, like so many others, had joined the gold stampede to California—aboard the *Humboldt*, by way of the Isthmus of Panama. One of his traveling companions on the *Humboldt* was Collis P. Huntington, also young and seeking his fortune.

For a while the first Irvine had worked as a miner, but he soon became disillusioned with gold as an avenue to wealth and joined a relative in San Francisco who had a prosperous grocery business. With what money he could save, Irvine began investing in San Francisco real estate, and soon he too was prospering modestly. But his fortunes took their most dramatic turn when he made the acquaintance of three former New Englanders, the brothers Benjamin and Thomas Flint and their cousin, Llewellyn Bixby. Having made some money in gold, the Flints and Bixby had acquired some ranch land in Monterey County, which they had decided would be ideal for raising sheep. Accordingly they had gone to Iowa to purchase a flock and, in 1853, had returned with a herd of nearly two thousand sheep, eleven yoke of oxen, two cows, four horses, two wagons, and the cumbersome camping equipment needed to cross more than half the continent—plains, rivers, the Rocky Mountains and the Sierras. Daunting as this shepherding project was, the three young men had made it back to California without a mishap, though the journey had taken them eight months. Their feat impressed James Irvine. Clearly these were tough men. So was he.

There had been no money to be made in sheep raising. Wool was in great demand, because the cotton industry in the South had been devastated by the Civil War. At the same time, the annual cost of herding, pasturing, shearing, and caring for a herd of sheep was only thirty-five cents a head. Each animal yielded an average of six and a half pounds of wool a year, which could be sold for anywhere from eighteen to thirty-five cents a pound.

By 1864 two facts had become apparent to Irvine, the Flints and Bixby. It was the worst—and would turn out to be the last—year of the Great Drought in southern California. The huge herds of cattle that had once roamed the grand ranchos in the south were all but decimated, and the Spanish-descended rancheros were desperate for cash. Vast tracts were being taken over by mortgagors, and other lands were for sale at a fraction of their former worth. Also, the four men noted that for some reason the sheep had fared somewhat better than the cattle in the drought. Three adjoining parcels of land particularly interested James Irvine and his friends—the Rancho Lomas de Santiago, which belonged to Teodocio Yorba, the Rancho San Joaquin, which belonged to José Sepulveda, and part of Rancho Santiago de Santa Ana, which belonged to José Antonio Yorba and Juan Pablo Peralta. Pooling their resources, Irvine, Bixby, and the Flints bought it all for about thirty-five cents an acre, or roughly fifty thousand dollars—120,000 acres, stretching from the Santa Ana mountains to thirteen miles of virgin Pacific coastline.

Because Irvine had been able to invest an amount equal to that of the other partners combined, he became the dominant partner and the group's financial mainstay. Soon the Irvine-Flint-Bixby group was grazing 30,000 head of sheep on the new ranch. Within a few years there would be more than 50,000 head. In 1866, James Irvine married Nettie Rice, who came from Cleveland and brought with her a small dowry. The following year their first and only child, James, Jr., was born, and, by 1876, James Irvine, Sr., was able to buy out his partners for $150,000. Now all the land was his.

The first Irvine's acquaintance with Collis Huntington on the boat had not immediately blossomed into friendship. Nor did it later.

In the 1870s one of the popular methods the Southern Pacific employed to obtain land for its roads was simply to march in and take it—with or without the owner's permission and often against his express wishes. Often this would be done on weekends, when the courts were closed and owners could not obtain injunctions against the land-grabbers. By Monday morning, when the tracks were laid, protests were futile, since in most communities the railroads' resources for buying judicial opinions were superior to those of the ranchers. The Southern Pacific had been trying for some time to obtain a right-of-way through the Irvine ranch in order to lay track between Santa Ana and San Diego. Irvine had refused to countenance locomotives charging through his herds of easily frightened sheep. One Saturday afternoon, after the courts had closed for the weekend and when a Southern Pacific crew had arrived at the ranch to begin putting down track anyway, James Irvine formed a posse of ranch hands, and with shotguns and rifles blasting, drove off the railroad crew. It was the last time Huntington's men tangled with James Irvine.

When Irvine died in 1886 his nineteen-year-old son James, Jr.— or J.I., as he was called—inherited the big ranch. J.I. did not get his land without a fight, however. According to his father's will, he could not claim his inheritance until age twenty-five, and the will gave the trustees of the estate the option of putting the property up for sale at public auction. This they attempted to do, and J.I. very nearly lost his land—for $1,385,000—and would have except for some confusion in the bidding process. The case languished in the courts until 1892, when, at last, J.I. was of legal age to claim the inheritance.

J.I. was, if anything, physically even tougher than his father—tall, muscular, lean as a whip. He was also stubborn, autocratic, and something of an eccentric. He once rode a high-wheeled bicycle— its front wheel nearly as tall as he was—from San Francisco to San Diego and back again, just to prove that he could do it. J.I.'s nature was a collection of contradictions. As a disciplinarian on his ranch he was despotic. In 1912, when a farmer named Joe Matlock attacked the daughter of an Irvine ranch hand and then fled to the hills above the ranch, J.I. pursued him for six hours with a two-hundred-man posse, expending a deputy sheriff and incurring a number of wounded before finally killing the man with a shot in the head. J.I. was a self-proclaimed misanthrope who liked to say that most animals were better company than most people, and he was a crude practical joker as well. He enjoyed particularly setting off fireworks under the chairs of female guests, which, however, didn't prevent him from being an enthusiastic womanizer. And yet, for all his somewhat unpleasant traits, there was another side to J.I. He was a gifted artist and drew dreamily romantic pencil and charcoal sketches of landscapes and women's faces. He played the piano and he wrote poetry. Though a college dropout, he read extensively, particularly on scientific subjects. He became interested in the pioneering airplane developments of Glenn L. Martin, who used an Irvine pasture for his first takeoff in 1909. In 1925 he invited the Nobel physicist Albert A. Michelson to use a mile-long strip of the ranch for the celebrated experiment in which Michelson first measured the speed of light with high accuracy. And yet uninvited guests to J.I.'s ranch were sent away with broken guns or broken heads.

J.I.'s greatest passion was for his land and what he saw as its limitless possibilities. One reason why he had invested heavily in Associated Oil was the chance that oil might be discovered on it. It never was, but in time the ranch would support much else—not only enormous herds of sheep but also thousands of head of cattle, as well as vineyards, citrus orchards, walnut groves, persimmon and avocado fields, fields of beans, sugar beets, tomatoes, alfalfa, and a good deal more. For more than a hundred years the great Irvine ranch would remain in J.I.'s family, one of the largest unsubdivided pieces of property since the days of Henry Miller—an area four times larger than the entire city of San Francisco. The ranch would also, as we shall see, be the scene of more bitterness, dispute, hard feeling, bloodshed, and death by violence than has afflicted any other California family.

PART TWO

THE EASY SPENDERS

CHAPTER NINE
Throwing It Around

ONE OF the pleasant advantages of owning one's own silver mine was that one never had to worry about where one's flatware was coming from. When, in the 1880s, John and Louise Mackay decided to order a silver table service, Mackay had 14,719 ounces of silver sent from his mine to Tiffany's with instructions to make his service as heavy and ornate as possible. Tiffany's took him at his word and created a design so elaborate that not a single visible area of the surface was without ornamentation. Worked into the design were shamrocks, for Mackay's native Ireland, and thistles, for his wife's Scottish forebears. Each piece bore the Mackay monogram, as well as the Mackay "family crest," which Tiffany and the Mackays devised together. At the time, the Mackay silver was the most spectacular the store had ever produced, and much attention to it was given by the press. There were a few sly gibes about the family crest, since, before John Mackay, there had never been a Mackay family crest, but none of this fazed the Mackays.

A single Mackay celery vase, though only sixteen inches high, contained 150 ounces of silver. A pair of candelabra, thirty-six inches tall, held fifty-eight candles and weighed more than 40 pounds. The complete service, 1350 pieces in all,* was shipped to the Mackays' London house, where it "became a tradition to use it at stately receptions for members of the Victorian court and the families of the great houses of Europe." In Europe the press, as well as society, was much kinder to the Mackays than New York or San Francisco had been, and Louise Mackay was described as "a great lady in the tight circle of international society . . . mastering several languages and all the social graces of the newly acquired fortune."

Back in San Francisco, the reports of the Mackays' European successes were read with dismay, envy, and no small amount of confusion. What, after all, did the upstart Mackays possess that entitled them to dinner invitations from the Prince of Wales and Princess Alexandra? Try as it might to forget it, San Francisco kept being reminded that San Francisco was not London or Paris or Rome or Madrid, nor was San Francisco New York, Philadelphia, or Boston. San Francisco had been an almost overnight creation; its rush to big-city status had been too headlong, its rich families had emerged too rapidly, and there were still embarrassing rough edges. Compared with eastern cities, everything about San Francisco seemed painfully imitative and second-rate.

San Francisco avidly followed the doings of East Coast society, of New York's Mrs. William Astor and her arbiter, Ward McAllister, who had codified and delineated society by the simple expedient of limiting it to the number of people who would fit in Mrs. Astor's ballroom. He had created New York's Four Hundred, the unquestioned list of people who counted. San Francisco had no such list. Suddenly the mere spending of money—on houses and jewels and yachts—was not enough. Spending money was simply too easy.

* Against today's prices, the Mackays' silver service was a bargain—it cost only $125.000.

Money alone could not purchase either respect or respectability, nor did it define social class. The elusive ingredient that San Francisco lacked, of course, was *tradition*. But where could one find tradition in a city that had risen from mud streets in a little over thirty years? Could one buy tradition the way the Mackays had bought a family crest? There seemed to be no one in San Francisco who could answer these questions. Then, all at once, there was.

His name was Ned Greenway, and he was, of all things, a wine salesman. He had come to San Francisco in the 1870s as the West Coast representative of Mumm's champagne, and because Mumm's was a French company, serving Mumm's champagne quickly became a San Francisco status symbol. Ned Greenway not only sold his champagne to San Francisco society but also put away a good deal of his product himself. He liked to boast that nobody in America drank more wine than he and that he often tossed back as many as twenty-five bottles a day. The secret, he explained, was to intersperse the bottles of champagne with quaffs of beer. Because his large wine consumption tended to make him gain weight, he restricted his diet of solids to cookies and pickled limes. Insufficient though these traits might seem for turning Ned Greenway into the darling of San Francisco society, that is exactly what they did. Before long no gathering was considered important without Ned Greenway and his Mumm's.

To San Franciscans, at least, Ned Greenway seemed to possess an almost daunting sophistication. In the first place, he was from the East—from Baltimore, where he claimed an ancient and aristocratic lineage. And he knew how to *do* things, things San Franciscans had always wondered about. He knew how to use a finger bowl, and how to remove it, along with the doily, before the dessert was passed, and how to separate the fork and spoon that arrived with the plate. He pronounced it acceptable to eat asparagus with the fingers. He knew that if the wine was spilled at the table, it was not proper to try to wipe it up. He could read a French menu, and even spoke French, larding his conversations with it. He loved to dance and drink champagne all night. He never rose until four in the afternoon, and when he did he immediately put on evening clothes.

Ned Greenway dazzled. He dazzled even the beautiful Jennie Flood, and for a while it was rumored that he was engaged to her. In San Francisco, Ned Greenway spoke of the famous Baltimore tradition, its Cotillon—spelled always with but a single *i*—and lamented that San Francisco did not have a similar one. He, after all, knew how to perform all the traditional cotillion figures. By the mid-1880s, Ned Greenway's position in San Francisco society was so secure that he decided he himself would become San Francisco's answer to Ward McAllister. When he elected himself to this post, there was no one in San Francisco to dispute him. In fact, the idea was greeted with great enthusiasm.

What Greenway needed, first, was a West Coast equivalent to Mrs. Astor. The woman he chose was Mrs. Eleanor Martin. Eleanor Martin gave frequent though dreadful parties—but that was one of her qualifications. So did Mrs. Astor. Conversations at her dinner table were so stiff and difficult that they were agonizing, but her guests felt so fortunate to be invited that they dared not risk the slightest lapse of taste or manners for fear of being banished from her circle forever. Her rules of conduct were strict. Any woman who drank more than one glass of champagne was never invited again. Divorced persons were never permitted past her front doorstep. Socially, she claimed impeccable credentials, tracing her ancestry far back beyond that of the Huntingtons, Crockers, Stanfords, and Hopkinses. Her brother had been a governor of California, and her brother-in-law, Peter Donahue, had founded the San Francisco Gas Works. To Mrs. Astor that might not have sounded like much at all, but, after all, this was San Francisco. Mrs. Martin was not as rich as Caroline Astor either—her husband's money had been made in street railways and the gas company—but Eleanor Martin possessed that one rare ingredient so essential to any social leader: the power to intimidate, to make everyone in her presence feel immediately inferior. Her rudeness was legendary and her snubs were legion. One never knew when one might displease her or where one stood with her. Physically too Eleanor Martin was overpowering, an immense woman with a spacious *poitrine* capable of displaying an inordinate amount of jewelry. According to Frances Moffat in *Dancing on the Brink of the World*, "She sailed through San Francisco society with the serene authority of a battleship."

When Ned Greenway approached her and suggested that the two of them might "organize" San Francisco society, Eleanor Martin agreed that this was a splendid idea. What they needed next was a list, a tabulation of who amounted to how much, and who would be in and who out. This did not take them long to complete. Mrs. Martin's immediate circle of friends had to be included, along with certain obligatory Crockers and Huntingtons and good customers for Mumm's champagne. Thereafter the invitations went out to San Francisco's first annual Bachelors' Cotillion.

By 1887 a number of San Francisco houses had ballrooms, but none was deemed sufficiently spacious for the event. Once again, San Francisco was not New York, and the Odd Fellows Hall was selected. On the night of the Cotillion, Greenway and Mrs. Martin led the quadrille—Greenway blowing a whistle and announcing loudly how to execute the elaborate figures—and were followed by a confused but enthusiastic assemblage of guests. Although San Francisco had never seen anything remotely like it before, the evening, when it was over, was considered an unqualified success. At last San Francisco had a tradition.

Overnight San Francisco society became newsworthy. No longer did local editors need to rely on the East for stories of the gentry. Cannily, Mike de Young hired Ned Greenway to write a society column for the *Chronicle*, whereupon W. R. Hearst immediately hired an ex-Mississippi riverboat captain, William Chambliss, to perform the same function for the *Examiner*. Each journalist expended most of his energies deploring the activities and denigrating the subjects of his competitor's column. Mr. Chambliss had a particularly vitriolic pen, which Hearst adored. Attacking the Greenway-Martin list of worthies invited to the Bachelors' Cotillion, Chambliss averred that they should all be "relegated without unnecessary delay to the ranks of colored society," which by his definition included not only blacks but Orientals, Latin Americans, and most Europeans. The

Crockers, Chambliss wrote, had "Indian blood" and were therefore "foreigners." And a great deal was made of Mike de Young's being a Jew.

Very few of California's new millionaires had at that point considered trying to establish themselves socially through philanthropy, and none seemed less likely to try than Leland Stanford. Since the birth of his only son in 1868, Stanford and his wife had seemed interested in little else than the child. Leland, Jr., was unmercifully spoiled, pampered by nurses and parents alike, supplied with all manner of toys, entertainments, and pets. Nevertheless, with the passage of time he showed promise of becoming a bright and attractive young man, with far more intelligence than his mother or father. But at age fourteen, while traveling with his parents in Italy, he was stricken with typhoid fever. Two years later, just short of his sixteenth birthday, he died.

His parents were inconsolable, and according to a persistent tradition, Leland Stanford cried out to his wife, "The children of California shall be our children!" Whereupon he resolved to donate a great university "To the Memory of Leland Stanford, Jr., and the Glory of God." According to another tradition, God himself— through a New York spiritual medium, Maud Lord Drake—ordered the Stanfords to create the university. Whatever the case, all the care and devotion that the Stanfords had lavished on their son they soon lavished on their university.

The Stanfords' grand plan was not greeted enthusiastically. The chosen location struck most Californians as peculiar and impractical. Stanford wanted to build near his country house in Palo Alto, overlooking the gardens where his son had once played. The San Francisco Chronicle retorted that the University of California at Berkeley, just across the bay from San Francisco, had never attracted more than three hundred students. Northern California, it was felt, had no need for another university, and anyway, the best education for a red-blooded Californian was the school of hard knocks. Eastern newspapers were even less kind, one commenting that "there is about as much need for a new university in California as for an asylum of decayed sea captains in Switzerland." Even educators offered Stanford little encouragement, pointing out to him that the name itself, the Leland Stanford Junior University, would cause people to think it was a junior college.

Still, Stanford proceeded with his plans. The great landscape architect Frederick Law Olmsted, who had designed New York's Central Park, was commissioned to design the campus. David Starr Jordan, a distinguished eastern educator, agreed to serve as the university's first president. And when the university opened its doors on October 1, 1891, the first student to register was a young man named Herbert Hoover.

Notwithstanding these auspicious beginnings, there was trouble ahead. Two years later Leland Stanford died, and his estate was found to be seriously depleted. His battle with Huntington, it transpired, had cost him more than the presidency of the railroad. All at once, new contracts for the salaries of Stanford professors had to be amended to read "or as much of it as shall be available." To the rescue came Stanford's widow. While her husband was alive Jane Stanford had seemed a colorless figure, except for her jewelry collection. Now she emerged as a woman of energy and resourcefulness. She sued Collis P. Huntington to recover sums that, she claimed, he had wrongfully transferred from her late husband. She carried her case through the courts and ultimately received from the California Supreme Court a decision in her favor. She persuaded, one by one, all of the major American railroads to haul her private car without charge while she went on an extensive cross-country fund-raising tour. She trimmed her own expansive style of living and sold her big houses, turning over what she realized from the sales to the university. She journeyed to England to pay a personal call on Queen Victoria to see whether the queen might be interested in buying the famous Stanford jewelry collection. The queen was not, but Mrs. Stanford was able to sell her jewels, including the four sets of diamonds that had been Queen Isabella's, elsewhere. The beneficiary of all this cash was the university.

Jane Lathrop Stanford had been the recipient of one of Eleanor

Martin's famous snubs. The Stanfords, Mrs. Martin had decreed, were "below the salt," and they had not received invitations to the Bachelors' Cotillion. Now Mrs. Stanford was proving herself to be by far the more important and influential lady. She even decided finally to bury the hatchet in the longstanding Stanford-Huntington feud. Not long before her death in 1905, according to Oscar Lewis in *The Big Four*, Jane Stanford presented herself in Collis P. Huntington's office, held out her hand, and said, "Mr. Huntington, I have come to make my peace with you." The flabbergasted Mr. Huntington took both her hands in his, sat her down in a chair, mopped his brow, and said, "Well, I declare!"

CHAPTER TEN

Prince and Pauper

AMONG THE disputatious members of San Francisco's new-rich upper crust there was one couple who had an unusual distinction: practically everybody in San Francisco liked them. They were Mr. and Mrs. William Ralston. William Ralston was a six-foot-tall handsome Ohioan who had worked as a clerk on a Mississippi River steamboat, come to California in 1848 with all the others, invested in railroads, vineyards, and real estate, and in the 1850s, when he opened his Bank of California, had become one of the richest men in the city. Thanks to William Ralston, a number of other San Francisco families became rich through banking—the Breckenridges, Tevises, Newlandses, and the Millses, to name a few, most of whom were collaterally related to the man Ralston made richest of all, William Sharon. And yet, as a result of one of the most stunning instances of business treachery in the history of California, there was never to be a Ralston family fortune at all. In fact, William Ralston's widow would be left without so much as a house to live in.

Ralston must certainly be classed among the robber barons of the era, but one tends to forgive him because he was such a pleasant man. He and his wife loved to entertain a hundred house guests at a time in their enormous house in suburban Belmont, and Ralston was notoriously generous with his money as well as his hospitality. He lent millions of dollars to friends and was known as the softest touch in town. He built the spectacular Palace Hotel in San Francisco, which had 800 rooms and was at the time the largest and most expensive hotel in the world. (It was much larger, actually, than San Francisco really needed—having then a population of only 200,000—but Ralston had faith in the city's growth.) By the 1860s the press was calling William Ralston "the father of San Francisco."

In 1864, William Sharon, down-and-out, drifted into town. Sharon was on the rebound from unsuccessful gold and silver speculations in Nevada, but his father-in-law knew William Ralston and took the mendicant to see the city's famous Good Samaritan. It was a meeting that changed the destinies of both men. As he did most people, Ralston liked Sharon immediately and asked what he could do for him. Sharon replied that he needed a loan and a job.

He got both—$15,000 in cash and an assignment to conduct some bank business in Nevada. Will Sharon completed the mission successfully and returned to San Francisco, where he suggested to his new boss that the Bank of California open a Nevada branch. Ralston liked the idea, and presently Will Sharon was put in charge of the operation across the Sierra. Now Sharon was on his way. Since he was able to keep in closer touch with the diggings in and around Virginia City, his mining investments were now much more sophisticated than they had been before. Besides, he had the financial backing of Ralston's Bank of California. Presently William Sharon's investments were yielding him an income of two thousand dollars a day. Ralston placed more and more trust in Sharon's judgments, and in the process the two men became, as far as could be discerned, the closest of personal friends. Among the most frequent guests at the Ralstons' Belmont mansion were Mr. and Mrs. William Sharon.

Once Sharon had money, he decided to acquire some respectability, and, accordingly, he purchased a United States senatorship from the state of Nevada by bribing the Nevada legislature with shares of one of his silver stocks. This was a common practice, although at the time there were indications that Sharon's manipulations were less than usually trustworthy. Once "elected" to the Senate, Sharon quietly sold his own shares of the stock, thereby driving the price down for all the others. The Nevada legislators were outraged, if clearly in no position to complain.

On August 26, 1875, there was a run on the Bank of California. Such occurrences were not at all uncommon. Whenever the volatile gold and silver markets fluctuated sharply, or when rumors of an important new strike circulated, depositors descended on the banks to withdraw cash for other investment. But the August 26 run was particularly heavy, and the bank was forced to close its doors half an hour early, leaving hundreds of customers outside the pseudo-Roman bank building on Montgomery Street still shouting and clamoring to get in. The run on his bank had come at a particularly bad time for William Ralston. He had been lending money to himself for his hotel as well as to support his own opulent life style. The house of cards he had built out of his borrowing now seemed about to collapse, and the rumor in the financial community was that the Bank of California would never open its doors again. This seemed confirmed when, the following day, the bank remained closed.

That day, the twenty-seventh, William Ralston did two things. First, he drafted and signed a "deed of trust," the purpose of which was to convey all his property, real and personal, to a trustee who, if all else failed, could use the instrument to reach a settlement with the bank's creditors. The deed of trust would serve as a last-ditch form of insurance. The trustee named was William Sharon. Whether Sharon was privy to the details of this instrument at the time has never been clear; doubtless he was aware of its existence. In fact, it is possible that the deed of trust was prepared at Will Sharon's suggestion. Next, around noon, Ralston called a meeting of his board of directors, which included Will Sharon, and grimly outlined the situation to them. He owed the bank four million dollars. He owed

Sharon two million. And to a group of other creditors he owed something more than three and a half million. His own assets amounted to only four and a half million, less than half of what he owed. But Ralston urged calm. He had weathered other such panics and knew that runs on banks were prompted primarily by emotional and psychological factors, the result of hysteria more than anything else. He asked for time. He suggested that the Bank of California remain closed for an indefinite period while it waited for the business climate to improve. Then the bank would open its doors again and proceed with business as usual. He asked his directors to have faith in him.

The directors listened to Ralston's recital glumly. They then asked for a few minutes in which to consider the situation and requested that during their deliberations Mr. Ralston leave the room, which he did. William Sharon then leaped to his feet and demanded that Ralston be asked to step down. A vote was taken and a majority of the directors agreed. Then, although Sharon had initiated the vote, another director, Darius O. Mills, was delegated to bear the bad news. Mr. Ralston took his directors' decision calmly. He penned a brief letter of resignation. Then he left his office and went directly to the Neptune swimming club at North Beach, where he often exercised, put on a bathing suit, and swam out into the Bay. Two hours later his dead body was carried ashore.

The immediate assumption was that he had committed suicide. But Ralston's wife and family were not at all sure. Ralston, they said, had assured his wife the morning of his death that even if he should lose everything, he was ready to start all over again, that, if necessary, they would live on as little as a hundred dollars a month, as they had once done. After all, he was still in his prime. To be sure, the family said, the shock of Sharon's betrayal at the board meeting coupled with the shock of the cold water of the Bay might have brought on a heart attack or stroke. But they did not think so. An autopsy revealed that there was no water in Ralston's lungs, indicating that he had not drowned, and that there was "congestion" in his brain, indicating that he could have been suffocated. The New

York Life Insurance Company agreed with Mrs. Ralston that there was no question of suicide and promptly paid the widow the benefits of a $65,000 policy.

Mr. Sharon is said to have reacted to his friend's death in two quite different ways, both of them recorded in George D. Lyman's *Ralston's Ring.* According to one report: " 'All I have I owe to him [Sharon cried out] and to protect his name and memory I will spend every dollar of it.' Suddenly Sharon laid his head upon the mantelpiece and sobbed like a child." According to the other, he was much less grieved: Several days after Ralston's death Sharon is said to have been approached by John Mackay. (Mackay himself might have had reason to feel guilty about Ralston's death; two of his partners, Flood and O'Brien, had helped instigate the run on the bank by announcing a day or so earlier that they intended to withdraw their funds to start a bank of their own.) Mackay is said to have asked Sharon, "Couldn't they revive him?" And Sharon is said to have replied, "For a few minutes I was afraid they would."

Whatever the truth of the matter, the deed of trust provided that everything that had been Ralston's was now William Sharon's, to do with as he wished. And now that the Bank of California was his, Sharon took his late friend's advice—and waited. A few weeks later the bank quietly opened its doors again. The atmosphere of panic that had existed in August was over, and the bank's business of handling deposits and withdrawals proceeded quite normally. To the fickle press William Sharon was a hero, "the man who saved the Bank of California." Though Ralston's widow sued Sharon over the deed of trust, in an out-of-court settlement of her lawsuit she was persuaded to accept $250,000. That, plus her insurance money, was all she ever got.

CHAPTER ELEVEN
Wedding Bells

PERHAPS AS a result of Ned Greenway's efforts to place the battling stars of San Francisco's upper crust into some sort of fixed planetary system, by the turn of the century intermarriage among San Francisco's wealthy families began to be surprisingly common, with marriages tending to take place "within the set." The Newhalls married Spreckelses and O'Briens, the Metcalfs married Huntingtons, the Hendersons and Redingtons married Crockers, the Nickels married Morses (of the Code family), and the Meins married Nickels. To be sure, no Spreckels ever married a de Young, nor did a de Young marry a Hearst, nor did a Huntington ever marry a Stanford, but the Tobins married Fays and de Youngs, the Thieriots married Tobins and de Youngs, the Olivers married Fays, the Millers married members of the Folger family (of Folger's coffee), and the Fays married Millers, Meins, and Tobins. Spreckelses married other Spreckelses.

Perhaps the most startling interclan marriage occurred within the Huntington family. Collis Huntington, like Leland Stanford, had spent much of his later life collecting residences. He had three large houses in California, a country home in Throgg's Neck, New York, and a $250,000 "camp" in the Adirondacks when he decided that he also needed a New York City address. At the cost of several millions, an imposing pile was erected for him at the corner of Fifth Avenue and Fifty-seventh Street. When the New York house was completed, however, Huntington could not be persuaded to live in it, having begun to subscribe to the superstition that men built houses only in order to die in them. He had already begun to prepare for this eventuality by ordering for himself in New York's Woodlawn Cemetery (for another $250,000) a huge marble mausoleum, an edifice that took eight years to construct. (When in the end Mr. Huntington moved into the mausoleum, his widow moved into the Fifth Avenue house. She used it periodically until her own death in 1925, when the property was sold for $3,800,000 and razed to make way for a commercial building.)

Huntington had been married twice. His first wife, the former Elizabeth Stoddard, was so shy and retiring that for years San Francisco was not sure whether Huntington had a wife or not. They had no children, but adopted a daughter, Clara Prentice, who was the daughter of Mrs. Huntington's dead sister. When the first Mrs. Huntington died, Huntington—with what seemed like unseemly speed—married again, this time a pretty widow named Arabella Worsham. Again there were no natural children, but the Huntingtons adopted the new Mrs. Huntington's son by her previous marriage. Thus Collis P. Huntington became the legal father of his first wife's niece and his own stepson. When Huntington died, a large share of his estate went to his widow, and some two million dollars was bequeathed to the adopted Clara. A much larger sum, however, was willed to Huntington's favorite nephew, Henry E. Huntington, the son of Collis Huntington's older brother, Solon Huntington.

Henry Huntington had in the meantime married Mary Alice Prentice, the sister of his uncle's adopted daughter, thus turning two sisters into cousins by marriage as well, and making Clara Prentice

Huntington's stepmother her aunt. The complicated, near-incestuous Huntington family relationships seemed about to fall apart when Henry and Mary Alice Huntington were divorced. But the centrifugal forces were contained when Henry Huntington then married his uncle Collis' widow. This had the effect of consolidating two large shares of Collis Huntington's fortune, as well as turning Henry Huntington's ex-wife's sister into his own stepdaughter. "It is all," said Henry Huntington at the time, "perfectly legal." It did, however, make sorting out the kinships within the Huntington family something of a chore. And if Henry Huntington and Arabella Huntington Huntington had had offspring (which they did not), their children's mother would have also been their great-aunt, and their father their second cousin. (San Francisco's upper-crust Jewish families were equally intramural when it came to marriage. Two Neustadter brothers, Jacob and David, married two sisters, Dora and Josephine Dannenberg. Daniel Koshland married his first cousin, Eleanor Haas, of the Levi Strauss family, and went to work for the company that gave the world blue jeans.)

When the second-generation members of California's new-rich families were not marrying each other they were scouring the capitals of Europe in search of titles to marry. The second generation had discovered two sad and interrelated facts: first, that when one had "arrived" in a city such as San Francisco, there was hardly any place to go, and second, that as far as New York was concerned, Californians might be rich but they had no class. An invitation to Ned Greenway's cotillion might mark the capstone to a social career in San Francisco, but it meant nothing to Mrs. Astor, whose doors remained closed to Californians. Once again Californians looked abjectly to the East for inspiration and instruction on how to glide out of the cocoon of San Francisco and into the glittering world of the international butterflies.

One thing was quite clear about Caroline Astor: she loved titles. A count, archduke, prince, or earl immediately found himself invited to her house. Even an undistinguished British baronet was included in her original list of four hundred by virtue of the fact that his name was Sir Roderick Cameron. If Californians could acquire titles through marriage, then perhaps they could be accepted, not only in Europe, where, if the Mackays were an example, it was easy, but, so much more important, in the East.

The American vogue of exchanging American-made fortunes for European coronets is sometimes said to have started with Jennie Jerome, the daughter of a New York stockbroker, who married Lord Randolph Churchill in 1874, but actually this sort of thing had been going on for some time on the East Coast. In 1798, Anna Louise Bingham, the daughter of a wealthy Philadelphia merchant, married Alexander Baring, later to become Lord Ashburton. A few years later her sister Maria, not to be outdone, eloped at the age of fifteen and married the Count de Tilly. In 1824, Elizabeth Astor (daughter of the first John Jacob) had married Count Vincent Rumpff. Following Jennie Jerome's example, a number of other American heiresses had made titled marriages. Consuelo Vanderbilt married the Duke of Marlborough; Jay Gould's daughter Anna married, first, Count Paul Ernest Boniface de Castellane and, second, the count's cousin, the Duc de Talleyrand-Périgord. Alice Thaw of Pittsburgh married the Earl of Yarmouth. True, not many of these marriages worked out very happily for the women involved, and in nearly every case they cost the women—or their parents—considerable sums of money.

It was clear that East Coast women of noble rank outweighed those of the West Coast, and California was determined to catch up. By contrast, the social scene in San Francisco did seem a little primitive. For the debut of John D. Spreckels' daughters, Grace and Lillie, in 1899, the party was held at the Native Sons' Hall. Five hundred and fifty guests danced to the strains of Rosner's Hungarian Orchestra, which was hidden behind a bank of palms and ferns. In 1905, in the announcement of Grace Spreckels' engagement to Alexander Hamilton—no kin to the American Revolutionary statesman but a member of the family that owned the Baker & Hamilton Hardware Store—it was noted that the bride-to-be had "mastered the art of safely and successfully driving an automobile."

The first San Francisco woman to outfit herself with a foreign title was not, as it turned out, a member of one of the Big Four families or even a member of Eleanor Martin's set. She was none other than Flora Sharon, Will Sharon's daughter, whose father now owned the Palace Hotel. An aging Briton named Sir Thomas George Fermor-Hesketh had arrived in San Francisco aboard his yacht, the *Lancashire Witch*, had checked into the Palace, and, according to the story, had spotted Flora Sharon in an elevator. Sir Thomas made inquiries, and when the *Lancashire Witch* departed for England, Flora was Lady Hesketh, wife of the seventh baronet of Lancaster. Before the marriage William Sharon had settled a dowry of five million dollars on Flora. The year was 1880, and San Francisco saw how easily titles were acquired. One just bought them.

In the years that followed Flora Sharon's triumph San Francisco went on a regular title-shopping spree, going about it—in typical California fashion—with cheerful abandon, with money no object, throwing caution to the winds. Eleanor Martin's sister, Anna Donahue, decided that her daughter Mary Ellen needed a title and set about interviewing likely bachelors from the *Almanach de Gotha*. In 1883, Mrs. Donahue settled on the Prussian Baron Heinrich von Schroeder. At this point the Crockers, not to be upstaged, arranged for Mrs. Crocker's sister, Beth Sperry, of the little river town of Stockton, to become the Princess Poniatowski, wife of a prince who claimed descent from the kings of Poland. Clara Huntington, Collis Huntington's adopted daughter, and John Mackay's daughter, Eva, were friends—on the surface at least. When it came to men they were fiercely competitive. Both now wanted titles, and their mothers agreed that they should have them, though John Mackay was far from enthusiastic about the whole title-hunting craze. For a while the two young women were in a neck-and-neck position to capture the prize of Prince von Hatzfeld-Wildenberg. Clara Huntington got him in 1889, for a reported price of five million dollars, which seemed to have become the going rate. Eva Mackay was next reported engaged to Philippe de Bourbon, but this rumor turned out to be false. Eventually it was announced that Eva would marry Prince Fernando

Galatro-Colonna of Naples, which she did, and both new princesses agreed that they had come out equally, though Princess Eva ran away from her prince eight years later and never returned.

Perhaps the most astonishing California success story of the kind concerned Maud Burke of San Francisco. Tiny and plain, with an enormous nose and mouse-colored hair, and, according to a contemporary report, a fondness for wearing "more *maquillage* than her poor, pointed face could bear," she was nonetheless extraordinarily ambitious. Having failed socially in both her native city and New York, she followed the Mackay example and tried London, backed financially by a wealthy uncle. Here, having changed her name from Maud—which she had always hated—to Emerald, she became enormously popular. Despite her appearance she had discovered that all-important key to social success—a kind of perpetual motion. She was so intensely animated that she could not be overlooked in any gathering, and her rapid-fire, almost nonstop manner of speaking—coupled with a fine mastery of the art of gossip—quickly earned her a reputation as a wit. No lexicon of the *bons mots* of Emerald Burke survives her, nor is it likely that one will be compiled, because nothing she said was really funny. The secret was in her delivery.

Unlike her California sisters who had to pay for their titles, Emerald found one, in the elderly sportsman Sir Bache Cunard (of the steamship-company Cunards), who was not only a peer of the realm but also an extremely rich man. As the fabled Lady Emerald Cunard she became, over the next forty years, one of the dominant social forces in England and one of London's most powerful and popular hostesses. In the early 1930s she was a pivotal figure in "the Prince of Wales set" and was one of the principals in the heady swirl of events surrounding the prince's romance with Mrs. Wallis Warfield Spencer Simpson. Following Edward VIII's abdication, most of his former set quickly turned their backs on him and transferred their allegiance to the new monarch and his wife. But Emerald Cunard's position was more secure. In fact, the new queen is supposed to have said, shortly after George VI's succession to the throne, that she was afraid she and her husband would never be included in any of Emerald Cunard's entertainments. "You see," she said, "Emerald has so often said that Bertie and I are not fashionable."

In San Francisco all these marital developments drew a mixed reaction from the press. On the one hand, the titled marriages were always fully reported with as much enthusiastic detail as might be used to describe a great American victory in a major war. But some sour notes were sounded too. From his society-gossip columnist's desk at Hearst's *Examiner* the irascible William Chambliss was particularly acid. To Chambliss, these marriages to "foreigners" represented a grave economic threat to the state of California, if not to the entire country. He saw good red-blooded American money being leaked out of the country in which it had been made. He wrote:

A complete list of all the marriages of American women to titled men, for the past thirty-five years, shows that at least two hundred million dollars have gone away from this country in that period. . . . California has had more than her share to bear. Seven California girls have taken away from this state alone nearly twenty millions of dollars, or ten per cent of the entire amount, in exchange for seven titles, most of which are both shabby and shop worn.

Prince Colonna has probably cost, up to date, in the neighborhood of five million dollars. Prince Hatzfedt [sic] an equal if not larger sum. Prince Poniatowski came cheaper: a quarter of a million was about his price. Viscount Deerhurst and Lord Hesketh cost in the neighborhood of two and five million dollars respectively. The *dot* of Lord Wolesley's California bride was probably something under a million, but with moderate luck Sir Bache Cunard will get some two millions of old man Carpentier's accumulation of dollars, as his bride, Miss Burke, is the Outland Capitalist's favorite niece and should come in for a large slice of his estate.

At the time the above was written the granddaughter of Darius Ogden Mills (the director of the Bank of California who had carried the bad news to William Ralston) had not yet married the Earl of Granard. Had that happened sooner, Chambliss would doubtless have accused Californians of contributing an even larger share of cash to the European money drain.

And yet the infusion of aristocratic European blood into the roughhewn stock of the California pioneers may have had at least one desired and desirable effect. It may have helped Californians acquire, or at least make them aware of, such Old World qualities as gentility and taste. It may have helped them appreciate quiet understatement, whereas before that the California rich had relied primarily on garish ostentation and flashy shows to make it clear that they had money. The 1880 wedding of Flora Sharon to Sir Thomas Fermor-Hesketh was a glaring example of the latter. Held at Belmont, the huge white palace near San Mateo inherited by the bride's father, it took place in the inevitable music room, 70 feet long and 24 feet wide, lined with floor-to-ceiling mirrors and lighted by three thirty-branch crystal chandeliers in an attempt to put the Hall of Mirrors at Versailles into the shadows. The Sharon house, which, like the hotel, had once belonged to William Ralston, contained other interesting features. It had an even one hundred bedrooms. All the doorknobs were of sterling silver. In Ralston's day he had loved pointing out to his guests the features of the house, such as the clever device that opened the main gates. When one approached the house, across a short bridge, the weight of the carriage on the bridge triggered a mechanism that swung open the heavy iron gates into the big entrance courtyard. All of this, along with the furnishings, now belonged to the Sharons.

One hundred and fifty guests had been invited to the ceremony, and eight hundred more to the reception following it, and preparations had been made to handle thousands of the general and curious public who were expected to line the drives and fill the lawns of the estate for a glimpse of the proceedings.

The weather was terrible. "The winds whistled through the little valley," the *Examiner* wrote. "The swiftly falling rain was blown in slanting sheets against the windows of the mansion and along the wide, hard driveway to the village. In the shadow of the hills the great trees quivered and shed their load of vaporous surcharge." Notwithstanding the rain, and whatever the vaporous surcharge was that was coming from the trees, throngs of people showed up. Two special trains had been engaged to carry the guests to Belmont from San Francisco. At the San Francisco station a woman guest, magnificently dressed in white silk from head to toe, tried to jump from the running board of her carriage to the curb and landed on her hands and knees in a pool of mud. Before the press could identify her she had climbed back into her carriage shouting unprintable words. At the Belmont railroad station forty carriages stood in readiness to convey the guests to the house. When the trains arrived at Belmont, there was a mad and furious rush for seats in the carriages, with much pushing and shoving. In the confusion one woman guest was pushed through some trestlework and landed in a gravel pit six feet below.

The Sharon house had been overpowered with decorations for the occasion. As the *Examiner* described it: "How profuse were the decorations may be inferred when it is stated that all the rarest plants of the greeneries, covering more than a city block in extent, had been gracefully disposed and festooned round the rooms. Every pillar of the many in the house was invisible for the smilax and camellias with which they had been covered. Boxes of evergreens, hanging baskets of shrubs and cut flowers had been again gracefully disposed in all the rooms."

The *Examiner* then filled two more columns of breathless print with what the guests ate, and still more with the wedding presents, one of which was a painting by Humphrey Moore: "Entitled 'El Bolero,' it represents a scene in a room of the Alhambra; a lover, whilst playing the guitar, is at the same time gazing with pleased admiration upon a beautiful animated creature in the graceful attitude of the dance. To place this inspiration upon canvas required but the work of three days, very wonderful proof of the eminent artist's dexterity."

In striking contrast, a generation later, was the 1909 celebration of another of San Francisco's intramural marriages. Flora Sharon's brother Fred, who had been an usher at the Sharon-Hesketh wedding, had married Mrs. Witherspoon Breckinridge, who had been a Tevis, the daughter of San Francisco's Lloyd Tevis. Thus Fred Sharon became the stepfather of Miss Flora Louise Breckinridge.

Flora Louise was now marrying the elder son of Sir Thomas and Lady Flora Hesketh, thus joining in wedlock Lady Flora's son and her stepniece. The wedding took place in Paris and was attended only by the bride's mother and stepfather, the groom's parents, and a small handful of Tevis relatives.

San Francisco's rich seemed finally to be learning how to relax with their money.

CHAPTER TWELVE
Mother and Children

ALMA SPRECKELS seemed to thrive on building museums. In addition to the Palace of the Legion of Honor, she built the Maryhill Museum in the state of Washington and contributed a large collection to it. She next built the San Francisco Maritime Museum and gave *it* a collection. At the time of her death, even though she cared little for music, she was working on assembling a collection devoted to the dance and theater, which was to form the nucleus of yet a fourth museum.

Alma Spreckels always became deeply and personally involved with all her projects. While developing her Maritime Museum, for example, she heard of a retired seaman who built ship models. She found him, appropriately enough, in a waterfront bar; they became friends, and she spent many afternoons in the bar with him while he whittled. When he died, Mrs. Spreckels went to his funeral, where

she met his widow, and offered to pay for the burial. The widow
demurred, but Mrs. Spreckels thrust a wad of bills into her hand
anyway. Then she went back to the old sailor's favorite saloon haunt
and bought drinks all around.

During World War II she was a virtual dynamo. The cavernous
garages of her Washington Street house were turned into a salvage
shop, which she ran for the benefit of at least five different causes and
which, among other things, raised over $170,000 for the Red Cross.
When the Nazis overran Denmark, Alma Spreckels organized an
appeal to the people of San Francisco and raised millions of dollars
for medical supplies and relief funds. During the war her doctor,
William Lister (Lefty) Rogers, was a naval medical officer, and at
one point, when his ship was in port in San Francisco, Rogers complained to her of the ship's lack of much needed surgical supplies.
Immediately Mrs. Spreckels ordered the required equipment. It had
not arrived by the time Rogers's ship was due to depart, but it did
arrive a few hours afterward. Mrs. Spreckels dispatched a speedboat
to catch up with the navy battleship in the Pacific and deliver the
equipment.

Throughout the war Mrs. Spreckels and her San Francisco League
for Service Men entertained San Francisco–based servicemen and
their wives. She furnished every service wife with an electric wash-
ing machine from what was apparently an inexhaustible supply. To
the servicemen she gave thousands of footballs, baseball bats, and
radios. She also provided musical instruments for no less than one
hundred and seventy-six military bands. Still, her primary interest
remained art and artists. During the First World War, for example,
she became interested in an impoverished sculptor named Putnam.
Through a friend Mrs. Spreckels arranged to have Putnam's sculptures shipped to France to be cast—despite the U-boats.

She was not, for all her philanthropy, a very practical woman. The
mainstay of her fortune was a trust amounting to about $10,000,000,
which had been created for her by her husband and from which she
received an income of about $750,000 a year. ("Remember, pet, I'm
in trust!" she would warn people who came to her for contribu-

tions.) She frequently overspent her income and was forever borrowing from banks to make ends meet. Once her trustees came to her and suggested that the trust sell a certain stock in which it had a strong position. Mrs. Spreckels opposed selling the stock, but the trustees outvoted her. She thereupon bought up the stock in question with her own money. It went down. She often seemed to have only a vague idea of the value of things. Accompanying her for a drive in her car one day, a friend commented on a pin Mrs. Spreckels was wearing, saying, "My dear, what beautiful jade!" Mrs. Spreckels studied the pin as though she had never seen it before and finally said, "God damn it, those are *emeralds!*" She did indeed have quite a large collection of jade pieces, and once, at a party, a guest in a festive mood slipped into his pocket a jade carving displayed on a table, thinking that this would be a great joke. Typically, the hostess never noticed the missing object, and, the next morning, thinking better of his prank, the guest returned the jade piece to her in the center of a flower arrangement. Mrs. Spreckels gave the flowers a cursory glance and sent the arrangement off to a local hospital. A few days later she received a letter of thanks from the hospital, acknowledging the flowers and "particularly the exquisite jade carving which, we have determined, may bring in excess of ten thousand dollars."

On her ranch in the Napa Valley she was equally casual. As a special gift, one of her house guests gave Mrs. Spreckels a pair of prize laying hens. Her cook prepared them for Sunday dinner. When motoring on the Peninsula, Mrs. Spreckels was fond of stopping at a favorite French restaurant called L'Omelette near Palo Alto. She and her party were always given front-and-center treatment at L'Omelette, where, sweeping in through ranks of bowing waiters and captains, she was always placed at a special table. One night, however, a Thursday, Mrs. Spreckels and a guest arrived— as usual, unannounced—to find the restaurant filled to capacity, with a long waiting line for tables. Spotting her immediately—which was easy to do because of her height—the headwaiter hurried over to her with apologies, "I'm terribly sorry, Mrs. Spreckels, but it's Thursday—

cooks' night out." Mrs. Spreckels looked confused. "Do you mean," she said, "that all these people are *cooks?*"

Like many rich people who enjoy being philanthropic, Mrs. Spreckels did not enjoy being asked for money outright. No one knew this better than her Legion of Honor curator, Thomas Howe. But when the staff of the Legion was organizing a baseball team, it found itself fifty dollars short of the amount needed to buy uniforms. The team, wondering whether the Legion's wealthy benefactress might be willing to make the needed contribution, approached Mr. Howe. Howe, who had never asked Mrs. Spreckels for money before, had misgivings, but he knew that Mrs. Spreckels herself was a baseball fan, and the amount was small. He brought the matter up with her at one of their regular meetings, explaining that the team intended to call itself the Adolph B. Spreckels Memorial Baseball Team. Mrs. Spreckels nodded approvingly. Then Howe brought up the matter of the fifty dollars. "*What!*" cried Mrs. Spreckels. She flung open her reticule and poured its contents—lipstick, emery boards, matches, a few coins, a handkerchief—onto the table. "Where do you expect *me* to get fifty dollars?" she cried. "My God, you people have got my skin. Now you want my guts."

It was not that she neglected her children exactly. Like many children of rich parents who were not born wealthy, the Spreckels children were spoiled unmercifully, pampered and fussed over by nurses, governesses and servants. Their mother showered them with costly toys and gifts. She gave her daughter Dorothy a coming-out party unlike anything San Francisco had seen since Flora Sharon's wedding to Lord Hesketh. "Nubians" in gold turbans and loincloths lined the marble staircase of the Spreckels house. Inside, where the debutante's mother had kicked off her shoes and curled up on one of her French sofas with her familiar pitcher of martinis to watch the fun, huge mounds of caviar reposed in ice-sculptured bowls and champagne bubbled out of fountains. The party was so splendid that social San Francisco forgot all its newly acquired good manners and reverted to the claim-jumping days. A number of guests were seen leaving the party carrying dripping bowls of caviar. At the time—

coming as it did in the darkest days of the Great Depression—Dorothy Spreckels' coming-out party was sharply criticized in the press (particularly in the ever hostile *Chronicle*) for its lavishness and ostentation. In reply to the critics Alma Spreckels took the familiar, if somewhat lame, rich person's line and pointed out that the party provided employment for caterers, waiters, florists, dressmakers, the orchestra, et cetera.

Her one son, Adolph B. Spreckels, Jr.—"Little Adolph," as he was called—had early displayed certain personality traits that a discerning parent might have found disturbing. He had a sadistic bent and seemed to enjoy torturing small animals and other children. As a young boy he had been given, of all things, a home tattooing kit, and he made a game of chasing his young cousins—particularly timid cousin Wayne—through the house with his ink and needles, trying to pin them down and implant tattoos on their bodies. He had to be carefully watched in the presence of his little nephew John. Adolph had been discovered one day carrying the younger boy by his heels up and down a staircase, pounding little John's head on the stair treads as he went.

Alma Spreckels' older daughter, "Little Alma," would have had an extravagant coming-out party too, but much to her mother's displeasure, she ran away in her teens and got married. The marriage did not last long. In fact, the three Spreckels children were married a grand total of twelve times and had eleven divorces. (In southern California the John Spreckels line in the same generation was not doing much better, with eight divorces.) Leading the family in the marriage sweepstakes was Little Adolph, who had matured into a not very pleasant young man, whose "mean streak," as it was called, had grown more pronounced. Adolph had six wives—or, by some counts, seven, although the seventh, with whom he was living at the time of his death, was one he had never bothered to marry. His third wife was his cousin, Geraldine Spreckels. His sixth wife, Kay Williams, was the most famous, because, after divorcing Adolph, she married Clark Gable.

Adolph had become an alcoholic, and at one point during his brief, stormy marriage to Kay he struck her on the head with a Scotch bottle. She charged him with assault, and he was arrested and sent to jail in Los Angeles, where he showed that he could be a gentleman. When he was released, shortly before Christmas, he sent Christmas gifts to all his fellow prisoners.

Little Adolph had a sense of humor—of sorts. During World War II he kept a photograph of Hitler on his desk, which he had inscribed "To Adolph from Adolph." Following his first marriage, he invited a large group of family and friends to a luncheon at the Waldorf-Astoria in New York, where the bride and groom were staying. Guests arrived to find the streets outside the hotel swarming with police cars and fire trucks. Adolph, it seemed, had constructed a lifelike dummy out of pillows and bedclothes, dressed it in a man's pajamas, and had tossed the "suicide" out the window. On a later occasion Adolph was thrown in jail again, on a disorderly conduct charge, this time in San Francisco. It had something to do with an altercation he had had with a taxicab driver whom Adolph had kept waiting an inordinate amount of time outside a bar and had then refused to pay. At the time, a well known local madam was on trial on prostitution charges. When Adolph was released from jail, reporters asked the scion of the Spreckels fortune what he was doing in town. "I am here to give moral support to my favorite madam," he replied. When the reporters asked if they could take his picture, Adolph declared, "No photographs until the people from the *Daily Worker* come." He was then asked how he would compare the San Francisco jail with that of Los Angeles. "No comparison—San Francisco's is by far the better jail," he said.

To be sure, the Spreckels children's mother may not have set them the most perfect example in regard to marriage. In 1936, twelve years after her husband's death and while her children were still in their twenties, Alma de Bretteville Spreckels, after an evening of partying, ran off to Reno with a ranch hand named Elmer Awl and married him. She was then fifty-five and he was some ten years younger. San Francisco society was stunned. No one had ever heard of Elmer Awl. "How does he spell his name?" a society editor wanted to know, to which someone is said to have replied, "A-w-l, as in the tool used for punching holes in old leather." For a while Elmer Awl cut a striking figure in San Francisco society. On opening nights of the opera Mr. Awl appeared in white tie and tails, to which he added white high-heeled boots and a huge white ten-gallon hat. The new Mrs. Awl had meanwhile brought one of her poor relations from Denmark to California, a young niece named Ula. It was not long before it became apparent that Elmer Awl was more interested in Ula than in Alma. Alma and Elmer were divorced, and Elmer married Ula and moved to Santa Barbara. Alma resumed her marriage name of Spreckels.

AFTER DIVORCING John Rosekrans, the man with whom she eloped, Little Alma Spreckels married James V. Coleman, a descendant of William O'Brien, the silver king. After divorcing Coleman she married Charles Hammel—and this union was to prove even more disastrous than the others. Hammel, a former merchant marine captain, was fond of sailing, and so Little Alma bought him—for $89,000— a forty-foot sloop-rigged motor-sailing yacht called the *Berylline*. Though Little Alma was a tournament bridge player and an expert horsewoman, she knew nothing at all about boats. Still, saying, "I believe in God and I believe in Charlie," she set out with her new husband in 1970—with no crew other than themselves—to cruise from San Francisco to Hawaii, with a freezer full of food.

On the second day out the *Berylline* headed into a storm with twenty-five-foot waves and fifty-mile-an-hour winds. First the freezer snapped a retaining pin and began to crash around alarmingly in the galley. Next, a broken bolt in the generator knocked out the entire electric system, including the motor needed for steering lights, radio communication, the toilets, and, of course, the freezer. The wheel chain broke repeatedly, making steering impossible, and new leaks in the hull appeared daily. The storm was followed by breathless doldrums, which were restful but of little use to a sailboat without a motor. At home in San Francisco it was reported that the Hammels had been lost at sea, but they were merely battling more storms and leaks. At one point Little Alma was thrown from a seat in the galley. She was knocked in the head at least five times. All the spoiled food in the freezer had to be thrown overboard, and eventually the only thing operating aboard the *Berylline* was a flashlight.

Somehow the pair made it to Hawaii, where they found themselves in Alenuihaha Channel, between the islands of Hawaii and Maui, notorious for treacherous weather and tides. Here the rudder chain broke, and the *Berylline* drifted inexorably toward the rocks. Finally the boat's distress flag was spotted and rescue came. The *Berylline* was towed into the harbor of Kawaihae after twenty-nine days at sea.

The Hammels managed to get home from this excursion, but early in 1972 both Captain Hammel and the *Berylline* disappeared, leaving Mrs. Hammel quite at a loss for an explanation. At one point Hammel and the yacht were reported to have been seen in Mexico, but then they disappeared again, supposedly for South America. By March, Alma Hammel had engaged a group of international lawyers to issue a barrage of lawsuits, injunctions, and restraining orders, not only to return Captain Hammel to his wife but also to return her yacht. The yacht had been registered in both their names, but, said Alma in her complaint, "At no time did I in any way indicate other than by joint name registration that the boat was his. At no time did I authorize him to take the boat from the Bay Area." She also added: "On recent occasions Mr. Hammel exhibited a tendency to violence as well as irrational behavior." A receiver was authorized by the court to return the sloop to its home port. Alma also sued Captain Hammel for divorce, asking only for the *Berylline* in settlement. She got the divorce and, eventually, the boat. After playing hide-and-seek with it for five months, Hammel finally surrendered it to her in Ensenada. Alma then asked the court to restore her maiden name of Spreckels.

Little Alma's sister, Dorothy, married, first, Mr. Jean Dupuy and, second, Mr. Andrew McCarthy. Her third marriage, to Charles Munn—who made millions by inventing the racetrack totalizer (the device that flashes on a board the numbers of the horses, their changing odds before the race, and the results afterward)—is the only one of the twelve marriages of Alma de Bretteville's children that did not end in divorce, and this must be considered something of an accomplishment. The Munns never set off alone in a yacht, but they did make news of sorts in 1971 when they spent eighteen thousand dollars to charter a Pan Am 707 jetliner to fly them from Paris directly to Palm Beach in order to avoid the "mishmash" of customs and changing planes at Kennedy Airport.

When Pan Am's publicity people released the news of this record-breaking charter, Mrs. Munn couldn't understand why so much fuss was being made. "It didn't cost more than people pay for a Rolls-Royce to charter that plane," said she. The analogy was a little weak. When one buys a Rolls-Royce, one gets to use it for at least a year or so. When chartering a 707, one does not get to keep the plane. As for Rolls-Royces, it was pointed out that the Munns at the time had four—one in San Francisco, one at their Palm Beach house, and two in Paris, where they maintained an apartment.

When Little Adolph Spreckels died in 1968—he fell in a hotel in Arizona and fractured his skull—his mother took his death very hard. Though all of her children had given her heartaches, and Adolph more than the rest, the death of her only son seemed to devastate her. Her famous energy seemed suddenly to desert her, and she became a virtual recluse in her Washington Street house. Sometimes at night, after the Palace of the Legion of Honor had closed, she would ask her chauffeur to drive her out to it. She would stand in the dark park and look at it for a while, then get back in her car and be driven home. She saw few of her old friends, and when her daughters came to see her, there were inevitably quarrels. From time to time she would try to ease the bitterness between herself and her children— all of whom she felt had led utterly wasted lives—with great conciliatory bursts of generosity. Once, after a visit with her daughter Alma that had gone reasonably well, Mrs. Spreckels called out to Alma, who was going out the door, "Need any furniture, pet?" Alma stepped back into the room and mentioned a commode of her mother's that she had always admired. "Take it!" cried Mrs.

Spreckels. Alma replied that she would see about getting a mover in the morning. "No, take it now!" insisted Mrs. Spreckels. "You can put it in the back of Jimmy Coleman's car." Alma replied that this was hardly practical; it was too valuable a piece not to be moved by experts, and besides, they had no movers' blankets. "Take some blankets off my bed!" said Mrs. Spreckels, and all at once the two women were quarreling again, over a piece of furniture.

Alma and Dorothy Spreckels Munn now own, in joint tenancy, the Washington Street house, that fantastic white-stone sculpture with so many carved garlands and furbelows on its façade that, in the San Francisco sunshine, it glitters like a confection of spun sugar —which, when one remembers where the money to build it came from, perhaps it really is. Was it all worth the candle? It should probably go without saying that the two sisters are now in a bitter legal battle over who will finally possess the house. In the fray for a while was also Kay Spreckels Gable, who claimed a share of the property on behalf of her two children by Little Adolph.

The house is one of the last great turn-of-the-century San Francisco mansions still owned by the family that built it. It is empty much of the year. Little Alma Spreckels has built a large new house for herself in Pacific Heights. The Munns spend their winters in Palm Beach, their springs and autumns in Paris, and visit San Francisco only briefly in between. When they are alone in the house, the watchmen and caretakers report strange night noises and are convinced that there is a ghost. If so, it is doubtless the restless shade of Alma de Bretteville Spreckels, searching for her children.

Her daughter Alma says, "She did a lot of wonderful things for us. But she didn't really take care of us."

CHAPTER THIRTEEN
Tempest About a Teapot

AFTER Edward Doheny's high-handed attempt in 1915 to buy up the Union Oil Company from the Stewarts and the other shareholders had been defeated by the Union's board, Doheny turned his hand to other matters. Los Angeles was still not quite a place. It was a small town of two hundred thousand souls and consisted mostly of bungalows. No notable public building of any sort would exist until 1925, and it would not be until the decade of the 1920s that the population of Los Angeles would leap to over a million, nearly twice that of San Francisco. When Alma Spreckels was planning the museum that was to become the Palace of the Legion of Honor, she had first considered building it in San Diego and had consulted her brother-in-law John D. Spreckels on the subject. He had advised her that San Diego was "not ready" for such an elaborate cultural center. He would have considered Los Angeles even more unready.

One important thing had, however, happened in Los Angeles. In 1914 the city's harbor had opened at San Pedro. With the Panama Canal open, this created the possibility that Los Angeles might become an important world port.

From California, Ed Doheny turned to Mexico, where he had prospected for gold as a young man, this time in search of more oil. He found a promising site inland from the gulf, in the jungles beyond Tampico, where he leased over a million acres. Doheny's Mexican Petroleum Company cleared the jungle, built roads and railroads, docks, pipelines, shops, and houses for his native laborers, and as a result of generous bribes to Mexican officials, had the great good favor of the Mexican government. By 1922, Doheny's accrued income from his Mexican company alone was $31,575,937, and his total worth was reported to be more than a hundred million dollars. By 1925 he was reliably reported to be even richer than "the richest man in America," John D. Rockefeller.

As a rich man the former southwestern gunman affected a monocle, a walrus mustache, British tailoring, and an autocratic manner. He also became devoted to prodigal spending and bought a large portion of what is now downtown Los Angeles, which he converted into a huge park and estate called Chester Place. His yacht, the *Casiana*, was one of the most luxurious in the country. He surrounded himself with an entourage of servants and bodyguards, and Chester Place was so heavily protected that once, when a fire broke out in one of the estate's many outbuildings, the Los Angeles Fire Department had trouble getting through the security at the main gate. His second wife, who had been his secretary, arrayed herself in ropes of sapphires, emeralds, rubies, diamonds, and pearls. Mr. Doheny was not particularly philanthropic, but he did contribute heavily to the Democratic party and the Irish Freedom Movement. In fact, it was probably his wife—or "Ma D.," as she was called—who was responsible for conserving Ed Doheny's fortune and for seeing to it that the money was not spent as rapidly as it was made. In later years she enjoyed reminding her family of this fact, and once, at a gathering of her children and stepchildren, she announced, "If it weren't for me, none of you would have a penny. I'm responsible for everything, right down to that big diamond ring on Lucy's finger."

While other California women were marrying titles, Ma D. purchased one of her own. As a result of a large contribution to the Vatican she was made a papal countess and enjoyed being introduced as Countess Estelle Doheny. At Chester Place she behaved more like a reigning empress. Physically she resembled Queen Victoria—small, plump, ugly, and imperious—and she had a decidedly Victorian manner. When one entered Chester Place one descended a long, wide marble staircase lined with footmen and maids and was ushered into a kind of throne room, where Her Grace, Ma D., received her guests seated on a throne. Though she became almost totally blind, no one was permitted to comment on or remind her of her affliction. Small carpeted ramps were built across the thresholds of doorways and up steps so that Ma D. could move through her house unaided.

For all her grand ways Ma D. had a middle-class American's love of showing off her home to visitors, leading her guests along the vast marble corridors, into the Pompeian Room, where she pointed out the vaulted ceiling covered with gold leaf and drew attention to her priceless collection of antique watches, and into the conservatory, which was big enough to contain large trees—including a beaucarnea tree, one of the largest tropical trees that grow, imported from Mexico—as well as her prize-winning collection of rare orchids. For her dining table a long silver centerpiece was designed just to contain the blooms of the specimen orchids, which were changed daily. Before each dinner party Ma D. and her head gardener rehearsed the names of the varieties in the arrangement and their order of position in the centerpiece. With this list memorized, Ma D. could recite the full Latin names of all the blooms that she could not see. Inevitably each tour of Chester Place ended with an elevator ride up two stories to Ma D.'s private chapel, with its magnificent reliquary and where the Eucharist was reserved. Outside the chapel, two tall Spanish armoires contained a variety of hats, scarves, shawls, and mantillas in all styles and colors so that women would have a selection of head coverings to put on in the presence of the Host.

One of Pa D.'s cronies from his prospecting days was a young man from Kentucky named Albert Bacon Fall. Like Doheny, Fall had had almost no formal education and had behind him a checkered career after heading west as a youth. He had worked as a cowboy, a farmhand, a prospector, and a miner, and had wound up in New Mexico when it was still a territory. There, after studying law in his spare time, he had passed the rather relaxed requirements for admission to the bar and had gone into politics. Fall had supported Grover Cleveland for the presidency and had been rewarded by him with a judgeship on the Supreme Court of the Territory of New Mexico. It was here that Fall first displayed a tendency to take the law into his own hands, as happened one day when he leaped down from his judge's bench to lead a posse of gunmen that was out to lynch a bandit. When word of this incident reached President Cleveland's ears Fall was summarily relieved of his judicial post.

Unlike his friend Doheny, Albert Fall never had the luck to strike it rich. With the outbreak of the Spanish-American War, Fall joined the infantry, reached the modest rank of captain, and at the end of the war came back to New Mexico, where he announced that he had switched political parties, from the Democratic to the Republican. When New Mexico was admitted to the Union in 1912, Albert Fall ran for the Senate and was elected New Mexico's first United States senator.

As a senator, Albert Fall provided Washington with almost a caricature of the western hombre. He had cold blue eyes and thin lips, from which there usually drooped an unlit, well-chewed cigar. He spoke with a heavy western drawl and wore wide-brimmed hats, even on the floor of the Senate, and shoestring ties. His appearance alarmed some observers. One Washington newspaperman wrote of him: "With a long drooping moustache, he looks like a stage sheriff of the Far West in the movies. His voice is always loud and angry. He has the frontiersman's impatience. From his kind lynch law springs." Though Fall and Doheny were now on opposite sides of the political fence, the two men shared a number of beliefs. Both were strong advocates—Doheny with particularly good reasons—of armed intervention in Mexico to protect American investments there. Both were also ardently in favor of the immediate and complete exploitation by private interests (such as Doheny's) of the nation's natural resources (such as oil). Doheny, in fact, had a grand plan that was as ambitious as any in a James Bond novel. He knew that the pools of oil that lay beneath the American subcontinent would not last forever. What he wanted to do was to pump it *all* out as quickly as possible; then he planned to store his oil, to keep the price up, and dole it out at his own rate of speed to an oil-thirsty country.

In the Senate, because he spoke a little Spanish, Albert Fall represented himself as an expert on Mexican affairs; because he was a friend of Ed Doheny's, he represented himself as an expert on the petroleum industry. In Washington, Fall became a card-playing chum of another senator, the easygoing Warren Gamaliel Harding from Ohio. When, in 1920, Harding became one of the most unlikely candidates for President in American history, Albert Fall was one of his staunchest supporters. So, at Fall's urging, was Ed Doheny, who contributed twenty-five thousand dollars to the Harding campaign. Doheny also paid for a controversial national newspaper advertising campaign that featured full-page photographs of Harding's parents. The point of this was to counteract rumors that Warren Harding had "Negro blood." The ads showed Harding's parents to be unmistakably white.

When Harding was elected to office by an overwhelming majority—carrying thirty-seven of the forty-eight states—Harding asked Fall if he would like to be his Secretary of the Interior. It was said at the time that Harding had at first considered making Albert Fall Seceretary of State but had been persuaded by his advisors that the Senate would never accept a southwesterner for the top Cabinet post. In offering Interior to Fall, Harding is supposed to have apologized for not giving him the juicier plum. But in view of what was to happen, he needn't have bothered. As Secretary of the Interior, Fall would be in a position to be of great assistance to Doheny; as Secretary of State, he would have been of no use at all. What is more likely, and characteristic of Harding, is that Harding asked Fall to take his pick of Cabinet posts and that Fall, after consulting with Doheny, selected Interior. Interior was known as one of the government departments most susceptible to graft, where important money could be made on the side. It was also already rumored that Interior was "owned" by the big oil interests.

Fall's appointment was greeted with cheers and applause on both sides of the Senate floor, and Fall went sailing into the job without the usual formality of having the appointment sent to committee for approval. This was, after all, the dawn of the carefree decade of the 1920s. At the time, Harding announced that it was his policy to pick "the best man" for each government position. *The New York Times* commented editorially that Harding was not appointing the best men so much as his best friends.

About three years before Harding's election Ed Doheny had had a meeting that would prove pivotal in the series of events that was to come. His son, Edward L. Doheny, Jr., had been serving as a lieutenant in the navy aboard the U.S.S. *Huntington* (named after another wealthy Californian), and while the *Huntington* was docked in Pensacola the elder Doheny, vacationing in Florida, came aboard for a paternal visit. The presence of the famous oil millionaire did not go unnoticed by the crew, and Ed Doheny was invited to meet with the ship's commanding officer, Captain John Keeler Robison. Doheny's meeting with Robison lasted a full two hours, and the topic of conversation was, quite understandably, oil. Oil had become tremendously important to the navy. Nearly all of its fleet had been converted from coal to oil burning, and to be sure that the navy would have an ample supply of fuel—and at a price considerably lower than it would have to pay on the open market—the Department of the Navy, under President Taft, had been given some 78,791 acres of oil lands. These were situated in three principal locations: at Elk Hills and Buena Vista Hills, in Kern County, California, and at a place in Wyoming quaintly named Teapot Dome. Ever since the Taft order, the private oil interests, including Doheny's, had been trying to obtain leases to drill and exploit this rich acreage of oil reserves, but thus far their pleas had been successfully resisted by the Naval Fuel Oil Board, which maintained that the land should be kept by the navy for navy use.

Captain Robison was an Annapolis graduate and a career navy officer, so he cannot have been expected to know much about the oil business. But he was devoted to the navy, and in his conversation with Doheny, Robison commented proudly on how well the navy was maintaining its oil reserves. Doheny responded with the sort of indulgent smile that a parent bestows on a child who has asked if the moon is made of green cheese. "Well, it is being handled very well for the people you have for neighbors," he said, "but you are not going to have any property there in a very few years." Captain Robison asked him what he meant by that, and Doheny explained that, while the navy was jealously guarding its untapped oil reserves, other drillers, on the periphery of the navy lands, were pumping oil out of the ground and systematically "draining" away all the oil from under the land the navy owned. Doheny pictured the oil situation underground as a series of large bathtubs with interconnecting canals. Empty one tub of oil and oil from the next one would simply flow into it. The navy, Doheny said, would be far wiser to get its oil out of the ground while it still had a chance.

The question of drainage from one well into another was not a new one to oilmen or to the navy's petroleum engineers. It had been studied by Woodrow Wilson's Secretary of the Navy, Josephus Daniels, with inconclusive results. Oil, it was decided, might occur in isolated pockets or it might also occur in connected pools, where some drainage might take place. But the science of geology in oil exploration was still in a fairly primitive state, and the fact was that, lacking a subterranean telescope, no one really knew for sure what was going on beneath the earth's crust. Still, Captain Robison was appalled by Doheny's information and by the vision of the navy's precious oil being sucked away by neighboring drilling companies.

It opened his eyes, he said later, to a problem he had never dreamed existed. Testifying before a Senate investigating committee, Robison said that Mr. Doheny's words carried particular weight because they had not come "from some $2,500 clerk," but from a man "who had made millions knowing how." He assured the senators, "That is the kind of information I believe." Doheny's warning, of course, was based as much on guesswork as on expert knowledge, but, more than that, it was part of his plan. He had planted the seeds of doubt in the mind of a high-ranking naval officer about the security of the navy's precious oil reserves.

President Harding's appointee as Secretary of the Navy, replacing the able Josephus Daniels, was a man named Edward Denby, whose principal qualification for the Cabinet post seemed to be that he had seen service as a marine in the First World War. Like Harding's other appointees, Denby was one of Harding's friends. There is no evidence to indicate that Edward Denby was a dishonest man, but he was lazy and not very bright. It became Denby's task to appoint a new chief of the navy's Bureau of Engineering, and the man he chose was none other than Captain John Keeler Robison, who was given the temporary rank of rear admiral. Whether Doheny or Fall had a hand in this appointment was never made clear in the subsequent investigation. But in retrospect it seemed likely. It fitted in so neatly with Doheny's plan. Robison now was in complete charge of the naval petroleum reserves.

There remained only a few loose ends to be tied together as Doheny and Fall closed ranks against the government of the United States of America. First, it was considered important to get the navy's oil lands—and Robison, who supervised them—out of the control of the Department of the Navy and the unreliable Mr. Denby and under the jurisdiction of Fall's Department of the Interior. Of course some explanation for the move would have to be given to Denby, and some persuasion would have to be exercised on the President to get him to authorize it. But Fall foresaw no problem on either front, and he was right.

As a President, Warren G. Harding may not have been the worst, but at his best he was never clear about what the highest office in the land entailed. The most that could be said for him was that he *looked* like a President—tall, ruggedly handsome, a tobacco-chewing Main-Streeter from Marion, Ohio. Once, when a problem involving taxation had come to his desk, Harding complained to an aide, "John, I can't make a damn thing out of this tax problem. I listen to one side and they seem right, and then—God!—I talk to the other side and they seem just as right, and here I am where I started. I know somewhere there is a book that will give me the truth, but, hell, I couldn't read the book. I know somewhere there is an economist who knows the truth, but I don't know where to find him, and haven't the sense to know and trust him when I find him. God, what a job!" He also once said, "It's a good thing I am not a woman. I would always be pregnant. I cannot say no."* Most administrative decisions, he admitted, gave him a headache. He would much rather be playing poker or out on the golf course, and he eagerly delegated as much authority as he could to the members of his Cabinet, most of whom were his poker-playing cronies. At his nightly White House poker parties, meanwhile, he was extra-ordinarily lucky, and friends like Fall and Denby were more than happy to let the Chief Executive win.

When Fall approached Denby about shifting the navy oil lands to Fall's department, Denby—always pleased when a piece of work that was on his desk could be placed on someone else's—was de-lighted. Not to have to run the oil lands gave him one less job to do. The only other person needed to approve the switch was the President. True to his word, he could not say no.

Others in the Department of the Navy were less cheerful about what was about to happen. Admiral R. S. Griffin, who was a former chief of the Bureau of Engineering, reminded Denby that the navy had been struggling for over a decade to keep its oil, and said that if he "turned the administration over to the Interior Department we might just as well say good-by to our oil." But Secretary Denby

---

* *Pictorial History of American Presidents* by John and Alice Durant.

explained that the President had already approved the scheme, and within a few days Fall was able to write to his friend Ed Doheny in California:

> There will be no possibility of any further conflict with Navy officials and this Department, as I have notified Secretary Denby that I should conduct the matters of naval leases under direction of the President without calling any of his force in consultation unless I conferred with himself personally upon a matter of policy. He understands the situation and that I shall handle matters exactly as I think best and will not consult with any officials of any bureau of his department but only with himself and such consultation will be confined strictly and entirely to matters of general policy.

Originally Doheny had wanted the entire naval oil reserves for his own company. But Fall, it turned out, had other plans. Doheny was not Fall's only friend in the oil business. Another was the eastern oil magnate Harry F. Sinclair, who headed the Mammoth Oil Company. Fall decided to split the pie two ways. He comforted Doheny with the reminder that, after all, if *all* the navy lands were turned over to Doheny for development, someone might think that something a little fishy was going on. And when one was doing something illegal, one had to be fair about it. The Teapot Dome acreage in Wyoming was turned over to Sinclair and the two big California tracts to Doheny.

Now all that remained to do was for Fall to arrange compensation for what he had accomplished. In this connection, it seemed that Sinclair was not as close a friend as was Doheny, because Sinclair's bill was considerably higher. For a smaller number of acres Sinclair paid Fall close to four hundred thousand dollars in cash and bonds. He also gave Fall six prize Holstein heifers, a yearling bull, two six-month-old boars, four sows, and an English thoroughbred horse for the Secretary's New Mexico ranch. Doheny, meanwhile, somewhat mollified navy officials, who were horrified over the transfer, by promising to build the navy some oil-storage tanks in Pearl Harbor, Hawaii, tanks that the navy had long wanted but had been unable to get from Congress. Now it was time for Doheny to pay Fall for his good services or, as Fall put it in a telephone call to Doheny, "I am now prepared to receive that loan."

Doheny sent for his only son, Edward L. (Ned) Doheny, Jr., and instructed him to go to the offices of Blair & Company in New York (where both father and son had brokerage accounts, and in which the former owned a considerable interest) and to withdraw from the younger Doheny's account a hundred thousand dollars in cash, giving two checks for the money. Doheny told his son to take the bills, wrap them in paper, put them in a small black valise, and carry them personally to Secretary Fall in Washington. In November 1921 Edward Doheny, Jr., carried out his mission and arrived with his little black bag full of banknotes at Secretary Fall's apartment in the Wardman Park Hotel. The younger Doheny, with his male secretary, Robert Plunkett, as witness, watched as Fall counted out the money and then—or so he claimed later—received Fall's note for the amount. At the time, Doheny said, he pointed out to Fall that no interest rate had been placed on the note. Fall airily replied that his old friend Ed Doheny could insert any rate he wished to.

Within days Secretary Fall was back home in New Mexico, where he paid cash for a large piece of property adjoining his Three Rivers Ranch. During this visit, his daughter testified later, she walked into her father's room and saw large piles of money lying on his desk. She snatched up one of the piles and cried, "Here's my trip to Mexico!" and started out of the room with the cash. But her father ordered her to come back and return the money, saying that it was reserved for paying off the mortgage on their house. Secretary Fall's New Mexico neighbors were somewhat surprised by the Fall family's sudden affluence; a relatively hardscrabble ranch was suddenly transformed into something of a showplace, with prize cattle and thoroughbred horses. But, then, it was known that Albert Fall had many rich friends and occupied a high position in the government.

On January 9, 1923, after completing all his various deals, Fall announced his intention to retire from his life of "tireless public service." To the press President Harding expressed profound sorrow at Fall's decision and said that, to keep him in Washington to continue to serve the nation's needs, he had offered to appoint Albert Fall to the United States Supreme Court. But Fall had turned down even this lofty post, saying that he wished to return to the land and to the humble life of tending his little southwestern ranch. And well he might have wished to get out of Washington, where various busybodies in the press were trying to figure out why and how the U.S. Navy's oil lands had made their way from the Department of the Navy to the Department of the Interior and, finally, into the hands of Doheny & Company, in a matter of months. Already there were dark mutterings about corruption, and though he did not show it, Fall may have been one of the most frightened men in America. He had collected some half a million dollars in payoffs and bribes, and he may have begun to wonder whether or not he had sold himself too cheaply. At the time, when for a mere hundred thousand dollars Doheny had acquired roughly 30,000 acres of oil lands, whose contents were estimated to be between 75 and 250 million barrels of oil, Doheny had commented, "We will be in bad luck if we do not get one hundred million in profit. But that will depend on the price of gasoline."

There were other indications that Fall may have been frightened that his machinations could be exposed and his bubble burst. There had been a curious meeting between Mrs. Fall and the President when Harding was passing through Kansas City. Mrs. Fall had appeared at Harding's hotel, unannounced, and asked to see him; she looked distraught and agitated. She was admitted to the President's suite, and after a private conversation that lasted about an hour she emerged looking even more troubled, red-eyed as though from weeping. When the President himself emerged he looked haggard and grim. What they talked about was never disclosed, but it cannot have been pleasant, and one might speculate that a presidential pardon for her husband might have been one of the topics. The next day, in an interview with William Allen White, the celebrated editor of the Emporia, Kansas, *Gazette*, Harding remarked to White, "In this job, I am not worried about my enemies. I can take care of them. It's my friends who are giving me trouble."

Publicly, meanwhile, Harding accepted Fall's resignation "with deep and sincere regret," and Fall departed, but not without one final bit of flimflammery. He ordered that the elegant Jacobean antique furniture, with which his Washington office had been furnished at taxpayers' expense, be shipped to his home in New Mexico. The transfer was all perfectly legal. Fall wrote out a personal check for $231.25 to the United States government to pay for the furniture. It was worth about $3000.

All through the early months of 1923 public criticism of the Harding administration mounted, not only against Fall but against others of the Harding Cabinet. Increasingly Harding began turning to his wife, Florence, for advice, and, as usual, Florence Harding formed her responses after consultations with her astrologist. What the stars did not foretell was that, on the evening of August 2, 1923, while Mrs. Harding was attempting to raise her husband's spirits by reading aloud a eulogy to him in the *Saturday Evening Post*, the fifty-seven-year-old President's heart would simply stop. He had been in office less than two years. Officially the cause of his death was said to have been some bad crab meat he had eaten on a trip to Alaska, though most food-poisoning cases give their victims a bit more warning before the onset of death. (At the time, of course, there were dark rumors that one of the President's "friends," made desperate by the fear of exposure, had poisoned him.) Now all the untidy mess of the Harding administration descended on the shoulders of his taciturn successor in the White House, Calvin Coolidge.

Slowly and laboriously, under President Coolidge, the legislators in Washington began to investigate some of the goings-on of the Harding era. The Senate Committee on Public Lands and Surveys, organized to look into what had happened to the naval oil reserves, held its first meeting on October 23, 1923. The chief examiner was Senator Thomas J. Walsh, a Democrat from Montana, and the first witness called was Albert Fall.

As a witness Fall was arrogant, contemptuous, and evasive, taking the position that everything he had done had been done for the good of the country and, furthermore, had been done on instructions from the President. He repeatedly and loudly demanded that Walsh "look at the records"—which, it turned out, were quite confused. Indeed, the records of the Harding administration had been so haphazardly kept that it was impossible to tell what the President had ordered and what he had not. Walsh pressed Fall to admit that in such matters as the navy's oil lands, which involved national security, it was proper to consult the Congress and not high-handedly take matters into one's own hands. He did succeed in getting Fall to admit he had not sought any legal opinions in connection with his maneuvers, though Fall countered by saying, "But I'm a lawyer myself." Fall then added that "law or no law," he would have done anything in his power to prevent the navy's oil from leaking away into neighboring fields. Asked why he had turned over the Teapot Dome fields to Sinclair without any competitive bidding, Fall's haughty reply was, "Well, I did it."

He told the first of many outright lies. "Did you ever get any compensation at all?" Walsh asked him. "I have never suggested any compensation at all and have received none," Fall answered. Not a penny from Sinclair. Not a penny from Doheny. "So long as I was in an official position," he said piously, "I did not feel I could accept any gift of any kind." No heifers, no sows, no boars, bulls, or thoroughbred horses. "I shall go into no further detail discussing this matter," he concluded. "The entire subject, of course, is more or less humiliating even to refer to." When asked about his obviously improved style of living, Fall did admit that he had received a hundred-thousand-dollar "loan" from a friend, but when asked who the friend was, Fall lied again and said that it was not Edward Doheny or anyone else in the oil business. The hundred thousand dollars, he said, had been lent him by the Washington publisher Edward B. McLean, husband of Evalyn Walsh McLean of Hope Diamond fame. (Having thus testified to the senators, Fall hastily contacted McLean and asked him to "back me up in this." McLean promised, but Fall had made a poor choice here. McLean, an alcoholic, promptly forgot the promise and later testified that he had never lent Fall any money at all.)

Ed Doheny made his first appearance before the Walsh Commit-

tee on December 3. He was then sixty-seven years old but still full
of restless, bristling energy. Unlike Fall, Doheny made a much more
likable and convincing witness. Poised and coolly professional, he presented himself as one of the world's leading experts on the petroleum
industry and petroleum science. He began his testimony with a professional lecture to the senators on the dangers of oil leakage from one
well into another. If lands under which oil lay were not exploited,
they could be pumped dry by neighbors. A single hole punched in
the earth's crust, he implied, could in time siphon away all the oil on
the continental shelf. He stated that he "knew" that the navy had
lost at least a hundred million barrels of oil prior to the Doheny take-
over. It had simply leaked away. He, he said, had stepped in out of
the sheerest patriotism to save America's oil for her fighting boys.

When Senator Walsh, at the Walsh Committee hearings, asked
Doheny why the engineers at the Bureau of Mines had not been
aware of this grievous loss of oil through leakage, Doheny replied
immodestly, "No man on earth has access to the same information
I have, because my information comes from twenty-nine years of
close study of the proposition, such as no other living man has given
to the business. That sounds egotistical, I grant you, but that is absolutely the truth, since you have asked me the question." Doheny
admitted that, though a Democrat, he was "sometimes a Republican,"
and that he had contributed twenty-five thousand dollars to the
Harding campaign and had paid for the advertising campaign por-
traying Harding's lily-white parents. But there was nothing wrong
with that. Asked whether he had ever given Fall any money, Doheny
replied, "Not yet. I want to say right here, though, that I would be
very glad to take Mr. Fall in my employ if he ever wanted to come
to us." This was stretching the truth a bit, but technically it was so,
since it had not been Doheny himself but his son Ned who had
handed Fall the bag of money.

The hearings wore on, with more witnesses called; they would
consume, all told, the better part of four years, filling thousands of
pages of printed testimony. As the scandals of the Harding days un-
folded, they would become known collectively as "Teapot Dome,"
after that Wyoming settlement where an odd-shaped hill had re-

minded early settlers of the top of a teapot. Fifty-odd years later the
Watergate scandals of Richard Nixon's administration would be
compared with Teapot Dome, but there were actually few simi-
larities. The complexities of Watergate were such that much of the
American public had trouble comprehending them. But the details
of Teapot Dome—graft, bribery, and corruption—were almost clas-
sically simple, and the hearings and trials that ensued, and the characters who populated them, had an almost burlesque quality of
opéra bouffe.

In January 1924, for example, Ed Doheny appeared before the
Senate hearings again. He came voluntarily, and because it was
widely reported that he was now about to "tell all," the Senate
caucus room was packed to capacity. He did not tell all exactly,
but he told a bit more than he had told before. Yes, he admitted, he
had lent Fall $100,000, because Fall was an old friend who needed
money to improve his ranch. He told about the cash and the little
black bag. But, Senator Walsh wanted to know, wasn't that an unusual way for a businessman to carry out a transaction? Not at all,
said Doheny. In the last five years alone he had carried out at least
one million dollars' worth of cash transactions in Mexico because it
was difficult to deal with banks from one country to another. But,
Walsh pointed out, they were not talking about an international
transaction here—this had been merely a transfer of funds between
two nearby cities, New York and Washington. Doheny countered
by saying that, after all, $100,000 to him was the equivalent of small
change and amounted to "no more than $25 or $50 to the ordinary
individual"—hardly a sufficient sum to warrant writing a check.
Walsh replied somewhat dryly that while he could see Mr. Doheny's
point, $100,000 was still a lot of money to a man like Mr. Fall. "It
was indeed," Doheny admitted, "there is no question about that."
Then he added, "And I am perfectly willing to admit that it probably caused him to favor me" (in terms of granting the oil leases).
Was the loan directly responsible for the leases, the committee
wanted to know. Doheny replied that he didn't think Fall was "more
than human"—a remark that drew laughter from the spectators.

Pressing on for more details about the loan, Walsh wanted to know whether Fall had paid Doheny any interest on it. No, Mr. Doheny said, he had not, and Doheny then repeated his earlier assertion that he would be perfectly willing to hire Fall for his company and let him work off the indebtedness. Had the loan been secured by a note, the senator wanted to know. Yes, Doheny said, Fall had given him a note for the loan, but Doheny had misplaced it somewhere and couldn't find it. Once more there was laughter in the hearing room.

Doheny's appearance before the committee ended with an odd scene. Walsh asked him if he had communicated with any member of the Senate committee prior to the hearing, and Doheny replied that he had not. "I was told that Senator Smoot handed you a note as you were coming in the room," Walsh said. Doheny hesitated and then admitted that this was true. "Let us see the note," Walsh demanded. Certainly, said Doheny, smiling broadly, and reached into his jacket pocket and withdrew a clenched fist. With a dramatic gesture, he opened the fist and scattered a small snowstorm of shredded paper onto the green baize table. The contents of the note, he said haughtily, would make "very painstaking" reading. "Can you *tell* us what was in it?" the senator asked him. "Yes," said Doheny. " 'After we finish, I would like to see you in my room.' " In disgust, Senator Walsh dismissed the witness.

Pieces of paper had a curious habit of getting destroyed or torn or lost when in Edward Doheny's possession. When he made his second appearance before that January session of the committee he had found Fall's note for the loan. It had, it seemed, been in his wallet all along. But for some reason the lower half of the document, where Albert Fall's signature would have been, had been torn off and was missing. Why was this, the senators wanted to know. Doheny offered a strange and rambling explanation. Before leaving New York for California after receiving the note, he said, he and Mrs. Doheny had begun to be afraid that their train might have an accident. If that happened and he and his wife were killed, it had occurred to Doheny that the executors of his estate might find the note and demand immediate payment on it from his old friend Fall. This of course would be a dreadful state of affairs—disaster piled upon disaster—and so he had torn the note in half and given the lower portion to his wife to carry in her reticule, and she, unfortunately, had lost it. As evidence Fall's note—if indeed it was Fall's note—was worthless. The senators remarked that they felt they had been "very greatly misled" by Doheny, who shrugged and said he was sorry they felt that way.

On June 30, 1924, a Washington grand jury handed down four indictments against Fall, Sinclair, Doheny, and Doheny's son. Fall and the two Dohenys were charged with felony in entering into a conspiracy to defraud the government of the United States in an effort to control the Elk Hills oil reserves in California. Fall and Sinclair were charged with a similar conspiracy in connection with Teapot Dome. The third indictment charged Fall with accepting a hundred-thousand-dollar bribe from Doheny, and the fourth charged Doheny with giving the bribe to Fall. The first civil case involving the oil scandals came to trial in Los Angeles on October 21, 1924.

Doheny's attorneys were delighted that Los Angeles had been chosen for the trial. After all, Mr. Doheny was one of that still rather small town's leading citizens, a local favorite son. A street cutting across Beverly Hills had been named after him. In Los Angeles, Ed Doheny was not only much loved but also much feared. It seemed most unlikely that a Los Angeles jury—or judge, for that matter—would vote to convict such a powerful local figure. A few months earlier, meanwhile, there had been a lurid murder in the Doheny family. Young Ned, Doheny's only son, had been shot and killed by his secretary, Robert Plunkett, who had assisted him in the cash payment to Fall. In Los Angeles it was whispered that the murder occurred because young Doheny had resisted Plunkett's homosexual advances. But, then, it might have been the other way around, because shortly afterward Plunkett put a pistol to his temple and killed himself. In any case, the suicide-murder effectively removed important witnesses—the two men who had actually delivered the cash to Fall—and there was even speculation that Fall might have had something to do with the killings. In Los Angeles the tragedy had created even greater sympathy for the Doheny family.

No one could help noticing that the Los Angeles press was treating the Dohenys very kindly indeed. Partly this was because Doheny's chief attorney, Frank J. Hogan, saw to it that all bits and pieces of evidence favorable to Doheny were delivered to the press table as soon as they were offered in court. Also, Mr. Doheny's physical appearance worked in his favor: elegantly tailored and shod, distinguished-looking, the picture of self-confidence and sincerity. Hogan and his large staff of lawyers had all been put up in luxurious quarters at Chester Place, where they led an active after-hours social life, making use of the Doheny's private gymnasium, bowling alley, and swimming pool. Members of the press were invited to Chester Place for parties and their journalistic output showed their appreciation. But one Los Angeles reporter admitted that his editor had given him strict instructions to write only nice things about Doheny. The newspaper did not want to lose the advertising revenue it received from Doheny-controlled oil companies.

After nine days of testimony the government rested its case, and Doheny's lawyers embarked on his defense, relying heavily on pathos, patriotism, and even bringing in the "yellow peril." The defense made much of the claim that Doheny's oil tanks in Pearl Harbor, which had been built for the navy as part of his deal with Fall, provided a vital national force to protect the Pacific—including the California coastline—from America's "enemies" in Asia (enemies who would not materialize until nearly twenty years later). In a ringing voice one of the Doheny lawyers told the court, "America can sleep tonight secure from danger of being overrun by a Mongol country because of the patriotism of such men as E. L. Doheny, Edwin Denby, and Admiral John K. Robison and their work in establishing a great naval oil base in Hawaii. These men have been humiliated and vilified because they endeavored to save you and me and our country." The trial lasted about two weeks and ended on November 12, 1924, after a five-day summation. Judge Paul J. McCormick retired to deliberate the case.

The judge's deliberations took him until the following May. In his 105-page decision he decided that the leases to the Elk Hills land were null and void, and that the contract for the Hawaiian storage tanks was equally illegal and had been obtained through fraud. He also held that President Harding had exceeded his authority when he turned over the navy's oil lands to Fall's Department of the Interior. Doheny's payment of a hundred thousand dollars to Fall, the judge decided, was "against good morals and public policy, and tainted with fraud." He ordered Doheny's company to pay the government for all the oil it had taken out of Elk Hills. It was a clear and unexpected setback for Doheny, but there was some comfort in it since the judge also ruled that the government had to pay Doheny for the storage tanks. The Doheny lawyers immediately appealed Judge McCormick's decision, which may have been a mistake. Reviewing the case in October, the Court of Appeals not only upheld McCormick's decision but took away Doheny's reimbursement for the storage tanks. Once more the lawyers appealed, this time to the United States Supreme Court.

Both Doheny and Fall would have to stand trial again, in Washington, on the bribery charge, which, since it was a criminal case, might end up not only costing them money but also sending them to jail. Still, Ed Doheny was undaunted, convinced that the power of his wealth would eventually prevail. For his Washington trial, which opened in November 1926, he was even better prepared than he had been in Los Angeles. His lawyer, Frank Hogan, marshaled an even larger staff of lawyers. A huge suite of rooms was leased on the third floor of the Columbia Building, opposite Judiciary Square, and this was fitted out as a private club for the Doheny legal aides. Once more the press was regaled. A chef and a staff of waiters were hired, and in addition to ample amounts of food and drink, the men and women of the press were fed a steady stream of releases, all taking the Doheny side. A personal press agent now accompanied Doheny into the courtroom to facilitate the flow of laudatory news.

But there were sinister notes as well. A few days before the trial was to begin, several jurors complained of threatening and other disturbing telephone calls from strangers. One juror reported that a caller who had identified himself as "the court" had telephoned to ask questions about his bank account, his real estate holdings, his social and religious affiliations, and his relationships with women other than his wife. Because of all this, the presiding justice, Adolph

A. Hoehling, ordered that the jury be sequestered during the entire lengthy proceedings. And so, while the defendant and his lawyers partied in the Columbia Building, the jurors languished in locked hotel rooms guarded by marshals. The jurors were not even permitted to join their families for Thanksgiving dinner, nor could they go to church on Sundays. Instead they were given Bibles to read. At the time, someone from the press slyly commented that the jurors were the only ones involved with the whole Teapot Dome mess who had thus far been placed behind bars.

Edward Doheny was now seventy years old, and when he took the stand on December 9 it was for the first time noted that he looked shaken, exhausted, and ill. He had been suffering from an infection in his arm, was wearing a sling, and rested his arm on a small cushion. Before her husband testified, Mrs. Doheny was called to the stand and repeated her strange story of the torn note and the missing signature.

Her husband's testimony, when he reached the stand, once again stressed his patriotic intentions. He was merely trying to "save" the navy's oil to keep America safe and strong. He insisted that he expected no profit at all from his deal with Fall, despite the fact that he had once announced that he assumed his profits would exceed a hundred million dollars. He explained that he had selected his son as the courier to deliver the cash to Fall because "I was endeavoring at the time to work him into every phase of the business of handling the fortune that I expected sometime or other he would handle all of." Doheny was asked whether he considered his son's rather simple mission to Washington an important part of the young man's financial education. "Yes, sir," Doheny replied. "Even if he had been held up on the way he would have learned something. He would have had something in experience." Doheny's was a mind that seemed frequently to contemplate disaster.

After some three weeks of testimony Frank Hogan was ready to sum up for his client and to demonstrate his particular mastery of the Irish gift of oratory. With flashing eyes and a voice that filled the courtroom, Hogan told the jury that what it had heard against Doheny amounted to "as wholesale and as vicious vilification as ever polluted the atmosphere of a court of justice." He asked the jury: "Do you think that man who has left his home at the age of sixteen and followed the trails of the pioneer West, who dug in mother earth for the minerals hidden therein, who with pick and shovel sunk wells that he might bring out the gold and liquid that today mean safety for worlds, would, even if he himself could, stoop so low as to bribe an official of his government, the friend of his youth and former days, a Cabinet officer of the United States of America, in order that he might swindle and cheat the land that had given him plenty?"

For more than five hours Hogan besieged the jury with his harangue, once becoming so overwrought that he had to pause and dry his eyes. He brought in the horrors of World War I and young Ned Doheny's valiant service in it. Doheny, Sr., had not only given America its riches from underground but had also "offered that young man's life upon the altar of patriotism. He went on the turbulent and submarine-infested oceans in his country's service—the only son. And you are asked to believe that when Edward L. Doheny, near the end of his life, corruptly intended to bribe Albert B. Fall, a Secretary in the Cabinet of Warren G. Harding, he deliberately used as an instrument therefor his son, the pride of his youth, the hope of his maturity, the solace of his old age!" He invoked the memory of the dead President, calling Harding "as able and loving and as fine-hearted a President as we have ever had, or will have," and saying that "from his sacred tomb in Marion, Ohio, I stand his splendid figure before twelve of his fellow men. . . . He stands here today as the best silent witness in this case." There was a hush in the courtroom as the spirit of the departed President was allowed to enter the proceedings. Before he was finished Mr. Hogan had compared his client's situation to the crucifixion in Jerusalem, and Edward Doheny to Jesus Christ himself.

After seven hours of deliberations the jury had not reached an agreement, and, as usual, the jurors were locked up for the night. At ten-fifteen the following morning they came in with their verdict: Not guilty.

Immediately a wild demonstration broke out in the courtroom, and chairs, tables, and desks were overturned. Lawyers, friends, and well-wishers rushed up to shake the defendant's hand. Old man Doheny wept with joy. His daughter-in-law also wept, as did Fall, Mrs. Fall, and the Falls' daughter, who had not yet got her trip to Mexico. In her hotel room, where she received the news, the blind Countess Estelle Doheny burst into tears as well, and, seizing a golden crucifix, she flung herself to her knees and cried, "My prayers have been answered!" The Doheny family returned in triumph to Los Angeles, where a welcoming crowd of some four hundred people had gathered on the station platform to meet their train. Doheny was given a huge testimonial dinner by the city to celebrate his victory. At the gala the mayor of Los Angeles spoke of "this great American patriot." Even the mayor of San Francisco—indicating that Los Angeles was at last becoming a metropolis worth recognizing—came down for the occasion to help extol the local hero.

It was a wonderfully Californian denouement: the scoundrel vindicated. It provided continued reassurance that the California rich could get away with anything, that skulduggery could be rewarded with laurels, honors, and prizes, and that checkbook justice worked just as effectively in the 1920s as it had in the days of the land-grabbers and the railroad robber barons. It proved conclusively that, in California, social and community status depended only on income. Morality was not even an issue. It didn't matter how one played the game. What mattered was how decisively one won it.

Of course there were some spoilsports who refused to see the Doheny acquittal as a great victory for American capitalism, the free enterprise system, and the power of California money to defeat all opposition. There are a few sour apples in every barrel, and one of these was Rollin Kirby, a topical cartoonist for the New York *World*. While all the celebrations and congratulations were going on in California, Kirby published a cartoon depicting a row of four prison cells, variously labeled "Rich Man," "Poor Man," "Beggarman," and "Thief." Three of the four cells overflowed with prisoners. The fourth stood conspicuously empty.

CHAPTER FOURTEEN

Final Curtains

EDWARD DOHENY's troubles were actually far from over. Within two months of the homecoming festivities in Los Angeles—on February 8, 1927—the United States Supreme Court upheld the California court's decision against him and ordered him to pay for all the oil he had extracted from Elk Hills. Initially a figure of $9,282,000 was placed on this, but later, through negotiation and compromise, the government's claim against Doheny was reduced to $5,500,000. The Supreme Court also declared that Doheny had no right to the $11,000,000 that he claimed the government owed him for the storage tanks his company had built at Pearl Harbor. The entire proceedings, the court declared, had been thoroughly stained with "fraud and corruption" from the beginning. It was a scathing opinion, and it was unanimous. Still, for a man to whom $100,000 was no more than pocket money, Doheny was getting off lightly.

But now it was Albert Fall's turn to stand trial, for accepting the bribe, and Doheny had an important stake in the outcome. If Fall were convicted of accepting the bribe, Doheny would have to stand trial again for offering it. As much to protect his own interests as Fall's, Doheny had urged Fall to engage Frank Hogan to defend him and had even made Fall a gift of $5,000 to help defray his legal expenses. To provide further help, Doheny had also purchased Fall's New Mexico ranch for $168,250, assuring Fall that he could continue to live there. And so, once again, the familiar cast of characters gathered at the Washington courthouse to play out yet another act in the long comic opera.

The curtain went up on a moment of high melodrama. Fall arrived at court looking terrible. He still wore his wide-brimmed western hat, but underneath it his face was gaunt and haggard. His color was bad and he looked much older than his sixty-seven years. A heavy overcoat and baggy trousers, looking as though they had been meant for someone else, hung on his emaciated frame, and he was in a wheelchair. A nurse and doctor were required to lift him, clutching a cane, from the wheelchair to a special leather easy chair that his doctor had ordered placed in the courtroom. The court proceedings had barely begun when Fall slid from the leather chair and collapsed in a heap on the floor. He was helped out of the courtroom by the nurse, the doctor, his wife and daughter, and Mr. and Mrs. Doheny. It was announced that he had suffered an "internal hemorrhage."

The next day, while Hogan and his staff were trying to obtain a postponement of the trial because of Mr. Fall's poor health, the doors to the courtroom suddenly swung open and Fall was wheeled in, looking even worse. With help he staggered once more to the leather chair, where a nurse covered his knees with a blue lap robe. He was insisting on going through with the trial because, as Hogan explained to the court, Fall wanted "vindication before he passes into the Great Beyond." Implicit in the whole scene of course was the possibility that Hogan had staged the whole thing in order to get the jury's sympathy for his sick, aging, and courageous client.

Hogan next tried to make emotional capital out of the murder of Ned Doheny. When Edward Doheny took the stand, Hogan interjected the son's name at strategic points. Each time he did so the elder Doheny broke down and wept, and the court had to be adjourned until Mr. Doheny had sufficiently recovered himself to go on. In addition, it seemed to many observers that Hogan continued to make excessive use of Fall's frail health in his remarks to the jury, a theatrical device reinforced by the fact that throughout his testimony Fall was solicitously hovered over by his wife, his daughter, the Dohenys, his doctor, and his nurse. Hogan also brought in, as character witnesses, a number of Fall's friends and neighbors from New Mexico. (Significantly, no one in Washington could be persuaded to perform this service.)

When the time came for both the prosecuting and the defense attorneys to make their respective summations to the jury, the prosecuting attorney was admirably brief. He reminded the panel that the state of Mr. Fall's health was immaterial to the question at hand. "It is all simple," he said. "There are four things of a controlling nature to remember. One is that Doheny wanted the lease of the Elk Hills. The second is, Fall wanted money. The third is, Doheny got the lease, and the fourth is, Fall got the money." As for the drainage of the oil lands, he said, "The only drainage in this case was from Doheny's to Fall's pocket."

In *his* summation Mr. Hogan seemed not quite able to repeat his past histrionic performance for Doheny, though he tried, and he even had Mrs. Fall bring the Falls' tiny granddaughter to court on that day. The child also seemed to be able to cry on cue. Hogan again tried to rely on pathos and the theme of patriotism. ("Patriotism," the prosecution had told the jury, quoting Samuel Johnson, "is the last refuge of a scoundrel.") Hogan spoke emotionally of Doheny and Fall as two old pioneering and prospecting pals, and chose one rather unfortunate simile when he said that national security ran "like a thread of gold" through the Elk Hills and Pearl Harbor deals. Finally the presiding judge, Mr. William Hitz, in charging the jury, said laconically: "Counsel has urged you to send this man back to the sunshine of New Mexico. Neither you nor I have anything to do with sunshine. You are here to decide this case on the evidence and nothing else."

The jury was out for eleven hours without reaching a verdict, before retiring for the night. This extended interval was regarded as a heartening sign by the Falls, the Dohenys, and their lawyers. But when the jury came out at eleven the next morning, its verdict was: guilty. Weeping, sobbing, and shouting filled the courtroom. The Falls wept, the Dohenys wept, and then Edward Doheny swore at the judge, saying, among other things, "this damned court." While the judge's gavel pounded for order one of Fall's many lawyers fell to the floor unconscious and was given a heart stimulant by Fall's doctor. Frank Hogan lost his composure as thoroughly as he had lost his first criminal case. He banged his fists on the table and shouted incoherently at the judge. The judge sentenced Albert Fall to a year in prison and a fine of a hundred thousand dollars.

Now the thing that Doheny had dreaded most would have to take place. Though he had been cleared of the conspiracy charge, he would now have to stand trial again on the criminal charge of bribing a public official. His prospects did not look good. With Fall convicted for his part in the transaction, how could the briber hope to fare better than the bribed? Once again he chose Hogan to defend him, and as the curtain went up on the final act of the drama, the audience hurried back to its seats.

Hogan stepped to the footlights. In a sepulchral tone he read from previous testimony of Doheny's dead son—"a voice from the tomb" —succeeding in imitating the young man's voice. Hearing him, the blind Mrs. Doheny cried out, "It's Ned! . . . It's Ned!" and collapsed in hysterical tears. Mr. Doheny wept along with her. The testimony contained almost nothing new and reiterated everything that had been said before, but Doheny did add one new wrinkle to his explanation of the hundred-thousand-dollar loan to Fall. Once, Doheny said, in the year 1886, he had fallen down a mine shaft and broken both legs. His old friend Fall had lent him some lawbooks so that he could study law while recuperating. For this favor, some thirty-five years later, he had helped Fall out with a hundred thousand dollars.

The trial lasted barely ten days, and Frank Hogan again provoked widespread weeping with his melodramatic summation to the jury. The jury was out for barely an hour before returning with a verdict of not guilty.

When the news reached Los Angeles, the town went wild. The favorite son had put the city on the map, and without disgrace. A reception committee even larger than the first turned out to meet the returning Dohenys when they stepped off their train. In the crowd were city officials, clergymen, commissioned officers from the army and navy, and a delegation of reigning motion picture stars. Not since Sarah Bernhardt's sweep through San Francisco had there been so spectacular a media event.

Edward Doheny's battle with the United States government had cost him quite a lot of money, perhaps $20,000,000 all told—which was a bit more than change. But he still had plenty more, at least $100,000,000. And he had not had to go to jail. His East Coast rival, Harry F. Sinclair, who refused to answer a question put to him by the Senate committee in 1927, had been declared in contempt and, partly on that account and partly on another, had been sentenced to jail and had served a term of six and a half months. On July 18, 1931, Albert Fall, after more than a year of unsuccessful legal maneuvering, went by police ambulance to the federal penitentiary at Santa Fe, where he became the first Cabinet member in American history to serve a prison sentence. Four months later, in November, he became eligible for parole, which, however, was denied him on the ground that it did not apply to the perpetrator of "so grave an offense against the government and civilization." Altogether Fall served more than nine months. But Doheny was free as air. The moral was clear: Californians were luckier than other mortals.

Though he had appeared to be at death's door at the time of his trial, Albert Fall survived for twelve more years after his release from prison, and died in March 1943 at the advanced age of eighty-three. Edward L. Doheny had died nine years earlier, on September 8, 1935, at age of seventy-nine, having been almost completely bedridden at Chester Place for three years. The last years of his life had been plagued by a welter of stockholders' suits as a result of his Elk

Hills and Pearl Harbor activities, and in all he had been required to pay $47,137,696.28 in settlements, taxes, interest, and penalties as a result of his involvement with Mr. Fall. But there was *still* plenty more. At his shrewd wife's suggestion he had, prior to his death, divided up his fortune between herself and other relatives, giving his family $75,000,000 in trusts and keeping $10,000,000 for himself.

Shortly after Doheny's death his estate, which owned the ranch in New Mexico, served an eviction notice on Albert Fall, a gesture that Fall and his family deemed unkind. But, then, Fall was no longer of use to the Doheny family, nor was he, in fact, to anyone else.

The Countess Estelle Doheny survived her husband for a number of years, living luxuriously in the vast reaches of her Los Angeles estate, surrounded by servants, guards, watchdogs, and occasional movie stars. Finally, taken ill, she was rushed to a Los Angeles hospital, where doctors advised the family she had only hours to live. A priest was summoned to administer the last rites and told to make all possible haste in getting to the hospital. He arrived within minutes and, informed that death was perhaps only moments away, ran down the corridor, swooped through the countess's doorway, skidded across a few feet of highly polished floor, and landed, elbows first, on the patient's stomach. With that, Mrs. Doheny expired.

THE UNITED STATES NAVY, meanwhile, had got its oil lands back. Periodically they were checked for leaks, which always proved to be minimal. As for the tremendous oil holdings of the heirs of Edward Doheny, they passed out of the family's hands in 1949. The purchaser had to borrow forty million dollars and issue 600,000 shares of stock to acquire them, because what was involved was in those days a great deal of oil—a production of 4,500,000 barrels a year, plus reserves of more than 48,000,000 barrels. The purchaser, ironically, was none other than the Union Oil Company of California, the company Edward L. Doheny had tried to buy out thirty-four years earlier.

CHAPTER FIFTEEN
Scandals

IT ONCE pleased San Franciscans to think that while people in Los Angeles were herding cattle on horseback, San Franciscans were riding to the hounds in hunting pinks. Certainly the northern city had come firmly to this view by the late 1920s. And while the Doheny oil scandals were going on in southern California, with all the sordid evidence of bribery, fraud, corruption, and even—if rumors about the Doheny murder-suicide were to be believed—deviant sex, San Francisco was embroiled in a much more genteel scandal of its own. It involved, not surprisingly, art. While news of the Doheny trials was buried in back pages of the San Francisco newspapers, the Great San Francisco Art Scandal received front-page banner headlines.

It all started in the summer of 1929, when Mr. James Duval Phelan took it upon himself to launch an attack on Alma Spreckels' Palace of the Legion of Honor, which was then less than five years old. Mr.

Phelan was a small, white-goateed, very proper gentleman of sixty-eight, who had been mayor of San Francisco and been called "San Francisco's first honest Mayor." He had then gone on to serve in the United States Senate from 1915 until 1921. He also wrote poetry and considered himself a connoisseur of art and antiques, and at Montalvo, his eight-hundred-acre estate in Santa Clara County which had an outdoor theater, he often entertained poets, writers, painters, and other artists. His particular friend was the San Francisco novelist Gertrude Atherton, who wrote romantic fiction about life in ancient Greece and Rome, and who more or less lived with him, though their relationship was assumed to be platonic rather than physical.

What first aroused James Phelan's ire was an exhibition at the Legion of Honor of the Huntington sculpture collection, part of the famous Huntington library and art gallery that had been assembled by Collis P. Huntington's nephew, Henry Huntington, after his marriage to his uncle's widow. Henry Huntington had recently died, and the thirty-million-dollar collection—considered one of the most important collections of rare books, paintings, and sculpture in the world—had been left, handsomely endowed, to the public. But the Huntington sculptures being exhibited at the museum, Mr. Phelan had discovered to his horror, did not include a single example of the work of the "famous" California sculptor Douglas Tilden. Tilden specialized in athletic subjects, and some of his more popular pieces were titled "The Baseball Player," "The Tired Boxer," "Football Players," and "The Indian Bear Hunt." Douglas Tilden had also executed monuments commemorating the admission of California to the Union, and others dedicated to the California volunteers and the mechanics of San Francisco. For failing to include a piece of Tilden in the show James Phelan publicly branded Mrs. Spreckels "ignorant and incompetent."

Alma Spreckels was not the only target of Phelan's broadside. He also attacked Herbert Fleischhacker, banker and philanthropist; William F. Humphrey, president of the Park Commission and an art critic; M. Earl Cummings, another art critic and also a sculptor; William Sproule, former president of the Southern Pacific as well as an art critic; and John McLaren, who had helped design Golden Gate Park. All these local worthies, in other words, represented at least one side of the Sàn Francisco art establishment (the de Youngs et al. represented the others). All were members of the board of the Legion of Honor.

In support of his diatribe Mr. Phelan issued the following windy statement:

> When the roll is called [at the Huntington exhibition of sculpture at the Palace of the Legion of Honor] unfortunately Douglas Tilden, one of the great native sculptors of California, will not be represented. He claims he was not invited. If, by charter amendment, we could only organize "art interests" under the stimulus of the Huntington collection, laid before us so magnificently, we would quickly assume our rightful place as an important art center.
>
> As it is, we have, virtually, the Park Commission in control and the Park Commission, figuratively speaking, consists, as it doubtless should, of gardeners and farmers. No one knows and no one cares.
>
> I have in mind the case of two distinguished artists, both exhibitors at the Paris Salon for years, who graciously vouchsafed to paint the lineaments* of two representative Californians, wearing the decoration of the Legion of Honor, and who were denied access for these paintings in the very hall of the Palace of the Legion of Honor itself by ignorant and incompetent trustees. What should be done, as a matter of poetic justice, with such commissioners but to reject them?†

Mr. Phelan then abruptly shifted the focus of his attack. In a non sequitur that perhaps would have made sense only in California, he stopped talking about art and began talking about swimming pools. The Fleischhacker Pool, then one of the largest outdoor pools in the world, donated to the city by one of the "ignorant and incompetent" directors of the museum, was, said he, "another folly in which nobody, speaking of the population generally, desires to swim because of our cool climate."

* An artistic word for "portraits."
† San Francisco *Call*, July 13, 1929.

In the indolent summer of 1929—the great stock market crash was still months away—the Phelan attack hit San Francisco like a bombshell. Eagerly, reporters scurried after statements from members of the museum board who had been subjected to Phelan's vitriol. Comments ranged from "most unfortunate" to none at all from those who "refused to dignify Mr. Phelan's statements." Across her copy of the San Francisco *Call*, which broke the story, Alma de Bretteville Spreckels wrote in her large, bold hand, "He overestimates his own value," and across the photograph of James Duval Phelan she wrote, "Some James!" And then, more or less quoting Robert Burns, she added, " 'That we could see ourselves as ithers see us.' " In the press the controversy was compared with the uproar raised by New York City women when Frederick MacMonnies' statue "Civic Virtue" had been placed in City Hall Park, depicting a muscular youth towering over a servile girl crouching at his feet. It was compared with the public outcry in London over Jacob Epstein's Hyde Park memorial to W. H. Hudson—a futuristic interpretation of Rima the bird-girl in *Green Mansions*.

The furor in the artistic community, and in the press, went on for days. Finally Park Commissioner William Humphrey was persuaded to issue a statement on behalf of the museum's board. Mr. Phelan's outburst, he pointed out, was simply a case of sour grapes. The person who had attempted to present the "lineaments" of a prominent Californian had in fact been Mr. Phelan. He had offered a portrait of himself to the Palace of the Legion of Honor, "but in the judgment of the trustees, based on competent advice, the quality of the painting as a work of art was not considered of such merit as to entitle it to a place in that gallery." Mr. Phelan's nose was out of joint, in other words, and Mr. Humphrey added, "The personal animus that prompted the statement destroyed the usual balance of Mr. Phelan. Evidently he did not investigate to ascertain the facts. His statement abounds in erroneous statements."* Mr. Humphrey then went on to rebut, one by one, the entire list of Mr. Phelan's charges.

Actually, the "personal animus" of James Phelan toward the

* San Francisco *Call*, July 13, 1929.

widow of Adolph Spreckels and the members of her museum board may have had its roots in events that had occurred more than twenty years earlier, in which Mr. Phelan and another member of the Spreckels family had been heavily involved. Rudolph Spreckels, Adolph's younger brother, had spent his time, when not quarreling with his father and brothers, amassing a large personal fortune of his own—including his First National Bank one—and working as an unofficial reformer of public morals. Like the other Spreckels men, Rudolph was tall and Teutonic-looking, with the bearing of a Hanoverian archduke, but unlike his brother John, Rudolph lacked a sense of humor. Indeed, he was a bore, because although everyone knew that everything he said about official malfeasance was true, no one wanted to do much about it. To San Franciscans, Rudolph Spreckels was righteous to a fault.

By the early 1900s, San Francisco had become as politically corrupt as any city in the world, corrupt beyond measure, beyond the wildest dreams of Edward Doheny. Corruption was so widespread and commonplace, in fact, that it was taken for granted. In order to obtain an ordinance, a building permit, an easement, a city contract, a change in the building code, money had to change hands. Even minor officials in the city government grew rich from selling licenses and permits, and, to the builder or the businessman, paying the necessary bribes had become accepted as part of the normal cost of doing business.

By 1901 the unquestioned boss of San Francisco, though he held no political office, was a man named Abraham Ruef. Ruef was a lawyer, and he had as his clients nearly all the most powerful corporations in the city, including the telephone and telegraph company, the water company, the gas and electric company, and the Crocker Bank. Ruef had never even met many of the men who ran these companies—socially, as a Jew, he was considered beyond the pale—and yet he had become a vital intermediary for them, since it was Ruef who seemed to know exactly which city official had to be bribed, and for how much, for whatever the businessman wanted to do. As the *Chronicle* put it—rather daringly, considering Ruef's enormous power to crush all opposition to his regime: "If you wish a job for yourself or your friend, you must see Ruef. If you wish a license for a grog-shop or a theater, you must see Ruef. If you wish to construct a building in defiance of the fire ordinances, you must see Ruef. . . . Ruef is by all odds the most dangerous boss this city has hitherto endured."

In 1901, having created his own political party, Abraham Ruef selected as his candidate for mayor a man named Eugene Schmitz, whose only political experience had been as president of the local musicians' union. Ruef's party was called the Union Labor party, and when Schmitz won the election handily—defeating both the Democratic and Republican candidates—there was considerable comment in the press across the country. No American city had ever had a Labor mayor, and it was widely assumed that San Francisco's Mayor Schmitz would soon be locking horns with the city's powerful capitalists. This, however, was not true. In fact, the opposite happened, and it was not long before the new mayor, a former fiddle player, was being invited to the perfumed gatherings of the city's most exclusive hostess, Eleanor Martin. Soon the mayor was building himself a new house, at a cost of $30,000—though his salary was only $6,000 a year—and gifts to help him furnish it were pouring in from the city's bankers and businessmen, including a $1250 Persian rug, which was a housewarming present from Eleanor Martin's son.

Before the 1906 earthquake and fire the city had begun laying plans for a street railway system. This could be built in either of two ways. The cheap way was to string overhead wires up and down the streets, but overhead wires were unsightly. A more expensive and esthetically pleasing system involved streetcars powered by cables buried under the streets. Rudolph Spreckels, then thirty-four, and James Duval Phelan, thirty-five, decided that for beauty's sake San Francisco deserved the more expensive underground system. Spreckels and Phelan were not only friends but brothers in the cause of good government and reform. The two men approached Mayor Schmitz and offered to build a street railroad for the city with their own money and then sell it to the city at cost, for they also believed that the city and not a private company should own and operate the transit system. Mayor Schmitz said he would think about it.

Los Angeles in 1853, with barely fifty American residents. It was "a sluggish, dispirited place where lynch law prevailed." *Culver Pictures*

The newer, more stylish homes in the outskirts of the city were surrounded by wild mountains filled with sagebrush and coyotes. *Culver Pictures*

Aerial view of sprawling Los Angeles in 1938. *UPI*

Hollywood has long served as an inspiration for dreams and fantasies.
This 1887 vision of a Hollywood subdivision was never built. *UPI*

Hollywood Boulevard in 1903, a mixture of rural and suburban. *UPI*

Los Angeles today, a spectacular view from the hills at twilight. *Culver Pictures*

This cartoon from a 1926 issue of *Life* magazine illustrates the California stereotypes that abounded even then. *Culver Pictures*.

Newspaper baron William Randolph Hearst indulged his passion for spending by building the palatial San Simeon. In this 114 room Moorish castle overlooking the Pacific he housed his awesome collection of art and furniture from all over the world. *Dept. of Transportation/State of California*

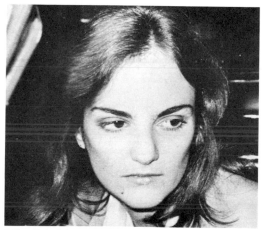

The Patricia Hearst trial made the same kind of sensational headlines that had been her grandfather's specialty. *UPI*

Coffee-fortune heiress Abigail Folger was one of the five persons killed in the Manson "family" murders. For months afterward, the rich of Southern California went into hiding. *UPI*

In 1950 alone, the annual output of California oil wells surpassed in dollar value the entire output of all the state's gold mines since the discovery of that precious metal at Sutter's Mill. *California Historical Society*

Lyman Stewart, head of the Union Oil Company, was a frugal Presbyterian who paid himself only $5 a day, even though his company produced about 5 million barrels a year. *UPI*

Edward Doheny (in straw hat) had been a mule driver, a fruit packer, a singing waiter, and a gunslinger before he became an oil tycoon who was "even richer than 'the richest man in America,' John D. Rockefeller." *California Historical Society*

Edward L. Doheny. "As a rich man, the former Southwestern gunman affected a monocle, a walrus moustache, British tailoring, and an autocratic manner." *UPI*

The home of Edward Doheny, Jr. *UPI*

Three generations of Dohenys. *UPI*

The tempest of the Teapot Dome Scandal swept the Secretary of the Interior and two oil magnates into a bribery and conspiracy trial that stormed all the way to the Supreme Court.

Secretary of the Interior Albert B. Fall (left) and tycoon Edward Doheny (second from left) with attorneys. *Culver Pictures*

Edward Doheny (seated third from right) testifying before the Senate investigating committee. He was the only man involved in the scandal who did not serve a prison sentence, proving that "Californians are luckier than other mortals." *Culver Pictures*

The Teapot Dome Scandal as
viewed by political cartoonists.
Culver Pictures

Oil operator Harry Sinclair (second from left) accompanied by his lawyers.
Culver Pictures

For the colorful Spreckels family of San Francisco, the road to riches began in a poker game with the King of Hawaii. With their fortunes they built mansions and museums—and much of San Diego.

Map of the port of San Diego dated 1782. *Library of Congress*

The San Diego skyline. *San Diego Convention and Visitors Bureau*

John D. Spreckels. *Culver Pictures*

Claus August Spreckels. *Culver Pictures*

John Spreckels' mansion in Coronado. *San Diego Historical Society*

The three Spreckels children were married a grand total of twelve times, and had eleven divorces. Pictured here is Adolph with one of his six wives, the former Lois Quantain Clarke DeRuyter. *UPI*

Adolph's most famous wife was Kay Williams, who later married Clark Gable. *UPI*

Of the third generation of California Spreckelses, "Little Alma," an expert horsewoman, is shown astride the champion horse at the Los Angeles Fifth Annual Horse Show. *UPI*

The original California Governor's Mansion, built in 1878, which Mrs. Ronald Reagan refused to occupy. "The house was on a corner facing two gas stations and a motel, and it backed up on the American Legion Hall, where I swear there were wild orgies every night." *Wide World Photos*

The Reagans settled for a state-rented home in the suburbs and construction began on this modern one-story mansion, which Governor Jerry Brown spurned as "too luxurious." *Wide World Photos*

The Irvine Ranch was established in 1864 when James Irvine and two partners bought 120,000 acres of land during a drought at 35 cents per acre.

James Irvine I. *The Irvine Company*

James Irvine II. *The Irvine Company*

James Irvine III. *The Irvine Company*

The Irvine mansion—a thirty-room ranch house in Orange County—was a setting for family strife and tragedy for nearly three-quarters of a century. *The Irvine Company*

Joan Irvine Smith, a twentieth-century heiress to the Irvine land legacy, waged—and won—a court battle with the private foundation that controlled her family's landholdings. *Wide World Photos*

The great-granddaughter of James Irvine then turned 77,000 acres of the original ranch into the largest and most elaborately planned housing development in the nation. Pictured here is one section of that profitable piece of real estate. *David Strick/The New York Times*

In the weeks following the fire, as the city struggled to rebuild itself, and while building permits and city construction contracts were being bought and sold like candy, the San Francisco Board of Supervisors, under the direction of Abraham Ruef, awarded the contract to build the street railway system, with overhead lines, to United Railways, a private company. The corporate counsel for United Railways was also Abraham Ruef, who was on United's payroll at a thousand dollars a month.

This flagrant conflict of interest was too much for Phelan and Spreckels. Certain that the Board of Supervisors would never order an investigation of its own improprieties, Phelan and Spreckels decided to use their own considerable funds to mount an investigation of corruption in San Francisco's city government. They hired Francis J. Heney, a well known attorney of the day, as their prosecutor, and William J. Burns, an equally well known detective, to gather evidence.

When Phelan and Spreckels announced their intention to clean up City Hall, their statement was applauded by the city's leading bankers, merchants, and businessmen, who had grown weary of paying bribes to city officials. But when Phelan and Spreckels subsequently announced that they would also bring to justice those bankers, merchants, and businessmen who were doing the bribing, they were castigated by the same group as traitors to their class. All at once they found themselves treated as pariahs, ostracized by San Francisco society.

In San Francisco, paying bribes had long since become socially acceptable. But taking them was not. The person who took a bribe was regarded as an extortionist, but it was unthinkable that the briber, his hapless victim, should be punished for his complicity. The double standard, to use a familiar analogy, decreed that the prostitute might go to jail but that her customer should go free. But Rudolph Spreckels was taking the unpopular position that all of this was wrong.

The business community was furious. Most furious of all perhaps were Rudolph's father and brothers, who no doubt had been guilty of paying a bribe or two in their day. Rudolph's motives were questioned by a suddenly hostile press. He was accused of wanting to run the street railway himself, of wanting to be mayor, of trying to dictate the morals of the entire city. But Spreckels and Phelan and their investigatory team pushed on undaunted. Evidence of wrongdoing at City Hall was almost ridiculously easy to find. The first to be indicted were Ruef and Mayor Schimtz, for extortion. Next came the chief of police, and the entire Board of Supervisors, who resigned en masse.

Now it was time to descend upon the business community, and indictments were handed down against the head of the telephone company, officials of the gas and water companies, a prominent real estate man, a leading lawyer. Suddenly it seemed as if every important person in San Francisco was under indictment or had a good friend who was.

In an effort to quell the rising public outcry against him Rudolph Spreckels issued an impassioned statement:

> I do not want to be mayor. I do not want the franchise of the United Railroads. The peculiar position in which I have been placed is distasteful to me. Do you suppose I enjoy prosecuting and bringing disgrace and public odium upon men who have been associated with me in business, and perhaps men who have been my dearest and best friends?
>
> In instituting this graft investigation, I was actuated by a broader motive than the mere punishment of wrongdoers and the moral cleaning up of a city. Any man who thinks can see that this country is in danger of a revolution. Our menace is the growth of bitter class feeling. Poor men are coming to believe that very rich men may break the law when and where they choose. Some rich men, I am sorry to say, are coming to believe so too.
>
> My greatest purpose in using my resources as a private citizen and bringing these rich corporations and rich bribe-givers to justice is to try to do something toward healing this terrible and growing breach between the classes. . . . I went into this resolved to let justice hit whoever was found guilty, be it my friend, my business associate, my enemy, or myself.*

* Frances Moffat, *Dancing on the Brink of the World.*

Why, the newspapers pointed out, this was right out of Marx and Engels ("In proportion as the antagonism between classes within the nation vanishes, the hostility of one nation to another will come to an end"). Now a new label was hurled at Spreckels: Bolshevik! And Rudolph Spreckels, although he denied wanting to be mayor, had indicated earlier his willingness to run for the United States Senate.

In the midst of the furor the press delightedly uncovered a juicy scandal, involving none other than Rudolph Spreckels in one of his periodic battles with his father. Claus Spreckels and his wife, Annie, had sued Rudolph to recover some five hundred thousand dollars' worth of sugar stock which, they claimed, was their community property and which Rudolph allegedly had malconverted. In his defense Rudolph and his lawyers maintained that the stock could not have been Rudolph's parents' community property, because, as far as Rudolph was concerned, he was not at all sure that his parents were really married. In other words, in order to keep his stock, Rudolph was prepared to go on public record as a bastard. And when he did so in open court, Claus Spreckels exploded. According to the court transcript, Claus cried out to his son, "You ingrate! You unworthy son! You are worse than an ingrate. I disown you. I don't want to have anything to do with you. You who would lie about your own father."

The press had a heyday. In a front-page banner headline the Oakland *Tribune* demanded to know, IS THIS THE RUDOLPH SPRECKELS CALIFORNIA WANTS TO SEND TO THE U.S. SENATE? The news of the sensational trial of Henry K. Thaw for the murder of Stanford White, which was being held simultaneously in the East, was buried in the back of the paper. Undaunted by the untidy publicity, Rudolph announced his determination to pursue his investigation.

At this point the proceedings got very ugly indeed, as people anxious to save their own necks began betraying and informing on their friends and business associates. Former supervisors had been promised immunity by prosecutor Heney if they would testify against others. One of these, James Gallagher, was to be a witness in a bribery charge against Ruef. Shortly before Gallagher was to testify, a bomb exploded in his house. A few days later another bomb went off, this time in an apartment house Gallagher had been scheduled to visit. Then Gallagher disappeared.

One afternoon, while prosecutor Heney was working in his courtroom, an unidentified man approached him, drew a pistol from a holster, and shot the lawyer in the throat. Miraculously Heney survived, but the motive of the assailant was never clear, because the next morning he was found in a jail cell with a bullet in his head. The police ruled his death a suicide, but a few days later, under heavy criticism for allowing a pistol in the prisoner's cell, the police chief was pushed, jumped, or fell from a police launch in the Bay and was drowned. The books of United Railways were subpoenaed, and on their way to the courtroom mysteriously disappeared. More witnesses vanished.

Still, the corruption hearings continued, and convictions began coming down. Mayor Schmitz was sentenced to five years in prison, and the head of the telephone company was found guilty of bribery. But as defense lawyers for the convicted men pressed on with appeals and other delaying tactics, one by one the verdicts of guilty began to be reversed. Mayor Schmitz's conviction was thrown out by the State Supreme Court on the flimsiest of technicalities—because the indictment against him had been addressed to "Eugene Schmitz" instead of to "Mayor Eugene Schmitz." The conviction of the telephone company head also was reversed, by State Supreme Court Justice Frederick Henshaw, who was later convicted of accepting a bribe of $410,000 from the heirs of silver king James Fair in their attempt to break Fair's will.

In the end only Abraham Ruef's sentence—for accepting a two-hundred-thousand-dollar bribe to arrange the street railway franchise—was allowed to stand. Perhaps it was because he was Jewish and had never been acceptable in Eleanor Martin's circle. He served a four-year-seven-month sentence in San Quentin. When he came out of prison he still seemed to have plenty of money, and one of the first things he threatened to do was to build an apartment house that would block Rudolph Spreckels' view of the Bay.

So much for reform and reformers in San Francisco. What the reformers had forgotten was that San Francisco had been built on graft and corruption and that by 1906 these practices had become as characteristic of the city as its precious views. The city's business leaders never forgave Rudolph Spreckels for trying to tamper with the established scheme of things, and—who knows?—he may have been lucky that he was not murdered himself.

As for James Duval Phelan, his bitter attack in 1929 on the board of the Palace of the Legion of Honor may have been his last-gasp attempt to get back at the San Francisco establishment, as well as at the Adolph Spreckels branch of the family, whom Rudolph had always hated and who had always hated Rudolph. And the art controversy that Phelan stirred up may have done him in. He died shortly afterward, in 1930, at the age of sixty-nine.

Meanwhile the crash of 1929 had brought on the collapse of Rudolph's First National Bank, which in its heyday was said to have provided him with an income of eighteen million dollars a year. In 1934 he was declared bankrupt. He moved to a tiny apartment in San Mateo, where he died in 1958 at the age of eighty-six. He liked to remind his few remaining friends that when *his* financial ruin had come, at least he had not jumped out a window.

PART THREE

BLOOD
AND
WATER

CHAPTER SIXTEEN
J.I.'s Land

THOUGH VERY few of California's "old" country and ranch houses are old in the sense, say, of old houses in Philadelphia or Newport or Boston, one way to recognize a California house that at least predates the era of air conditioning is to observe whether it is built high off the ground (sometimes even on stilts) and is approached by a long flight of steps—precautions against the seasonal floods that used to occur in Central Valley regions. Also, early California houses generally are surrounded by large trees, stout palms and tall stands of eucalyptus. These trees, planted close by, quickly over-reached the structures and eventually protected the houses from the dry, hot summer winds. This was the way James Irvine, Jr.—the irascible J.I.—landscaped the white frame two-story "mansion" that he built on his ranch in 1900. Some twenty-five years earlier J.I.'s father had bought out his partners for a hundred and fifty thousand dollars—a bargain, as the value of the Irvine ranch would eventually be placed as high as a billion dollars and would make J.I. one of the richest men in California. The mansion—really no more than a large, comfortably furnished ranch house that would grow, with additions, to contain thirty rooms—would become the principal setting for family discord, strife, and tragedy for nearly three-quarters of a century.

From the upstairs veranda of his mansion J.I. liked to survey his domain—one hundred and thirty-eight square miles of southern California land, the largest landholding in Orange County. He strolled the upper veranda like a sea captain patrolling the bridge of a great ship, ever on the lookout for poachers, trespassers, and other unwanted intruders. For all his gruff and unpredictable temper, he was a handsome man, and vain, proud of his broad shoulders, flat stomach, and Teddy Roosevelt mustache. In 1892 he had married a pretty Cleveland girl named Frances Anita Plum, who, like him, was an amateur painter, and she had promptly done what he expected of her and had borne him three children, two of them—much to his satisfaction—sons: James III, who was nicknamed Jase, Kathryn, and Myford, whom his parents called Mike. Though J.I. was a domineering husband and father, it was clear that his wife and children worshiped him. And it was clear that he loved them too, though he showed it in curious ways—such as bellowing noisy curses and imprecations at them when they failed to kiss him goodnight.

For the first few years of their marriage J.I. and Frances Anita and the children lived principally in a large house on Pierce Street in San Francisco, with J.I. making periodic trips to southern California to inspect the operations of the ranch. After the 1906 fire, however, J.I. decreed that the city was a perilous place to raise children. Also, he had begun to feel that the children—particularly the boys—were becoming too citified and needed the rigors of ranch life to toughen them up. So he ordered the family moved south, to the mansion, for at least six months of the year.

The ranch was then a vast and in some ways desolate place, plagued by drought as well as floods and scorched periodically by the strangely debilitating Santa Ana winds, which, when they occurred, seemed to take the life out of the air and penetrate the marrow of one's bones. In these hot, dry periods, fires in the hills were a constant danger, and a single spark could cause an entire mountainside to explode in flames. Except for the ranch hands and staff, there was little companionship. The nearest neighbors were miles away, the nearest town, Los Angeles, thirty-five miles distant, a three-hour drive over primitive roads. In this bleak scheme of things a rancher spent most of his days fighting the weather.

There were hard times. In 1888 another Great Drought had reduced the herds of J.I.'s sheep from 50,000 to 12,000, and J.I. decided to phase out his sheep-ranching operation and to concentrate on crops—hay and grain, lima and black-eyed beans, grapes, barley, walnut trees, and citrus, thousands of acres of Valencia oranges— and thereafter he grew steadily richer.

But then fate seemed to prepare a revenge against J.I. for his hard ways, and the first of a number of deaths occurred when Frances Anita Irvine died suddenly of pneumonia in 1909—three years after J.I. had moved her to the mansion—leaving J.I. a widower at forty-two. Soon afterward he left his three young children in charge of a governess and embarked on a trip around the world—the first, as it would turn out, of many solitary travels to distant places in an apparent effort to escape the memory of his young wife.

On his periodic returns to the ranch he would invariably bring with him exotic seeds and seedlings to see how well they would do on the land. But in other respects J.I. seemed to have undergone some kind of personality change. He had always been autocratic, but now he appeared at times demonic. His rages became legendary, and among his workmen he was hated and feared. Once one of his foremen, Raymond Willsey, came to him with a problem about laborers who were too drunk after payday to show up for work. "Weed 'em out!" said J.I. "But some of those guys have been with us twelve years or more," Willsey argued. J.I.'s answer was final: "I don't care if they've been here thirty years. If they're not on the job, get 'em off the payroll." When the men failed to heed Willsey's warning, sixteen were fired in a day.

J.I. developed a cruel streak and seemed to love to cause discomfort to others. He liked to hunt quail and was inevitably followed about by as many as half a dozen retrievers and their puppies. At one point J.I.'s pack of hunting dogs reached a grand total of fifty-six animals, and his ranch veterinarian would deliver five or six dogs each evening to the mansion, on a rotating basis, to keep him company. The Irvine hounds were not housebroken, and J.I. insisted on bringing his pack with him when he went on social and business calls and was greatly amused when the big dogs lifted their legs on rugs and furniture. Because he suspected that local hostesses invited him to their houses more for his money than his charm, he saw to it that the charm was nonexistent. When invited to formal dinner parties he would bring his dogs with him and, when seated at the table—with the dogs scrambling beneath it—he would toss them bones and scraps from his plate. The more the hostesses tried to lure this very eligible widower, the more antisocial and outrageous he became. One trick with the dogs was particularly unpleasant. At the occasional parties he felt obliged to give in the mansion, J.I. would bounce a tennis ball up and down until the animals were leaping and slavering with excitement. Then he would suddenly fling the ball into a lighted fireplace. The dogs would leap into the fire after it and quickly retreat, singed and howling. While J.I.'s guests looked on appalled, he would roar with laughter. As a long-time observer once said of him, "From the day J.I.'s wife died, he loved only two things, the land and himself. The rest of the world could go scratch."

This is not an entirely accurate appraisal, though J.I. was nothing if not autocratic. He neither smoked nor drank and would not permit anyone in his house or in his presence to do so. In 1922 his younger son, Myford, married a handsome Australian-born girl named Thelma Romey, whom he had known at Stanford. After spending the first year of her marriage living in her father-in-law's houses—in San Francisco and on the ranch—the bride quickly became accustomed to a rigid regimen governed by sounding gongs and ringing bells. To announce each meal and each day's scheduled activity a bell was rung. "At least in San Francisco they rang musi-

cal chimes," Thelma Irvine recalled many years later. "But at the ranch house a butler walked up and down the halls swinging a big cowbell. I remember my first morning at his house. A bell rang, and the housekeeper came into my bedroom to tell me that it was seven o'clock, time to get up. I was expected downstairs in the dining room for breakfast with my father-in-law, fully dressed, at eight on the dot. Anyone who was not there at eight would not be served. I simply said, 'I won't be down at eight. I'll have my breakfast later, on a tray.' You should have seen the expression on the face of that poor, terrified housekeeper! Actually, I got along well with him. We hit it off because I wouldn't always take his orders. To me, he was a very lonely man, one of the loneliest men I've ever known. He was too suspicious of everybody around him to have any real friends. He was always sure that people were trying to cheat him, and probably many of them were. Of course, in the end I began coming down for breakfast with him—just because it upset the housekeeper so when I didn't."

Though J.I. was abstemious in most respects, he was thoroughly addicted to bridge. Thelma Irvine had not been married long before she was ordered by her father-in-law to make up a fourth at the bridge table. "But, Father, I don't play bridge," she protested. "That's all right, just fake it," J.I. replied. Wisely, the new Mrs. Irvine refused to fake it, but she did find it prudent to learn the game. Later Charlie Cogan, who was in charge of sales for J.I.'s company, would say to Thelma Irvine, "You're the best thing that's happened to this family." "Yes," she replied tartly, "because he doesn't drag *you* out of bed anymore to be a fourth for bridge. He drags *me*!"

J.I. was also a man of deep private fears and anxieties, which he did his best to conceal and which only those closest to him sensed. When, during World War I, his older son, Jase, was sent overseas with the army, J.I. was certain that his heir apparent would be killed, and spent two years consumed with worry. It was during this period that he began rapidly losing his hair. Then, in 1919, his only daughter, Kathryn, married a man named Frank Lilliard and became pregnant with J.I.'s first grandchild. Though Kathryn begged her father to let her have her baby in a hospital, J.I. forbade it. He had been born on the ranch, he declared, and his first grandchild would be born on the ranch. Kathryn gave birth prematurely. The infant, a girl, survived, but Kathryn died. Thereafter J.I. was consumed with horrible guilt. He fell into a terrible depression, not marked by withdrawal but by bursts of violent anger. Because he was a tough and hardy man, he had expected his daughter to be as hardy as he, and she had betrayed him. Not long after his daughter's death J.I. suddenly lost all his body hair, including his exuberant mustache. The cause was assumed to be the emotional shock of Kathryn's death. From then on, wherever he went, J.I. covered his baldness with a hat, but the lack of facial hair and eyebrows gave his face an odd, waxen appearance. It pained him that his little granddaughter screamed in fright at her grandfather's appearance when he tried to lift her onto his knee.

But his land continued to be his primary concern. He would, he once said, do anything to protect his land—even kill for it. Still, despite the fact that, as one of his former employees once said of him, "His wages were low, his work hard, and he drained everything he could from you," he succeeded in building up his ranch to the point at which, on his hundred thousand acres, he was sustaining one of the largest Valencia orange groves in the world. To do so he fought off squatters, poachers, and other encroachers with a fury that became famous in Orange County. He was less successful, however, in his battles with governmental bodies, which wanted to condemn pieces of his land for one public purpose or another, though he made it a policy, whenever these forced sales occurred, to use the proceeds to buy more land. When, for example, the United States government requisitioned some 2300 choice acres for El Toro Marine Air Base, J.I. took the government's money and bought another hundred-thousand-acre ranch in Montana with it. With this "land for land" policy, he also was able to avoid any serious tax consequences.

Although he had become one of the richest men in California, he remained miserly with his staff. He did, however, occasionally reward longtime and trusted employees with gifts of land. And he could also be extravagant. He spent thousands of dollars on fireworks for his annual Fourth of July cookout and barbecue, and he was known to make lavish gifts of clothes, jewelry, and travel to a long series of lady friends. In 1931, to everyone's surprise, he announced his intention to remarry, choosing a bosomy San Francisco divorcée named Katherine Brown White. J.I. was then in his sixties and Mrs. White was some twenty years his junior. "Big Kate," as she was called (though not to her face), was the daughter of a wealthy San Francisco businessman and the former wife of a prosperous lumberman. She was a large, garrulous, very outspoken woman fond of oversized hats. Even during their engagement J.I. continued to see other women. At one point his bride-to-be paid an unexpected call at the ranch while J.I. was entertaining another friend called Sally. J.I. turned to his daughter-in-law, Jase's wife, for help. "Take Sally into town and keep her there," he ordered. Town in those days meant the Santa Ana branch of Bullock's, and the rejected Sally spent her time there well, running up over seven thousand dollars' worth of purchases against J.I.'s charge account.

Big Kate, according to one old friend, was "sort of a Diamond Lil kind of gal who liked to swish her sables, sweep into a room like a galleon under full sail, and make a big fuss." She was also, it seemed, able to match J.I. pound for pound, blow for blow, and dog for dog—almost—and brought into the marriage her own swarm of twelve tiny Pekingese. Added to J.I.'s hounds, they made the mansion sound like a boarding kennel. Big Kate quickly put a stop to J.I.'s ball-throwing-into-the-fire sport and made it quite clear to her husband that she intended to have some rights of her own. "She led him around by the nose," one family member recalls. "Nobody ever gave him hell before. I believe he liked it. Big Kate could be fun. I think J.I. admired her."

Though not as tall as her six-foot-two husband, Big Kate reminded others of an oversize Queen Victoria. For their honeymoon trip Big Kate and J.I. insisted that Mike and Thelma Irvine come along—not out of sentimental reasons, it turned out, but because the newlyweds wanted a bridge foursome. The four Irvines traveled by train—playing bridge all the way—north to Eugene, Oregon, and eastward to Cleveland. Somewhat to Big Kate's surprise, the trip to Cleveland *was* based on sentiment. With his new bride J.I. was making a pilgrimage to visit his first wife's relatives.

Big Kate was able to tame her husband, but only up to a point. For years, out of penuriousness, J.I. had refused to have the mansion centrally heated, claiming that the winter chill was healthy and good for the circulation. Once, at a party at Jase's wife's house, he had fetched a pail of water and doused the fire in her fireplace. "But, Father, it's cold!" the younger Mrs. Irvine had protested. "Why don't you wear long johns like me?" he had roared in reply, and his daughter-in-law meekly passed out sweaters to her other guests. Big Kate, however, succeeded in getting her central heating. She also succeeded in breaking his no-drinking rule and began serving cocktails to her guests. (Big Kate also smoked, though J.I. never knew about it.) He had also refused to build a swimming pool for the mansion, maintaining that a pool was nothing but a waste of good irrigation water. Big Kate not only got her pool but a tennis court as well—though J.I. managed to have the last word on the pool. As soon as it was finished he had it stocked with trout; if one wanted to swim, one had to swim with the fish. Next, both Big Kate and Thelma Irvine campaigned for central air conditioning for the house. On that, however, the women were never able to prevail. "I lived without air conditioning," J.I. would say. "So can you."

Still, as Thelma Irvine recalled many years later, life with Big Kate at the ranch was more fun—less lonely—than it had been.

But four years after J.I.'s remarriage the Irvine household was plunged into grief once more when J.I.'s older son, Jase, died suddenly of tuberculosis at the age of forty-two. J.I. was devastated. He had clearly intended Jase to assume the stewardship of the vast and growing Irvine empire. His only remaining son, Myford, had shown no interest in nor aptitude for ranching. Living in the north, Mike and Thelma Irvine had used the ranch mostly for summer vacations and Christmas holidays. Mike Irvine was musical—he composed and played the piano and a number of other instruments—and had begged his father to let him major in music at Stanford. But his father had forbidden it, and Mike had settled for a job at the Irvine office in the Crocker Bank building in San Francisco, where he helped manage the family's financial affairs. Now he was summoned permanently to the ranch to replace Jase, and Mike and Thelma Irvine gave up their big house in Hillsborough with its six servants, two gardeners, and private nine-hole golf course. "I also gave up all my San Francisco friends," Thelma Irvine recalled later. "Now all our friends were my father-in-law's friends." The mansion became a household of widows and half orphans. Frank Lilliard had re-married and moved away. His motherless daughter, Katie, was growing up on the ranch with a governess. There was also Jase's widow, and their little daughter. After Jase's death J.I. became solitary and withdrawn and spent most of his days on horseback, riding around his ranch.

Two years later J.I. drew up a trust instrument by which he established the James Irvine Foundation "to provide aid for educational and charitable institutions which were privately supported"; no institution receiving public funds was eligible for aid. J.I. was a fierce believer in private enterprise. Earlier, in the 1930s, he had handsomely endowed the ailing Santa Ana Community Hospital, to insure that it would be maintained as a *private* hospital, not one that was government-subsidized, but that was also nonsectarian and non-profit. To guarantee that the Irvine Foundation would have the final say in the Irvine Company's business, he specifically deeded to it a majority share of the company's stock. And to make sure that neither Myford nor Big Kate would control the foundation after his death, J.I. specified that the foundation be directed by four old friends, Loyall McLaren, Robert Gerdes, Arthur McFadden, and James G. Scarborough.

One summer day in 1947, J.I. and his general ranch manager, William Bradford Hellis, who had been working for Irvine since the age of twenty, and a real estate broker friend named Walter Tubach journeyed to Montana for a fishing trip at J.I.'s ranch, which he had named the Flying D. The three men roamed up and down the icy stream, and as Hellis and Tubach explained later, the three became separated. Eventually Hellis and Tubach found each other, but J.I. was still missing. When they found him at last he was floating face down in the river. The coroner's verdict was that he had died of natural causes, and, after all, he was then eighty years old. But some members of his family were never satisfied with that explanation. He had been in splendid health and was an expert mountain fisherman. He knew every rock and gorge of his Montana property as well as he knew his California land. And a few days earlier he had refused to lend Brad Hellis two hundred thousand dollars.

The presidency of the Irvine Company fell to Myford Irvine, who was then forty-nine, and Brad Hellis, who had been Mike Irvine's boyhood friend, was made second in command. But Mike Irvine, who knew next to nothing about agriculture, gladly turned the reins over to Hellis, and for the next ten years—in a style as imperial as old J.I.'s—Hellis ruled the Irvine ranch. Then suddenly, under circumstances in which, as we shall see, many troubling questions were raised, Hellis resigned.

Without Brad Hellis at his side Mike Irvine seemed to fall apart. He appeared to be having some sort of nervous breakdown. There was talk in the family of huge gambling debts incurred at Las Vegas and of threats from underworld figures, suggesting that he was entangled in a land deal involving the future site of Caesars Palace. In January 1959, Mike Irvine, in an agitated state, told the family that he had to raise $6,500,000 and that he needed at least $400,000 of that sum immediately. He was, he said, "sitting on a keg of dynamite." This was a Friday, and he needed the money, he said, by Monday morning at the latest. His relatives hastily began making arrangements to buy Mike Irvine's company stock, putting up their own stock as collateral for loans. At 5:00 P.M. on Saturday, Mike Irvine met with Paul Trousdale, the owner of the Trousdale Construction Company, a Los Angeles firm that was negotiating to buy some Irvine coastal land for subdivisions. "He offered to sell his stock to me for five million dollars," Trousdale said later. "It was very peculiar. I felt like I was a last resort. He wanted to sell that day, and he wanted cash. He was very nervous. I told him I would buy the stock Monday morning." The family was also ready to buy his stock on Monday, and on Sunday afternoon a niece telephoned him at the mansion to tell him so. But it was too late. Mike Irvine's body was found in the basement of the mansion with two shotgun blasts in his abdomen and the bullet from a .22 caliber pistol in his head.

Family members and friends reacted with shocked disbelief to the coroner's verdict that Mike Irvine's death had been suicide. He had left no note, and for a man to have used two different guns to shoot himself in both the stomach and the head seemed almost a physical impossibility. The family was convinced that he had been murdered and that it was a Mafia slaying somehow connected with Las Vegas. But a lengthy investigation by the California attorney general's office could turn up nothing. At one point in the grim proceedings Mike Irvine's body was exhumed and another autopsy was performed. But again the coroner's verdict came back: suicide.

If there was any comfort for the family, it was in the realization that at least old J.I. was no longer there to face the terrible circumstances of the death of the last of his three children. But Mike Irvine's bizarre death raised even more questions about his relationship with Brad Hellis and Walter Tubach, the third member of the fatal fishing party in Montana, who had become the principal real estate broker for the Irvine Company.

Mike Irvine died in 1959. Now, to gather up the other threads of the strange story, it is necessary to go back to the year of his brother Jase's death in 1935.

A FEW years before his death Jase Irvine had married for a second time (an earlier, childless marriage had ended in divorce). His bride was Athalie Richardson, and their only child had been named Athalie Anita Irvine, after her mother and her Grandmother Irvine. When her father died little Athalie Anita was only two years old.

She was a beautiful child, with blond curls and blue eyes, and she was also, from an early age, extraordinarily willful and precocious. After her father's death Athalie Anita and her mother went to live with her grandfather, old J.I., at the Irvine mansion. Old J.I. doted on the little girl and gave her everything she wanted, including a whole menagerie of pets, and she quickly grew to adore him. Unlike certain of her cousins, she was not frightened by her grandfather's bald head and hairless face. From the time of her father's death until J.I.'s death her grandfather loomed as the towering influence in her life. Even when she was a tiny child, friends used to comment on how strongly, in terms of temperament, she resembled him.

From an early age the little girl demonstrated an exceptional ability to get her own way and, if not to make friends, to influence people. At the age of five she decided that "Athalie" was hard to say and anounced that she had renamed herself Joan. She had gotten the name, she said, from a Mother Goose nursery rhyme:

> Here am I, little jumping Joan;
> When nobody's with me,
> I'm always alone.

The name stuck, and some people suspected that more than Mother Goose was involved in her choice, since as Joan Irvine she now had the same monogram as old J.I. At seven her grandfather gave her a pony so that she could ride around the ranch with him. He took her on fishing trips in the mountains and shopping trips to Europe. At the ranch she often visited him in his office, and he let her sit in on his business meetings. As a young girl she was quick to notice and point out to him that some of his staff and associates tried to take advantage of him, and together the two enjoyed plotting ways to outwit the schemers.

She spent her summers at the family cottage on the family beach at Irvine Cove, where she body-surfed, snorkeled, learned to play tennis, show horses, race sailboats, and, later, fly airplanes and paint. From the cove she would ride her horse or drive her jeep up into the golden brown hills and the green fertile valleys which, on much of the ranch, were really not used for anything—just beautiful, empty land stretching to the horizon and, beyond the horizon, more land.

Growing up in the 1930s and 1940s, she could not help being aware of the incredible, sprawling growth that was taking place in Los Angeles, where the population jumped from a little over a half million in 1920 to more than a million and a half in 1940. The war, with the burgeoning military installations and the importance of the aircraft industry, would add another half million people. Los Angeles was growing out of all control—northward into the San Fernando Valley, gobbling up Burbank, Glendale, and Van Nuys, threatening to push onward into Oxnard and Ventura. In Beverly Hills, where not much had been before—the Doheny family had owned one whole mountain—movie stars and motion picture moguls were building Italianate mansions. Eastward, Los Angeles was stretching out toward Pasadena, and southward the population push had passed Long Beach. But south of that the great press of people was stopped at the frontier of the Irvine ranch, which lay athwart the expansion path of one of the fastest growing metropolitan areas in the world. Here, where the builders along the increasingly valuable coastline met the undeveloped coast that belonged to the ranch, everything stopped. The great, empty wilderness of the ranch lay like a peacefully sleeping giant with its back against the city.

Growing up in this expansive era—and in the process becoming a tall, slender, athletic, and strikingly beautiful young woman—Joan Irvine on her horse or in her jeep, surveying the ranch, began to dream of whole communities, whole cities, that could be built there. In her mind she planned shopping centers, parks, apartment complexes, hotels, industrial parks, futuristic office towers, luxurious houses overlooking the sea, a university, marinas, yacht harbors. The land was there to contain all these things, a Utopian city of tomorrow.

More than anything, though, Joan Irvine had begun to dream that all this land—as far as the eye could see and beyond—might one day be hers.

CHAPTER SEVENTEEN
Tough Lady

ONE REASON why it was hard to take Joan Irvine as seriously as she obviously wished to be taken was that she was, after all, "only a woman." In the traditionally all-male world of big-time ranching a woman's function was supposed to be decorative and domestic. In fact, this was a rule that applied pretty much to the state of California, where the mentality of the mining camp died hard. (In the mining camp the miner was hardworking, hard-drinking, the boss; his women were simply whores.) In California, even in the 1950s, there were only a limited number of things considered acceptable for a moneyed woman to do. She could shop at I. Magnin. She could join her moneyed women friends for Monday lunch (the fashionable day) at the old Mural Room of the St. Francis Hotel. She could plan menus with her Chinese cook and pen invitations to little dinner parties and thank-you notes to her hostesses. Some volunteer work was expected of her, either for the Junior League or for something high-minded like art or something unquestionably worthy, such as the children's hospital. Beyond that was man's stuff. A woman was not expected to handle money or manage a checkbook, and all of her bills were placed, unopened, on her husband's desk. She was supposed to stay out of politics and certainly out of business. Otherwise she found herself in deep trouble in the California he-man's world. Which was exactly where Joan Irvine found herself in 1957—a big, beautiful blonde who couldn't possibly have a brain in her head, meddling in the affairs of men.

In fact, other than as a sportswoman and passable amateur painter, Joan had not displayed any particular talent. At the Westridge School, a private preparatory school for girls in Pasadena, she had been only an average student, who had a fondness for low-cut dresses and, according to her yearbook, "liquid luaus." Her exposure to higher education was brief—two dilatory stints at Marymount College, in Los Angeles, and the University of California at Berkeley. And yet, when Westridge was raising funds among alumnae for a new library, Joan responded by writing out a check for twenty-five thousand dollars. Since hers was the largest single contribution, the school christened its new building the Joan Irvine Library.

She had also made several quick passes at being married. At age nineteen she had married a man named Charles Swinden, who was a lifeguard at Laguna Beach. There was a son, James, but the marriage lasted only two years. Next she married Russell S. Penniman III, who was described as "a dashing Navy flier." Again there was a son, Russell IV, but again the marriage lasted just two years. Her third marriage was to Richard Burt, a contractor, and this lasted another two years but produced no children. Finally she married a Virginia horseman and gentleman farmer named Morton Smith, by whom she had a third son, Morton. Perhaps because Smith was nineteen years older than she and the first of her four husbands to be wealthy in his own right, this marriage seemed to take, and to provide her emotional life with some stability, at least for a while. But her marital record did little to mitigate the impression that Joan

Irvine was nothing but a typical spoiled, bored, rich girl who had no idea of what she wanted.

On the other hand, though there was much of her grandfather in Joan, there was also much of her mother. Athalie Irvine was a similarly independent sort who didn't mind bending the sexist regulations of California society. Mrs. Irvine was eventually remarried, to Judge Thurmond Clarke, a relative of South Carolina's Senator Strom Thurmond. The new Mrs. Clarke had flung herself enthusiastically into Republican politics in Orange County, a very Republican place. She had also taken a job, as publisher of a Spanish-language movie magazine that her husband owned.

When old J.I. died his company owned the ranch in Orange County, which consisted of about 82,000 acres (reduced from its original size by several forced sales, including two branches of the interstate highway system which traversed it), plus 90,000 acres in Montana, and a smallish—7000 acres—parcel in the Imperial Valley. Fifty-four percent of the stock in this demesne had already been deeded to the Irvine Foundation. In her grandfather's will Joan was left 22 percent of the stock. Smaller bequests went to his widow, his then one remaining son, and other grandchildren. Thus it was that though the foundation controlled the majority of the voting stock, Joan became the largest *individual* stockholder in the Irvine Company.

Which brings us to the summer of 1957, when twenty-four-year-old Joan, whose mother had acted as custodian of her stock up to that point, was given her stock and attended her first meeting of the company's all-male board of directors. She looked very pretty, her blond California hair in a casual California flip style. The gentlemen greeted her warmly, and of course a bit patronizingly, particularly her grandfather's old friend Loyall McLaren, whom, as a child, she had called "Uncle Loyall."

The meeting had been expected to be no more than a routine affair. But to everyone's surprise—and no small amount of displeasure—Joan started off the proceedings by asking a number of tough questions. These involved certain land dealings in the company's Imperial Valley properties. Brad Hellis, it seemed, had cut himself into partnership with some of these company investments and had also, Joan claimed, taken advantage of his corporate position to buy lands on his own account or in partnership with the company's real-estate man, Walter Tubach. She demanded that the board terminate these partnership arrangements. The stunned board of directors voted to postpone action on her motion until its next meeting, four months later.

For this meeting Joan arrived—fresh from having her second baby and fresh from a separation from her second husband—armed with lengthy documentation of nine complicated real-estate transactions between Hellis and the company, Tubach and the company, and Hellis and Tubach. In one of these, she alleged, Hellis would in effect be given the two-hundred-thousand-dollar loan that her grandfather had denied him before his death. She moved that the company remove Hellis and have no further dealings with Tubach. The first of many angry exchanges occurred between her and McLaren, who called her a "damned troublemaker." She responded by calling him "senile."

It was clear that Joan Irvine was out to depose the palace guard, headed by Hellis, which had run the company since her grandfather's death ten years earlier. It was also clear that she was out to settle old scores; she had never been convinced that her grandfather's death had been either natural or accidental. And it was finally clear that the debutante had turned into a Dragon Lady. When no one would second her motion Joan departed from the meeting in fury. As Loyall McLaren bewailed, "The camel has gotten into the tent!"

It was worse than that. At a special meeting of the board that was called a few weeks later Joan announced that she and her mother had engaged counsel and had taken legal action to prepare a stockholders' suit against the Irvine Company, Hellis and Tubach. She said that the Los Angeles Superior Court would soon subpoena the two men for pretrial testimony, along with several other directors, including Myford Irvine. A few days later Brad Hellis resigned from the company. In return Joan agreed to drop her lawsuit, saying also she didn't want the proceedings to uncover anything that might be damaging to her Uncle Myford, which suggested that a three-way conspiracy might be involved. Naturally she considered Hellis' resignation a personal victory and a tacit admission on his part of wrongdoing. Hellis, insisting that he had been guilty of no improprieties, also cited Myford as his reason for resigning, saying that he "decided he didn't want to fight. So I resigned."

This resignation, of course, seemed to lead to Myford's sudden decline and, two years later, to his extraordinary death.

Myford Irvine's "suicide" made a bad corporate situation much worse, for now the company's reputation was tinged with scandal. On the day of his funeral a hasty meeting of the board was called at the mansion. The immediate problem was succession now that the last adult male Irvine was gone. (In fact, the only remaining male Irvine was Myford's six-year-old son, James.) Joan vigorously proposed that a three-man executive committee be set up, with herself a member, but this notion was voted down by the board. Instead, while Joan accused them of old-fogyism, the board proceeded to elect its oldest member, seventy-seven-year-old Arthur McFadden, as president of the company, and another old-timer, Loyall McLaren, as vice president. McLaren was also elected president of the foundation.

The next item of business concerned the way the company was to make the inevitable transition from farming to urban development. It had to come, Joan argued, and she accused the board of dragging its feet. She produced population-growth studies showing that the company's Orange County land was the next logical extension of the urban growth of Los Angeles, and yet at the ranch very little had been done to prepare for this lucrative tide of building. The board replied that real estate development required careful study and should be approached with great caution and the advice of experts. Harvesting Valencia oranges was one thing, but building cities was quite another. There were also tax problems. Since most of the company's business was still agricultural, whatever sales of land had occurred had been taxed at the farm rate of 25 percent, rather than the higher corporate rate applied to housing and business.

Joan asked that a top flight architect or city planner be engaged to provide an over-all plan for the development of the land. She had other complaints. It struck her as absurd that on the company's balance sheet the property of the Irvine ranch still carried a value of less than a dollar an acre—the appraised value in 1894, when the company was incorporated—when the land was clearly worth much more than that. She claimed that the company's stock was greatly undervalued. (Later an Internal Revenue Service appraisal would prove her quite right.) But most of all she objected to the fact that, though the company had annual profits after taxes of $5,500,000, out of a total income of $28,600,000, only $2,400,000 was paid out to shareholders in dividends by an organization that was worth at least $200,000,000. This meant that Joan's stock in the company paid her only $496,000 a year, or just slightly more than 1 percent of the value of her holdings. Most other stocks, of course, pay at least 6 percent.

The board, which had begun referring to Joan as "the princess pretender" (while she referred to them as "McLaren and Company," and "the Foundation bozos"), countered by saying that Joan's real problem was that she was greedy.

It is always hard to feel sorry for a girl who has a yacht, and an attractive young woman with an income of half a million dollars a year has a hard time presenting herself as a figure for pity. But with Joan Irvine it was not easy to make the greedy label stick. She was, after all, merely asking for a return on her money commensurate with its earning power if invested elsewhere. At the most conservative estimate, her Irvine stock was worth more than forty million dollars, and in fact she had been offered a hundred million for it and had refused to sell. She pointed out that the Irvine Foundation, with its majority interest in the company, was also being grievously shortchanged. With a higher yield the foundation would have greatly increased funds to expend on its charitable operations.

She charged that the foundation had become merely a device by which huge sums of corporate money were being hoarded tax-free, since foundations pay no taxes. But more than just money was involved. There was also a spiritual side to her crusade and her girlhood dream on horseback of great cities rising out of the empty land. She had good reason to believe that she was her grandfather's favorite heir, and she believed that she was his spiritual heir as well, with a mission to carry his creation into the twentieth and twenty-first centuries, to deliver his land to what she saw—and felt he would approve of—as its manifest destiny. As his surrogate she was merely trying to express his will.

And in the process she was proving herself to be just as stubborn and strong-willed—and, yes, as difficult to get along with—as old J.I. The University of California had been casting about for possible sites for a new campus south of Los Angeles, and a search committee had settled on a one-thousand-acre stretch of the Irvine ranch. Some twenty other communities and property owners meanwhile had offered to donate land to the university, and Joan strongly urged the company's board to do the same. Her motives were not entirely altruistic. She had watched the University of California at Los Angeles being built and had noticed the building boom in the immediate vicinity that accompanied it. She had seen how the Janss family, among others, who had developed the Village of Westwood hard by the U.C.L.A. campus, had become very rich. But the board of directors, who now routinely voted against anything Joan proposed, said no. They would sell the land to the university, but they would not give it away.

So Joan Irvine, backed up by a small flotilla of public relations people, took her case to the public. She helped organize and attended a rally in Orange County at which she spoke out strongly in favor of the Irvine campus, citing all the benefits it would bring to the immediate community. She made more speeches and gave newspaper, radio, and television interviews. She proved remarkably skillful at manipulating the media, gathering them for formal press conferences as well as for chatty meetings, with drinks, at her house on

Emerald Bay in Laguna Beach. She succeeded in getting press coverage of normally closed board meetings through the whimsical device of issuing temporary proxy votes to reporters—infuriating the board, of course, in the process, a key reporter for the Orange County *Illustrated* was once assigned a thousand shares of voting stock, making him a tycoon for a day. She had also begun carrying a tape recorder tucked under her suit jacket in order to record the acrimonious and often chaotic proceedings at board meetings. In the minutes of its meetings the board had often failed to record her negative votes. Now she had them on tape. She once brought a radio transmitter to a board meeting so that the goings-on could be broadcast outside the board room, but the signal got picked up by a car radio and Loyall McLaren heard about it and installed a special generator to jam her signal—or so she claimed. In the course of her publicity barrage she charged the majority stockholders with illegally taking over the company after her grandfather's death, with mismanagement, with lack of leadership, and with setting up cozy deals with each other that benefited themselves more than the shareholders. She made the Irvine Company's directors sound like miserly curmudgeons, narrow-minded enemies of higher education and the public weal. Her pretty but unsmiling face was soon familiar to readers and viewers throughout southern California.

Whether or not her well-publicized efforts were directly responsible for embarrassing the company into capitulation is a moot point, but it finally announced that it would give the university most of the acreage it wanted, and in the end gave all of it. Joan, understandably, took this as another personal victory in her battle with the "bozos."

Two months after Myford Irvine's death Loyall McLaren reported to the board on a visit he had made to Roger Stevens of New York, one of the country's shrewdest real estate developers, and recommended that Stevens be retained by the company to draw up a development proposal. For once the board unanimously agreed. Stevens visited and toured the land and came up with a plan providing for the board to set up a separate development company, of which the Irvine Company would own 70 percent and the Stevens group 30 percent. The subsidiary would periodically buy land from the Irvine Company and pay the tax on the profits. Joan immediately objected. This, she said, would be fine for the foundation—which paid no taxes anyway—but it offered no tax shelter to her as an individual. She proposed an alternate plan, involving wholly owned subsidiaries that could be sold after five years with their shares distributed tax-free to shareholders. Once more the board voted her down.

After a hasty huddle with her lawyers Joan announced that she would sue to liquidate the Irvine Company if the board accepted the Stevens plan. Her lawyers had discovered an interesting loophole. For some reason that has never been quite clear to his heirs, old J.I. had had his company incorporated in the state of West Virginia. The lawyers had unearthed an arcane West Virginia law under which a shareholder of 20 percent or more stock could force the liquidation of a company if "sufficient cause" could be proved. Faced with this threat, the Stevens group withdrew from the rancorous arena, and Loyall McLaren angrily denounced Joan Irvine for disrupting the company's attempts to carry on an orderly business.

Joan's next important victory occurred in 1969. She had taken her case—along with her lawyers and public relations staff—to Washington, where, as a result of vigorous lobbying (and, reportedly, about a million dollars of her own money), she succeeded in getting certain clauses inserted into the Tax Reform Act of that year. According to the act as it pertained to foundations, a foundation could now own only a certain percentage of any given company—2 percent in the case of the Irvine Foundation's ownership of Irvine Company stock. Furthermore, the act stated that all foundations must contribute to charities an amount equal to at least 6 percent of its holdings every year. The Tax Reform Act was passed by Congress and signed into law by President Nixon. Joan was delighted.

But the foundation's lawyers then succeeded in postponing the foundation's stock-divestiture date until 1983, and Joan was less pleased. In 1969 the citizens of Orange County were surprised to learn that their airport had become the sixth-busiest in the nation. What the experts on population growth had predicted had been right. Orange County was being overrun by Los Angeles. In 1970 the Irvine Company announced its ambitious plans for the largest totally master-planned city on the North American continent—the city of Irvine, to cover 53,000 acres, with a population of 430,000 predicted by the year 2000. Designed by the celebrated California architect and planner William Pereira—who, among other projects, designed the Los Angeles County Museum of Art and the Houston Center—it sounded like Joan's visionary dream come true.

But throughout the 1970s, California building laws and codes changed so rapidly that often, no sooner had the ink dried on a builder's sheaf of permits than new rules had been laid down. Environmentalist groups had to be given their say about development. The Irvine Company and Pereira had originally envisioned a kind of Space Odyssey luxury city for the rich, or at least the upper middle crust. But new laws specified that in any development provisions had to be made for economic and ethnic balances. In all these new regulations the Irvine Company found itself caught in the middle, and development did not proceed as smoothly or as speedily as had been hoped. And on top of all the other nuisances, there were the proliferating lawsuits—many of them instituted by Joan—and each new lawsuit seemed to set off half a dozen other actions.

The foundation meanwhile was somewhat grudgingly going about its business of conforming to the new Tax Reform law and exploring ways to divest itself of most of its company stock. Just how carefully the foundation was examining its options was not clear because of the directors' fondness for secrecy; as one of the directors had once exploded to a reporter, "What goes on at Irvine is nobody else's business!" But in the spring of 1974 an Irvine Foundation spokesman hinted broadly that the foundation had decided to offer its shares for sale on the open market.

For Joan this sounded as though final victory was in sight. On the open market the foundation's holdings would certainly end up divided among many different buyers, and her 22 percent would very likely give her effective control of the company. But then, at the moment when her hopes were highest, they were dashed. The foundation spokesman, it seemed, had spoken with a forked tongue. Some months earlier the foundation had begun secret negotiations which, by the fall of 1974, had led to a tentative agreement with Mobil Oil for Mobil to buy out the foundation for $110,000,000. For Joan this spelled utter defeat. If the Mobil deal went through she would be forced into a merger and would have to accept Mobil shares in exchange for her Irvine shares. She would wind up as a small shareholder in a giant multinational corporation where she would have no power whatever. Naturally, the foundation had not apprised her of the pending Mobil deal; she had learned of it quite by accident. She promptly filed another lawsuit.

She alleged that the sale price was unreasonably low and therefore constituted a breach of faith with both the company's minority stockholders and the foundation's charity beneficiaries. Others joined her objections in Orange County. It was charged that Mobil was "fronting for the Arabs." The Sierra Club claimed that Mobil would promote sprawling, automobile-dependent suburban growth so it could sell more gasoline, though there was no real evidence that Mobil had such a scheme in mind. Other loyal Orange Countians protested that their county was being invaded by "New York city slickers and foreigners." (Mobil's land-development subsidiary had its headquarters in Canada.) Mobil raised its price to $200,000,000, and by May 1976 the rest of the minority stockholders, most of whom were Joan's cousins, had signed agreements to sell their shares to Mobil, thereby earning the boundless wrath of their embattled relative. It began to seem that "little jumping Joan"—now supported only by her mother, her stepfather, and her lawyers—was at last all alone and fifteen years of struggle had been for naught.

But then, just when things looked darkest, they suddenly turned brighter again. Unexpected support came from the office of the California attorney general, which joined Joan in a lawsuit of its own on behalf of the recipients of the charities. Mobil, the attorney general claimed, was trying to buy a billion dollars' worth of California assets for only two hundred million. The people of California, the state contended, would lose the difference. The courts declared an injunction against the sale; the foundation appealed to have the injunction reversed, and their appeal was denied.

In January 1977 the case was back in the courts again, with Joan doing her best to block the Mobil take-over. Meanwhile two other bidders had entered the fray. One was Cadillac-Fairview, Ltd., a Toronto-based real estate development company controlled by the Bronfman family of Seagram's. The second was Taubman-Allen, a group of investors headed by A. Alfred Taubman, a Michigan shopping-center developer, and Charles Allen, a New York investment banker. In addition to Messrs. Taubman and Allen the group included such heavyweight partners as Henry Ford II and Donald L. Bren, a wealthy California builder and developer.

In February 1977, suspecting that the key to success might lie in having Joan Irvine join forces with them, Taubman-Allen invited Joan to be a member of their consortium. It was intended as a gesture of goodwill toward her, and Joan graciously accepted the invitation. With that, Taubman-Allen became Taubman-Allen-Irvine. In the months that followed, a lively bidding battle for the company broke out among the three suitors. New bids were submitted every two or three days, and Mobil's original $200,000,000 offer inched steadily upward. In April, Cadillac-Fairview dropped out, and the bidding between Mobil and Taubman-Allen-Irvine became heated, with a new bid coming in each day by noon. Finally, on May 20, 1977, Mobil dropped out, refusing to top a bid of $337,400,000 by Taubman-Allen-Irvine. In July 1977 the sale was completed. Taubman-Allen-Irvine merged the Irvine Company into itself, as a Michigan corporation, and changed its name back to the Irvine Company.

At last, it seemed, Joan had achieved total victory, including her aim of ousting the directors of the James Irvine Foundation. She also won a commitment from the new directors to speed up the pace of development of the land, as she had wanted the foundation to do, and immediately a seven-thousand-acre planned development was announced, to include marinas, golf courses, a dozen shopping centers, scores of new industrial, residential, and agricultural sites. Two thousand new housing units a year would be built on the Irvine property. From the sale of her Irvine stock Joan received $72,000,000 in cash plus 10 percent of the new company, making her one of eleven charter owners, and she was given a seat on the new company's executive committee, where her "zeal and historical perspective" toward the Irvine property were intended to be put to full use. Surely, everyone thought, she must now be satisfied.

Alas, it seemed, she was not. The honeymoon with the new company lasted less than a year before she was back to her old habits, barraging the new board of directors with questions, challenges, accusations of mismanagement, and threats of lawsuits. Her activities placed a particular strain on the new company's president, thirty-eight-year-old Peter Kremer, who began receiving as many as ten hand-delivered messages a day from Joan; over an eighteen-month period in 1978 and 1979, Kremer's office had to cope with more than 1200 of her letters and angry memoranda. Her behavior on the executive committee was so uncooperative that she was removed from it. If anything, she was harassing the new board of directors even more enthuisastically than she had the old foundation.

In March 1979 she sued the company to block a $3,800,000 expansion of a pipeline designed to bring water to the development from northern California and the Colorado River. When a judge refused to grant her a restraining order, Joan sued Mr. Kremer and eight directors—who owned roughly 80 percent of the development company, including Mr. Bren, who owned 35 percent—for $1,000,000,000. All this friction came at a particularly bad time for the new Irvine Company owners, who, in spite of a refinanced debt of $240,000,000, were still not in the clear. A year earlier, trying to convince doubters that the heavy borrowing undertaken by the new owners was under control, Mr. Kremer had released glowing figures that showed a 60 percent revenue growth for the fiscal year 1978. By 1979, however, he was releasing no figures.

TODAY, JOAN IRVINE SMITH is approaching fifty, still slim and attractive but with a touch of gray in her blond hair and new lines of determination around her wide mouth and large, hooded eyes, which she inherited from her grandfather. She spends as much as eighteen hours a day preparing for the various hearings, giving depositions, going over the fine points of her litigations with her team of attorneys, dictating her endless stream of letters. Meetings of the board of directors of the Irvine Company are still stormy affairs, full of reproach and bitterness and insults. Joan used to fly back and forth—piloting her own jet—between her beach house in southern California and her horse farm in Virginia, her legal residence. But now she has more or less permanently settled in her California camp —an armed camp, literally—to fight the fight she says she will never give up while there is any fight left in her.

The battle has cost her a lot more than imposing legal fees. It has caused a deep rift between Joan and her ever-loyal mother and the rest of the Irvine family. By 1979 it had cost her her fourth husband, Morton Smith; after sixteen years of marriage the Smiths were in the divorce courts. In the process she has become more anti-social than old J.I. ever was, and people who once considered themselves her friends complain that she never answers their letters, never returns their telephone calls—in fact, will not come to the telephone except to talk to one of her lawyers. When she goes out she is surrounded by a brace of armed bodyguards.

"The ranch seems to have taken over her life," says her cousin, Linda Irvine Gaede, Myford Irvine's daughter. "She's become convinced that everyone is out to get her, that people are trying to do her in, that her whole family is trying to do her in. Why else the bodyguards? She thinks people are trying to kill her." Linda Gaede accepts her father's death as a suicide and attributes the dark talk of murder to Joan's "paranoia." Mrs. Gaede also believes that her grandfather died of natural causes on his fishing trip—"He'd had heart attacks before." Linda Gaede adds, "Even though Joan is seven years older than I am, we used to be fairly close. But I haven't spoken to her or set eyes on her in over a year, even though she lives right down the road. It is very difficult to remain close to someone in your family who keeps suing you." From her spectacular house perched high on a bluff overlooking the Pacific, where pods of whale periodically pass by, and with a splendid view of Irvine Cove, where the Irvine children used to swim and surf, Linda Gaede can see the roof of the family beach house that all the Irvines put up several years ago, replacing an earlier structure. "The beach house was the last thing we did together as a family," she says. "We all chipped in to build it—Joan, my cousin Katie, myself and my half brother Jimmy. But it's hard to think of it as really a family place anymore." Linda Gaede turns and points to a handsome jade horse that sits in a living room cabinet with other jade figures. "I managed to snap that horse away from Joan," she says. "She collects jade too, but fortunately I heard that the horse was for sale while Joan was out of town. She'd have bought it instantly. But now it's *mine*."

What is it, in the end, that Joan Irvine wants, this good-looking, obsessive, extremely rich woman? Linda Gaede says: "She seems to just want more money, and to control the company. Also, it's clear that she enjoys the fight for its own sake, just as our grandfather enjoyed a fight. She really should have been a man." Others say she would be satisfied if she were made president of the company. But there is more to it than that, and Joan Irvine herself has said, "Why should I want more money? I already have more than I could possibly spend in a lifetime." She has also often said that she sees the land as her "heritage" and that she sees herself as a "spiritual link" between the ranch's pioneering past and its billowing future.

To Joan Irvine the ranch conveys a sense of place, of home, of family. It speaks of a young unlettered Irishman, the first James, down from the poverty of Belfast, who crossed the isthmus on a mule in search of Eldorado. After the disappointment of the gold fields he became a grocery clerk, and then turned to the land—three Mexican grants, all told, picked up as cheaply as the dirt itself—and with it the floods, the droughts, the chores, the plowing-under of the carcasses of thousands of dead sheep. There was love, and there were kisses behind the cellar door with a shepherd's daughter, and more down by the bunkhouse where the ranch hands slept and got drunk on payday, then marriage to a pretty girl who came all the way from Cleveland, who gave him a strong son, the second James, whose feeling for the land was even more intense than his father's, who would take up a gun to fight off the poachers and trespassers and thieves, even the big railroads that tried to muscle their way across the land—his land. Land that stretched from the mountains to the edge of the earth, the sea—as far as it would go; that was its particular significance.

And then, at last, the golden door that opened onto the polished parquet of the front parlor, the jade and teakwood furniture from Gump's, the Spode and Baccarat and heavy tea services, the governesses for the children, the furs and the emerald earclips for Frances Anita's birthday, and the clothes with Paris labels. And the violence, and the illnesses, and the deaths, and the betrayals, and little Joan riding in the saddle beside Grandpa, who had lost his favorite son and could not rid himself of thinking that he had helped kill his only daughter. From old J.I. she had grasped the fact that none of this had come easily. So many things had been tried, and had failed, on the land; promises had been broken and hopes had been dashed—first the cattle, wiped out in the Great Drought, then the prize Merinos, destroyed in another drought. Next came the cultivation of grapes, followed in 1881 by the terrible epidemic of grape phylloxera which in the next five years killed more than a million vines in Orange County. No sooner had the phylloxera been brought under control than the vineyard owners were dealt another blow: Prohibition. Next came citrus fruits, and now the orange groves were being plowed under for the next risky experiment—urban development, housing, shopping malls and greenbelts and office towers. On such attachments and associations and connotations there is no way to put a price, no way to subject any of it to logic. They had all fought and worked too hard and surrendered too much for what they had to give it up without a fight. To fight was just to give the land and its dead their due.

Her detractors have called Joan Irvine hard-boiled and bullheaded and arrogant. Jim Sleeper, a former Irvine official, refers to her sarcastically as "Saint Joan" and adds, "She'd pour water on a drowning man." But she has also displayed traces of the kind of sentiment that her grandfather worked so hard to hide. Not long ago the Irvine Company proposed to drain the Peters Canyon Reservoir on the ranch. It was old and no longer used, and the lake bed could be put to more profitable developmental use. Understandably, the owners of homesites around the lake were not pleased with this proposal, and Joan took their side. She could remember, she said, the fun she and her grandfather had had fishing in the lake. She hoped the homeowners would be able to enjoy it with their grandchildren as well. The Peters Canyon Reservoir remained undisturbed. An Irvine Company official, struggling to compose his face to a rational expression when he speaks of Joan, says, "When she got her money we all thought she would pack up and go back to Virginia and raise horses and begin enjoying life." To this Joan Irvine replies simply, "The land is still here, and so I'm still here." She also likes to quote the comment of a real estate friend, Sandy Goodkin: "I would not say it is good land, but I happen to know that God dropped His option on the ranch only when Heaven came on the market."

Of course, a sense of the importance of the continuity of generations is probably even stronger for a woman than for a man. In her long fight with the company Joan Irvine was also following something of a western tradition, that of women who picked up where their men left off. Such women as Mrs. Leland Stanford, out stumping the countryside for money for her university; Mrs. Huntington, daring to marry her own nephew; Flora Sharon, determined to marry a titled Englishman; the indomitable Alma Spreckels, set upon having her museum; blind Estelle Doheny, memorizing the names of all her orchids and holding on to the strings of her spendthrift husband's fortune.

In the male world of California money, California women were showing the men that they could give them a run for it.

CHAPTER EIGHTEEN
End of the Battle

ALMA SPRECKELS, who loved her children in an abstract way and enjoyed visiting with them when there was time between meetings and appointments for her various museum projects, made periodic efforts to be on good terms with them, particularly the two girls. But these were never really successful. For too many years the children had resented their mother's outside-the-home preoccupations, which had left them in the care of governesses and nurses and other servants until they were old enough to fend for themselves. Little Alma's youthful elopement and marriage to John N. Rosekrans had been interpreted as an act of filial defiance, and of course the marriage did not last long. Late in life Big Alma decided to divide her Washington Street house into three large apartments so that her daughters could live with her. At least that was what she had in mind. She gave the top-floor apartment, with its ceiling of Tiffany glass, to her daughter Dorothy, but Dorothy rarely came to San Francisco to use it. The second, or "parlor," floor was for Mrs. Spreckels herself, and the ground floor was intended for Little Alma.

But Alma had no interest in living beneath her mother. She was involved in building her own huge modern house on Broadway, all decorated in black and white (the only colors that Little Alma—a tall, fair woman—ever wore), which had its own indoor swimming pool, among other amenities. So Big Alma offered the ground floor to the young man who had become her favorite grandson, Little Alma's son, John Rosekrans, Jr. Rosekrans was equally fond of his grandmother, whom he called "Gangy," and the span of another generation helped him appreciate her imperious manner and outspoken tongue that seemed only to startle strangers. Rosekrans' first wedding, for example, had been a garden affair, and Mrs. Spreckels' two daughters had been horrified to see their large mother take her seat in a gilt ballroom chair and drive its legs deep into the ground. It took two sturdy ushers to pull the chair out, while Mrs. Spreckels stood by muttering earthy expletives. Rosekrans had thought the whole episode quite funny. But about sharing the big house with his grandmother he had a few reservations. He was then in the process of getting a divorce, and he wondered how his grandmother might feel about the occasional lady friends who might visit him. "Don't think a thing about it, pet," she said. "Listen, you only live once, and when you're dead you're dead a long time. Your grandfather had a mistress, and when she died they turned her house into a mortuary. You do whatever you want." And so Rosekrans took the big apartment, which had at least sixteen rooms, for which his grandmother charged him a token rent of a hundred dollars a month.

She didn't snoop on him exactly, but she did like to pop in on him, usually unannounced. On emerging from her bath in the morning, at least one young woman who had spent the night was startled to see a tall, stout, elderly woman pottering about the apartment in bedroom slippers and a pink nightgown, helping John set up for a party he was planning that evening. "My God," bellowed Mrs. Spreckels, "who the hell are you?" Such encounters became rather common.

Even after her son, the much-married Adolph, who had been such a trial to her in his lifetime, had died, she remained loyal to his memory. Kay Spreckels Gable, his sixth and last wife, was suing the estate and asking to be a trustee on behalf of her Spreckels children. "No!" cried Mrs. Spreckels. "She's a bitch! Don't give her anything!" And to make sure he knew how she felt on the matter, she began making daily telephone calls to the judge who was weighing the case. Her lawyer, Mr. Bradley, who was also an officer in the trust, begged her to stop making these telephone calls, which were only damaging the family's position. She refused, snorting, "What does Bradley know?"

In later years she led a somewhat peripatetic existence, seeming to weary of the ongoing battle between her museum and the de Young Museum. She had never, of course, been really accepted by San Francisco society, which had become more or less dominated by the de Young sisters—an irony, considering the fact that their father had been one of the most dreaded and disliked men in town. At one point Mrs. Spreckels bought a house in Neuilly, outside Paris, and for a while had an idea of living permanently there. She also kept an apartment in New York at 1020 Fifth Avenue, where she sometimes spent her winters. But in the end she always came back to San Francisco, where, she liked to reminisce, she used to walk two miles to school to save the nickel streetcar fare.

Aside from her grandson, her favorite companion was probably Thomas Howe, the director of her museum, although she always was careful to address him formally as "Mr. Howe," and he in turn always addressed her as "Mrs. Spreckels." Her daughters clearly resented her relationship with him. ("She doesn't call you 'Mr. Howe' behind your back," one of her daughters snipped to him.) The two often traveled together to New York, to visit the art auction houses and the galleries—Findlay's, Knoedler's, and Duveen's—along Fifty-seventh Street. They traveled to Washington to visit the National Gallery, and on one of these visits Mrs. Spreckels expressed a wish to see Colonial Williamsburg. She could be miserly, and though accustomed to being driven around San Francisco in a Rolls-Royce by a chauffeur, she decreed that the trip to Williamsburg be made in a rented drive-yourself car, which Mr. Howe would drive.

Arriving at Williamsburg, they checked in at the inn, and were asked how long they intended to stay. "Oh, about a week," said Mrs. Spreckels. But by four o'clock that afternoon she had grown restless. "Mr. Howe, haven't we pretty much seen everything?" she complained. "Let's go back to New York." So they checked out of the inn and flew back to New York from Richmond. In New York she was soon restless again and wanted to go home to San Francisco, though Howe had museum business to conduct in New York and needed to remain a few more days. "How much money do you think you'll need?" she asked. Howe mentioned a modest figure—the year was 1940 and New York had not become an expensive place—and, somewhat grudgingly, Mrs. Spreckels peeled off a few hundred-dollar bills from the large roll she carried with her when she traveled. Three days later Howe was back in San Francisco, and he presented himself at Washington Street to deliver an accounting of his expenses. She received him, as usual, in her bedroom. Just back from a shopping trip, she tossed her large flowered hat onto one of the swan-headposts of her extraordinary bed ("A king made love in it, of course") and nonchalantly wriggled out of her girdle and stockings. Howe explained that he had about three hundred dollars left over. "Do me a favor," she said. "Put it into something for little Primrose." Primrose was Howe's young daughter. So she could be generous too —just as she could cause acute embarrassment to her friends. Once, at a dinner party where her guest of honor was Pierre Monteux, the celebrated conductor of the San Francisco Symphony Orchestra, Mrs. Spreckels boomed out, "You know, Mr. Monteux, Mr. Howe plays the piano!" Tommy Howe was then forced to go to the piano and deliver an awkward rendition of "Limehouse Blues."

Still, Tommy Howe was devoted to her. "She was a kind of Fafnir character, out of Wagner," he says. "People didn't always agree with her, and people didn't always like her. Her two daughters hated her heartily. But better than anybody I've ever known, she had the ability to sense the fundamental qualities in people, and cut through sham and pretense." Howe never made any pretense, either, of the low esteem in which he held the daughters. "Neither of them ever did anything for their mother's museum. We were raising money for some awards once, and I went to Dorothy and asked her for a contribution of two hundred dollars. She said she could only afford a hundred dollars. Practically in the next breath she was talking about an expensive necklace she wanted to buy. It was Dorothy too who once sent a hasty note to her mother from Palm Beach, enclosing a photograph of herself sitting next to the Duke of Windsor at a dinner party. "Look who I'm sitting with!" wrote the granddaughter of a man who had once won a large part of the kingdom of Hawaii in a poker game. Her mother wrote back, saying, "I give up. Who is it?"

Tommy Howe remained loyal to Mrs. Spreckels even after Little Adolph died and Mrs. Spreckels began to be more and more of a recluse—even after the time had come when Howe would arrive at Mrs. Spreckels' house to deliver copies of the latest museum catalogues and she would no longer want to see him. Her grandson, John, had been remarried—to a woman, fortunately, whom Mrs. Spreckels liked—and had moved into a house of his own, and John and Dodie Rosekrans were among the very few people whom Gangy asked to see. In 1964 she fell and injured her back. Later that year she had another fall and broke her hip. She recovered from that, but six months later she came down with pneumonia, and died at the age of eighty-three.

Immediately her two daughters fell to wrangling over the funeral services. Dorothy wanted the private family services at her house, and Alma wanted them at hers. Finally, when it was pointed out by the directors of N. Grey & Company, San Francisco's fashionable undertaking establishment, that the platinum-plated casket that Dorothy had insisted upon would not fit through the doors, Dorothy relented, and the services were held at Little Alma's huge black-and-white modern house (six years in the building; Alma had not wanted her mother to see it until every last black-and-white detail was finished). The service was small, just for family and close friends, and

Mrs. Spreckels reposed in the huge casket wearing a black dress, her famous pair of sunburst diamond clips, and some other stones. Tommy Howe read "When Earth's Last Picture Is Painted," and Dorothy Spreckels Munn whispered to him, "Doesn't she look *sweet*? Of course I'll take the jewels off before they close the coffin."

The public funeral the next day was something else again. It was held in the huge rotunda of the Palace of the Legion of Honor, in the center of which Mrs. Spreckels lay in state. It started at ten in the morning, and long before that hour the rotunda and the rooms and grounds beyond had filled with more than ten thousand people —friends, enemies, public officials, the press and television, and merely curious San Franciscans who wanted a glimpse of the legendary old lady who had lived alone in the block-long "Sugar Palace" in Pacific Heights. Just before the services were about to start a tour bus pulled up in front of the museum and disgorged a full load of out-of-town art lovers, who were quite unaware of what was going on. As the tourists entered the museum, noticing that the center of attention was obviously the platinum-plated casket, the tour guide announced, "Ladies and gentlemen, this is a wax effigy of the museum's founder, the late Mrs. Alma de Bretteville Spreckels." Immediately a museum guard stepped over to him and hissed, "That is not an effigy. That *is* Alma de Bretteville Spreckels." It was a moment Alma Spreckels might have enjoyed.

The moment the services were over, Dorothy Munn cornered Tommy Howe to say, "Quick, come with me to the mausoleum. We've got to get the jewels off before they close the casket!" Howe accompanied her to the mausoleum, where the clips, rings, and necklaces were quickly removed from the earthly remains of Dorothy's mother. Then the casket was closed and sealed.

IT HAD long been the hope of San Franciscans that the resources, revenues, and collections of the two battling museums could somehow be combined into one museum of art. But even though Mrs. Spreckels was gone, the de Young sisters continued vigorously to oppose a merger. More people would have to die before this could be accomplished, and the final opponent, Helen de Young Cameron, did not die until the early 1970s. With that the two museums finally agreed to join hands and marry. But even then the de Youngs seemed to have come out on top. When the new, combined museum, consolidated under a single director, Ian McKibbin White, became a reality at last in 1972, the de Youngs managed to get top billing on the letterhead, which read:

THE FINE ARTS
MUSEUMS OF
SAN FRANCISCO

M. H. de Young
Memorial
Museum

California
Palace of the
Legion of Honor

Of course one of the peculiar things about the de Young sisters, when all four were alive, was that they all actually seemed to like one another. That was unusual in San Francisco. More common were the Spreckels sisters, who, with their mother gone, now had only each other to quarrel with. Among other money-related issues was the question of which woman would control 2080 Washington Street—the enormous wedding-cake house in which even the servants' rooms had wall-to-wall carpeting, the house with its $30,000 French commodes, its $25,000 motor-operated movable glass swimming-pool enclosure and built-in radiant-heating system, and everything else, almost literally, that money could buy.

CHAPTER NINETEEN
Overnight Tradition

ALTHOUGH Alma de Bretteville Spreckels had never appeared to care whether or not she was accepted as a leader in San Francisco's fledgling society, it was clear that the de Young sisters did. In their social ambitions the sisters were inspired and directed by their mother, a gentle creature of cultivated speech and manners who, throughout her lifetime, did as much as she could to offset her husband's unsavory reputation. She also had to counter the galling fact that for many years the children of the city's "better" families were not permitted to enter the de Young house at 1919 California Street —the house that had mysteriously made its way out of the hands of the Crockers. Mrs. de Young tutored her daughters in the social graces—"Never point, except at French pastry"—and, though none of the girls was exactly a beauty, she had tutored them assiduously in acquiring that elusive element so important to an earlier generation —*charm.*

236

They all had it. They could enter rooms with pleasant expressions on their faces and move with light, quick steps to where their hostess stood to tell her how beautiful she looked, how lovely the flowers were, how pretty the house was. Though not notably intellectual or quotably witty, the sisters were all skillful at making light, engaging small talk about this or that, and when it came to party gossip they were attentive listeners. They had soft, light voices, they were punctual, they remembered names. On the street or lunching at the St. Francis, they were invariably gloved and often hatted, masters of the expensively understated elegance for which San Francisco women were becoming famous. There was nothing about these poised and gracious ladies to suggest that their father had been little better than a blackmailer. And the fact that he was Jewish was elaborately overlooked.

The de Young sisters were also certainly collectively—and perhaps even individually—far richer than their father had ever been. This was a state of affairs that was not uncommon in the second generation of California fortunes, and it had to do with the state's astonishing population growth between, during, and after two world wars and the resulting steep escalation of property values. For example, Helen de Young's father had given her "some sand dunes" on the southwest side of town. She had placed little value on this real estate and had hardly given it any thought at all until after World War II, when the sand dunes were being snapped up by developers for middle-income housing at many thousands of dollars an acre. The de Young sisters had also made impeccable social marriages— Yvonne to Charles Theriot, Constance to Joseph Tobin, Helen to George Cameron, and Phyllis to Nion Tucker, whose occupation was "sportsman." Unlike the Spreckels daughters, the de Young girls seemed capable of *staying* married.

Meanwhile, Mrs. Eleanor Martin, San Francisco's first real social leader, had died in 1932 at the age of one hundred and one, and her mentor, Ned Greenway, had long passed from the San Francisco social scene to the great ballroom in the sky, and the rituals of his Cotillions had been abandoned. San Francisco languished through the 1930s with no real polarizing force, but the de Young sisters were

waiting in the wings. In 1941, while America nervously watched
the war in Europe, Phyllis de Young Tucker decided that San
Francisco society needed a revitalizing shot in the arm. With
Stuart Nixon, an assistant manager of the Palace Hotel, and Mildred
Brown Robbins, society editor of the *Chronicle* (which, being a
de Young paper, was guaranteed to give any de Young project full-
est support), Phyllis Tucker announced plans to revive the San
Francisco Cotillion along the original Greenway lines. The revival
was a huge success. The guests paraded about the Palace ballroom
performing the intricate quadrille figures, and the climax of the evening was reached when the season's crop of debutantes, in long white
dresses and long white gloves, were presented, one by one, on the
ballroom stage. Soon afterward, of course, came Pearl Harbor, and
a moratorium was declared on coming-out parties, but as soon as the
war was over, Phyllis Tucker revived the Cotillion again—again
successfully. It was designed to be an annual affair, second only in
social importance to the September opening of the San Francisco
opera.

Debutante parties were enormously popular in the late 1940s and
1950s throughout the country, and, looking back, it is a little hard
to see why. Though based on the ancient custom of presenting the
eligible virgins to the males of the tribe—a custom that goes back
to the Stone Age and even before—they had more or less lost their
point by the mid-twentieth century. The eligible virgins all knew
the male members of the tribe anyway, sometimes only too well—
and how many of them were actually virgins was always open to
question. As parties, most debutante balls were not all that much fun.
It was hard to get the boys to dance with the girls—the boys preferred gathering in little knots to tell jokes or shoot craps—and for
that reason a debutante usually invited more than one male escort,
often as many as four or five. Still, despite the preponderance of
males over females, there could always be found at least one debutante sobbing in the powder room because no one would dance with
her. Most debutante parties were not given for the purpose of having
fun; their intent was to confer social status, not only on the debutante herself but on her parents.

The trouble was that the status conferred was in most cases illusory. Though the balls were touted as "exclusive," they weren't really exclusive in the sense that certain people were carefully excluded from them. Most American debutante parties of the era were produced for charities, for which they raised a considerable sum of money, and this meant that any parent capable of raising the required price could have his or her daughter made a debutante—provided of course that she was not black or Jewish or, in Boston, Irish Catholic —regardless of lineage, family background, social graces, or other credentials of respectability. All sorts of "outside" people had to be included too. The perfume manufacturer who provided the party favors had to be given a table at the ball for his executives and their wives, along with the distillers who had donated the liquor, the florist who had provided the decorations, and the hairdressers who had coiffed the young ladies. In other words, most American debutante affairs did not represent a gathering of real "society" at all. Most were commercial enterprises, fund-raisers, with more than a touch of Madison Avenue (including advertising sold for the programs), where places on the debutante list were bought and sold.

But some were not. In more firmly established eastern cities the coming-out ritual was quite different. Many eastern cities had been colonized by the British, who had brought with them the traditional British class system. And though America had no peerage as such, certain eastern families had joined to compose a strictly defined aristocracy, based not only on wealth but also on length of local residence and similarity of education, interests, manners, and tastes. In cities such as Boston, Philadelphia, Baltimore, and Charleston, there were families who could trace their descent for more than two hundred years in one place and who placed great emphasis on and took great pride in their ancestry, birthplace, and breeding, and who set themselves rigidly apart from outsiders and newcomers.

Just as it was in England, a family could live for fifty years in Philadelphia and still remain "a stranger to these parts," incapable of penetrating the tight stronghold of old-guard Philadelphia society. The Philadelphia Assembly had been started in 1748, and for a young woman to be presented at the Assembly she virtually had to be born to it. In Charleston the St. Cecilia Ball, which dated from 1762, was equally exclusive, and so was Baltimore's Cotillion. In Charleston certain young women could attend the St. Cecilia as "out-of-town guests," provided they lived more than a hundred miles from Charleston, but first their credentials had to be carefully checked by the ball committee. If a girl had lived in Charleston twelve months or longer, she was considered a "resident," and if she was not a member of St. Cecilia—and most newcomers weren't—there was no possible way she could attend the ball. Some new families moved out of Charleston, at least temporarily, after eleven months, just so their daughters could qualify as out-of-towners. In both Charleston and Philadelphia a divorce was considered a blot on the escutcheon, and there were cases in which certain Philadelphia parents were not even permitted to attend their daughters' presentations at the Assembly because they had been divorced. Obviously charity played no part in these venerable institutions. They were strictly private parties, their costs divided among the participating families of society.

Obviously, too, San Francisco could claim no families who had been prominent for more than two or three generations. The young Jimmy Floods could not conceal the fact that Mr. Flood's grandfather had been a bartender and his grandmother a chambermaid. In Phyllis Tucker's case, the rough edges of the de Young family had not been smoothed out until her own generation; and the Spreckels sisters had to accept somehow the truth that their father had not even graduated from high school. Phyllis Tucker was aware of all this. One could not deny the raw state of San Francisco's upper crust, but one could simply ignore it. Though San Francisco might he short of families whose ancestors had signed the Declaration of Independence or crossed on the *Mayflower*, one could still adopt the pattern set by such ancient eastern cities as Philadelphia and Charleston and thus achieve an effect of overnight tradition and instant old money. This was what Phyllis Tucker chose to do with her San Francisco Cotillion. It would be unquestionably a private affair, with no charity as beneficiary. Costs would be borne by the families of the debutantes invited to the party, and the invitation list would be strictly controlled by Mrs. Tucker and her committee. No debutante could buy her way in; she had to be chosen for the honor.

This policy insured the Cotillion's success—in the 1940s and 1950s at least. Parents of would-be debutantes who did not meet Mrs. Tucker's standards vainly knocked on her door, wrote her letters, and wooed her with lunches at the St. Francis and invitations to little dinners. Families who had friends who were also friends of Mrs. Tucker's tried to have the mutual friends intercede on their behalf, but nothing worked. Mrs. Tucker was always pleasant, always polite, but always firm. "I just don't think your daughter would be *happy* as a debutante," she would say with a sympathetic little smile, and that was that.

Needless to say, the San Francisco families that had been excluded from the little chosen circle of Floods, Folgers, Tobins, de Youngs, Crockers, Meins, Nickels, Millers, and Tevises were not happy with this state of affairs. After World War II many new-rich families had come to San Francisco and its suburbs, and these families also wanted debutante status for their daughters. Rather quickly a number of rival debutante balls were organized. Across the Bay, in Oakland, the Winter Ball, benefiting a hospital, was established. To the south of the city the Peninsula Ball came into existence, and in the new-money suburbs of Marin County, to the north, the Marin Ball presented debutantes for seven hundred dollars a head. Finally, a Cotillion rival was set up in the city itself, the San Francisco Debutante Ball, which benefited the Presbyterian Hospital and where it cost a girl a thousand dollars to be presented. But none of these had the cachet of Mrs. Tucker's Cotillion and, in fact, merely served to emphasize the superiority of the affair. When a girl was presented at anything other than the Cotillion, everyone in town knew she was settling for second best.

Through it all Phyllis de Young Tucker began, almost literally, to levitate to the top of San Francisco society. Though some hated to admit it, she had become unquestionably the leader. There was something almost other-worldly about her easy, smiling mastery of every social situation, as the city bowed and scraped and curtsied to

"Aunt Phyllis," and some spoke, a little bitterly, about her "elevation to sainthood." She was like royalty. Out of her creation, the Cotillion, satellite groups sprang up. There was the Spinsters, for example, a postdebutante club consisting mostly of Cotillion alumnae, which put on an annual ball, and the Spinsters' male counterpart, the Bachelors, which put on a ball of its own "to repay the Spinsters and certain debutantes to whom the Bachelors are indebted," and soon the Bachelors had a rival group of their own which called itself the Downtown Operators' Association. All these organizations owed their existence to the spiritual leadership of Phyllis Tucker. What no one realized of course was that Phyllis Tucker was making San Francisco dance to her tune just as effectively as her father had made it dance to his.

In her wake—but not very far behind—swam her sisters, but, alas, they did not have Phyllis' staying power. Mrs. Theriot went down on the *Andrea Doria*. Then Constance Tobin died, and then Helen Cameron, whose great estate in Burlingame, Rosecourt, was thereupon broken up. But Mrs. Tucker survived—survived, miraculously, the great revolution of the 1960s and 1970s that was to spell the doom of debutante parties across the country: the revolt of youth.

Suddenly it seemed that though it was still all right to be rich, it was no longer acceptable to show it. Though parents were still eager to continue the coming-out tradition, their assertive and outspoken children were not. Coming-out parties were condemned as sexist, irrelevant, wasteful, undemocratic, shamefully unimportant compared with the plight of Chicano workers in the grape fields, the poisoning of the environment by the internal-combustion engine, Jane Fonda, nuclear waste, and Cambodia. Boys replaced dinner jackets and sports cars with patched jeans, guitars, and motorcycles. Girls preferred to outfit themselves from thrift shops, and it was difficult to get a girl to put on so much as a dress, much less a long white ball gown and opera-length gloves. At parties, champagne was replaced by marijuana. The rites of passage from youth to adulthood seemed to have changed abruptly, and unkempt hair, clothes, music, and manners among the young were not only all at once permissible but the order of the day.

Parents of every economic stratum were dismayed by what their children had become and struggled to grasp the new ideology. The middle classes blamed everything from television to Vietnam and Kent State. The rich blamed, among other things, the schools and the servant problem; they saw a generation that had been brought up, unlike their own, without the reins and guidance and strict discipline of German governesses and English nannies. Clearly, coming-out parties were in deep trouble all across the country. All at once there were so few young women willing to make their debuts at the Marin Ball that it was canceled, never to be revived. The San Francisco Debutante Ball tried adding a rock group to enliven the traditional waltz and fox trot strains of such bandleaders as Meyer Davis, Lester Lanin, and Peter Duchin. Then it tried changing its name—dropping the word "Debutante"—and referring to the girls as "honored guests." But by 1972 only seven honored guests could be rounded up, by sheer coercion, for the occasion; and that ball too disappeared without a trace from the San Francisco social scene the following year.

Still, however uncertainly, the San Francisco Cotillion and Mrs. Tucker remained, undaunted through an entirely new social climate, hanging on by what seemed the slimmest thread. And Mrs. Tucker may have been right in sticking to her guns, because in the late 1970s the pendulum started to swing back again. It began to seem as if the youthful rites of passage had not changed permanently after all, and in cities across the country the ranks of debutantes, which had diminished to a trickle, began to swell again. Each year from 1977 on, a few more young women appeared not only willing but eager to come out, to cross the stage with white-gloved hands tucked in their fathers' arms and deep-curtsy to their peers. After all, every species has a mating dance, the rituals of which survive for centuries. In the jungles of New Guinea, fathers of girls who have reached puberty toss coconuts into the sea to announce the fact. The wealthier or more influential the father, the more coconuts he throws out to sea. In America the coconuts are dollars.

Some San Francisco people wonder whether the Cotillion will survive Phyllis Tucker when she is gathered to her ancestors—at least in its present by-invitation-only form. But it survives—in testimony, perhaps, to her unshakable belief in traditional modes and manners, as well as to the power of pure snobbishness and the siren lure of landscapes that only the Chosen, only the Elect, may set foot upon.

CHAPTER TWENTY

"Valley People"

ONE REASON why the San Francisco Debutante Ball did not flourish for long was that, in order to attract support, the ball included debutantes from the Central Valley or, more accurately, the two broad valleys formed by the San Joaquin and Sacramento rivers—a vast area of flatland stretching for some four hundred miles between Redding and Bakersfield. The ball honored young women from such towns as Stockton, Modesto, Lodi, and Sacramento, even from as far away as Fresno. Perhaps because of its peninsular physical shape and similarly narrow and insulated frame of mind, San Francisco and San Franciscans had long been accustomed to regarding themselves as a special breed apart from all others, superior in fashion, architecture, taste, and cultivation. This had nothing to do with money, because when you stopped to think about it (which San Franciscans didn't do very often), there was a great deal of money in the Valley, in oil and agriculture. Most of what San Francisco ate was raised in the

Valley, and perhaps that had something to do with it. San Franciscans had come to regard Valley people as purveyors of victuals for the table, rather like caterers, and therefore part of the servant class. San Francisco's feelings of superiority over Los Angeles were as nothing compared with their feelings toward residents of Stockton, Modesto, Lodi, and Sacramento.

The wealthy Valley families were well aware of this attitude, resented it deeply, and, as a result, developed classic symptoms of inferiority about their addresses. A Modesto woman, for example, traveling in the East, would seldom identify herself as being from Modesto. She would say, "I live about eighty miles inland from San Francisco." A Sacramentan might admit that Sacramento was his home—it was, after all, the capital of the state—but he would usually add, "But we often drive to San Francisco for dinner." A Valley woman might buy her clothes where her citified San Francisco sisters did, at Magnin's, Ransohoff's, and Saks, but when she attempted to join the Francisca Club, San Francisco's elite, all-woman answer to New York's Colony Club, she met resistance. A wealthy Valley rancher might own as many Brooks Brothers and Roos-Atkins suits as his San Francisco brother, but it was difficult for him to join the Pacific Union Club. Businessmen from New York, Chicago, Washington, and Atlanta had no difficulty joining San Francisco's exclusive, quasi-artistic Bohemian Club. But it was a different story for a banker from Stockton. One Modesto man was turned down by the Bohemian Club so often that he made it something of a crusade. When, after some twenty years of rejection, he received word that his membership had finally been approved, he was so excited that he suffered a cardiac arrest and died with the letter in his hand.

A wealthy Valley mother might send her daughter to San Francisco's fashionable Miss Hamlin's School for girls (where, as a boarder, she would immediately be marked as an outsider in a student body composed primarily of city day students) or her son to the Menlo School for boys, but that did not mean that the youngsters would ever be invited to Mrs. Tucker's Cotillion or, for that matter, to any other fashionable San Francisco parties. This was true simply because people from the Valley were, as San Francisco sneeringly referred to them, "Valley people," carrying the stigma of being farmers, hayseeds, country bumpkins, hicks.

There were, to be sure, certain disadvantages to living in the Valley. During a strike by the Teamsters Union the wife of a wealthy dairy farmer might find herself helping her husband lift twenty-gallon milk cans onto a flatbed truck to get the milk to the market-place, and the husband, driving the truck, usually placed a loaded pistol on the seat beside him, the Teamsters' reputation being what it was. At the height of the harvest season the peach grower's wife could often be found in the packing shed sorting and crating peaches. No matter how rich the farm, there were always certain duties that befell the farmer and the farmer's wife. Some of the wealthiest Valley ranchers worked in their shirt sleeves, Levi's, and muddy boots and carried their lunches in paper bags, even those who regularly changed into black tie for dinner.

The Valley landscape was not particularly inspiring; without hills, there were no real views or vistas, only a certain sameness in every direction. Perhaps because there was really nothing to look out on, the houses of the Valley rich (along with their gardens and swimming pools) began to encase themselves behind high walls of stucco or brick or redwood "privacy fences." This custom tended to give the residential streets of Valley towns a certain monotonous appearance, a squared-off, boxed-up look that offered the passerby no clue to the luxuries that might exist inside the boxes. Finally, there was the Valley climate—the damp, chilly winters (never really chilly enough to be *cold*), and the dense, almost impenetrable fogs that rose from the tule marshes along the riverbanks. In summer, there was the searing heat—temperatures as high as 120 degrees for days on end. And despite sophisticated efforts to control the considerable insect population of this agricultural region, even a short drive down a Valley highway could result in a windshield covered with the corpses of flying bugs. In San Francisco it was said you could spot a Valley person's car by the insect-deflector mounted on its hood.

Still, Valley people did their best not to be recognized as "Valley." In the days before air conditioning was standard equipment in California cars it was not uncommon to see a Valley woman, driving to San Francisco for a day at Gump's and Magnin's, wearing nothing but a slip and bra. Only when she had left the heat of the Valley and had descended the last foothill of the Diablo Range into the misty coolness of the Bay Area would she pull off the road in some inconspicuous place and with difficulty put on her little black suit with the mink collar, her hat, gloves, girdle, and stockings, in order not to be outdone by the San Francisco ladies having Monday lunch at the St. Francis—ladies, to be sure, most of whom she would never meet.

The Valley was the butt of all San Francisco's little jokes. Herb Caen, the popular columnist for the San Francisco *Chronicle*, would lead off a column with a snide aside: "Lodi's leading playboy (and that's funny right there) . . ." And the disparagement of Valley towns often reached a national level, as when a newsmagazine wrote (in a review of a novel by Leonard Gardner called *Fat City*): "The place is Stockton, California, a city filled with a litter of lost people, most of whom pile on urine-smelling buses each morning and head for the onion, peach, or walnut fields for a killing day on skinny wages." Such towns as Visalia, Yuba City, and Colusa fared no better in the national press. In the early 1970s the lyric of a popular song moaned, "Oh, Lord, stuck in Lodi again!" And so it has gone. Each time a new slur against the Valley towns has come to the surface, the Valley people, and the editorial writers of the Valley press, have reacted with outrage and indignation, but to no avail. The poor image of the Valley had jelled.

Even Mrs. Ronald Reagan, during her tenure as First Lady of California, spoke scornfully of her forced residence in Sacramento, not only the capital but also the Valley's largest city. "Thank heavens we can escape to Beverly Hills on the weekends," she told a journalist, adding that she had to go to Beverly Hills at least once a week to have her hair done. "No one in Sacramento can do hair," she sweepingly asserted. Like most people from San Francisco and Los Angeles, Nancy Reagan had never spent much time in the Valley and had never set foot in Sacramento until her husband was elected governor. When she did, she was horrified by what she found.

The California governor's mansion at the time was a huge turreted affair of Victorian gingerbread built in 1878, painted a glittering wedding-cake white. An exuberant house from that exuberant period of California history, it was reminiscent of James C. Flood's wedding-cake mansion in Menlo Park, and previous governors and their ladies, including the Earl Warrens, had found it charming. It recalled the old days of the spring floods, built as it was high above the level of the street and approached by a wide flight of snow-white steps. But to Mrs. Reagan it was immediately unacceptable. "There were seven fireplaces, none of which could be lit," she said. "The house was on a corner facing two gas stations and a motel, and it backed up on the American Legion Hall, where I swear there were vile orgies every night. The house was condemned fifteen years ago. I said to Ronnie, 'I can't let my children live there.' " When she saw the mansion Mrs. Reagan refused to occupy it, and the governor indulged "Mommy," as he calls her, and settled on a state-rented house in the suburbs of the city. (It was during the Reagan administration that construction of a new, modern California governor's mansion was begun, which Governor Jerry Brown refused to occupy because it was "too luxurious.")

In Sacramento, Mrs. Reagan also said that she was "too busy" to get to know any of her Valley neighbors. She made one trip to the Sacramento branch of Magnin's and found its merchandise inferior to that in the stores of Beverly Hills and San Francisco, where she preferred to shop. "Here everything is scaled down for these Valley farm women," she said.

These, needless to say, counted as nothing less than fighting words to the men and women of the Central Valley, who, among other things, had been Ronald Reagan's staunchest Republican supporters. Valley people, after years of put-downs by citizens of the coastal cities, wear their psychological scars as chips on their shoulders and have become vociferously, pugnaciously defensive about the Valley. In their counterattacks Valley people usually use money as their chief weapon of defense, pointing out how much sheer wealth has been amassed there, thus giving San Franciscans further ammunition with which to claim that Valley people are coarse and *nouveau*.

It is certainly true that a great deal of money has been made in the Valley. There is the case, for example, of the late Mrs. Tillie Lewis of nearby Stockton, typical of the new, post-robber-baron fortunes that have been made in California. Tillie was a Jewish girl from Brooklyn, New York, born in 1901, the daughter of Jacob and Rose Ehrlich. Tillie started out in the wholesale grocery business in Brooklyn and went into the canning business in 1935. With her second husband, Meyer Lewis, she founded and developed Flotill Products, Inc., a cannery, in Stockton, that took advantage of the area's expanding reclamation—through the construction of levees—of rich Sacramento Delta land, which was given over to tomatoes. Her enormous fortune built up when Flotill's canneries developed a way to take sugar out of canned tomatoes and juices. In 1951 the Associated Press newspaperwomen named Tillie Lewis—or "Tillie Flotill," as she was now known locally—as Businesswoman of the Year. Naturally she was taken into the Stockton Golf and Country Club and the Tennis and Racquet Club of Palm Springs—but not into the Francisca Club of San Francisco or the Burlingame Country Club. She might be a savvy city lady from the East, but she was still a Valley farm woman.

At the same time, there are a number of Valley families that have been established longer than families in San Francisco and Los Angeles and that could count themselves among the oldest of California's old guard. In Bakersfield, for example, the landholdings of the Tevis family were almost as large as those of Henry Miller, and the Tevises and Millers represent a long-standing money feud. In the 1930s, while the heirs of Henry Miller were battling with one another over their shares of his estate, the Tevises found themselves land-poor. In order to raise capital the Tevis family interests formed the Kern County Land Company, and shares were sold to the public, thereby departing from Tevis family control. Not long afterward a bonanza in oil was discovered beneath Kern County Land Company acreage. Kern County Land Company shareholders found themselves rich overnight, and at least one man, Mr. C. Ray Robinson, the lawyer who had handled the Land Company's affairs, made himself a million dollars in legal fees alone, not counting what the jump in the value of his stock had netted him.

The Tevises moaned and gnashed their teeth, but, alas, there was really nothing they could do. Though still very rich, they saw a whole additional fortune slip through their fingers. At one point the Tevis mansion in Bakersfield had had its own private golf course, and the Tevises had entertained foreign royalty in their home. In 1870, Lloyd Tevis had built one of the first great castles on Nob Hill in San Francisco, where his library contained (or so he liked to boast) the largest collection of books in the West. Later the Bakersfield house became the clubhouse for the Stockdale Country Club, and still later the country club was purchased by George Nickel, a San Franciscan and Henry Miller heir. None of the Miller-Lux heirs today feels the slightest guilt about gloating over the fact that the Millers still outweigh the Tevises in terms of financial leverage.

Farther north, in Fresno, the county seat of what is called "the richest agricultural county in the United States," the Giffen family has been hugely wealthy for several generations. Today Russell Giffen, from an office furnished with museum-quality eighteenth-century American and English antiques, directs a ranching operation with acreage in the hundreds of thousands—so much land that he is not quite sure how much he owns—raising cotton, barley, wheat, safflower, alfalfa seed, melons, tomatoes, and a good deal more. Still, for all their money, old-family background, and elegant life-style, the Giffens have never been invited into the *Social Register*, because they are Fresno.

In San Francisco such Italian American families as the Baldocchis, Aliotos, Cellas, Gianninis, Ghirardellis, and Petris have all made their way into the *Register*. But eighty miles away, in Modesto, the Gallos, the largest wine producers in the world, have not, despite the fact that the homes of the brothers Ernest and Julio Gallo are local showplaces. (Of course it was not always thus for the Gallos.

At the height of the Depression the Gallo brothers' father, convinced that he was a ruined man, led his Italian-born wife by the hand out into the vineyard and put a bullet through her head before putting a second bullet through his own.)

There *is* something about the Valley people that seems to set them apart from city folk—a certain manner and a certain cast of mind. Being farmers—or, in the current vernacular, being in the "agribusiness"—the Valley men are tough, pessimistic, politically conservative, fiercely independent, contentious, and hot-tempered. If there is one thing a Valley rancher resents it is "folks from outside trying to tell us what to do." The folks from outside are usually from the federal government, and at the heart of much of the continuous grumbling is the Central Valley irrigation project, and what kind of water will go where from which dam, and the fact that it is a U.S. Department of the Interior project—representing outsiders from Washington.

Though Stewart Udall long ago departed from his post as Secretary of the Interior, mention of his name still raises the hackles of Valley farmers. After all, Udall was an easterner (from way back east in Arizona, where water from the Colorado River has long provided a bone of contention for the two states that share its banks), and he came out representing Washington and tried to change things around. Former Secretary of Labor Willard Wirtz is held in even lower esteem. (A Valley rancher was found floating face down in his swimming pool—supposedly for putting in a good word for Wirtz.) It was Wirtz who did away with the *bracero* program, which ranchers—now that it is no more—tend to speak of today as one of the great humanitarian achievements of the twentieth century. The *braceros* were Mexicans brought into the Valley during peak picking seasons to perform the "stoop labor" of gathering low-growing fruits and vegetables. "Why, the *braceros* were the greatest boost to the Mexican economy there ever was!" one rancher insisted not long ago. "The Mexicans who came up here loved the work, and they were wonderful workers. A good picker could make anywhere from sixty-five hundred dollars to ten thousand dollars in a season! But then the Government came out here and said we should put heaters in the bunkhouses—*heaters*! A Mexican's not used to a heater! Doesn't want one, much less know how to use it! They said to us, 'Why aren't you feeding them meat? Why aren't you feeding them eggs?' My Lord, don't those damn fools in Washington know that a Mexican eats tortillas and beans?"

Valley ranchers admit that they may have used the wrong public relations tactic when Secretary Wirtz came out to California in the 1960s to look over the conditions under which the Mexican laborers worked and lived. For one thing, one rancher had the misfortune to say that Mexicans were ideally suited for stoop labor because they were "short and built close to the ground"—and to be widely quoted across the country. For another, the ranchers, hoping to woo Mr. Wirtz to their point of view, put on a big party for him, which may have been a grave mistake. Wirtz was a teetotaler—or at least he frostily refused the many stiff drinks that were urged upon him— while Valley ranchers pride themselves on their capacity for alcohol. Wirtz also made a point of not eating a single bite of the elaborate barbecue that was spread before him, leaving the implication, very strongly, that he would prefer to see the Mexican workers offered similar fare. He went back to Washington, where he promptly canceled the *bracero* program.

There are other complaints related to agriculture. As one Valley rancher puts it, "The national farm program has been conducted as a relief program for the South. Farm legislation on a national scale has been controlled by the South and the Midwest. California keeps getting the short end of the stick. For years the chairmen of both the House and Senate agricultural committees were Southerners, and now we've got a goddamned Southern farmer in the White House. Meanwhile, we're caught here in a cost-price squeeze. Our taxes go up, but our customers have concentrated their buying power. There used to be, for example, hundreds of canneries for the cling-peach people to go to. Now there are nineteen or twenty. Those of us who used to sell direct to markets—well, there used to be thousands of little ones to shop from. Now there are just a few big superchains. So it's harder for the farmer to fight for his price."

Adding to their woes is the fact that the farmers have lost control of the California Assembly and state Senate. The large landholders used to have great power in both, but under the one-man-one-vote system their voice is much less effective. Now, though the Valley ranchers remain resolutely Republican, the Valley counties often go Democratic. Needless to say, Valley ranchers have few kind words for Cesar Chavez and his striking table-grape pickers, whose headquarters was in Delano, some seventy-five miles south of Fresno. "We weren't *about* to have some labor organizer tell us what to do," one rancher says. "Why, California pays the number-one farm wage in the country, and the grape pickers are paid the best! Why couldn't he pick on states that were behind?" Mrs. William Harkey, the wife of a wealthy peach rancher in the little town of Gridley, says, "You bet I bought plenty of grapes during that whole darned thing. I didn't buy them to eat, of course, because they're terribly fattening. I fed them to my pet raccoon." Senator Edward M. Kennedy's support of the table-grape boycott produced the somewhat sick California joke: "Confucius say, 'Man who boycott grapes should not play in Martha's Vineyard.'"

Valley ranchers, pessimistic by nature, are endlessly gloomy about their labor problems, and some insist that there can be no solutions. "The only people making money here are the developers," one rancher claims. "They're buying land at five thousand dollars an acre and selling it for housing at five thousand a lot. Twenty-five years from now this whole Valley will be nothing but houses, and all our fruits and vegetables will be coming from Africa." Still, despite the cities' sprawl, California's harvest acreage continues to increase. Another rancher says, "When they took away the *braceros*, they forced us to use the winos. Those decent, hardworking Mexicans have been replaced by the dregs of society." It is true that during the harvest seasons the trucks gathering up winos from the slums, skid rows, and backwaters of Valley towns for work in the fields are not a pretty sight and make the image of "urine-smelling buses" an apt one. At the same time, the labor shortage has forced the farmers to increase the mechanization of their farms. More and more, computers are feeding cattle and machines are shaking peaches out of trees, replacing human hands. This has meant that though the California farmer may not have been able to raise his prices by much, and though his machines are expensive, they have enabled him to increase his yields enormously. California farmland grows increasingly valuable. It seems likely that California farmers will be able to afford their air-conditioned cars, their heated pools, their air-conditioned houses and pool houses, their private planes, and their wives' regular forays to I. Magnin's for some time to come.

Though the Valley farmers continue to curse the federal government and the trade unions, one of the most difficult things, perhaps, for them to understand is why the average laborer is not willing to work as hard as they, the farmers, do themselves. During the harvest season the farmer rolls up his sleeves and goes into his fields, where he will work for fifteen or twenty hours a day, seven days a week. His wife will put in the same hours in a 120-degree shed as a weighing master, and his sons and daughters will stoop and pick in the hot sun side by side with the winos. When floods threaten the levees of the Sacramento Delta, the Delta ranchers will work all night lugging and hoisting sandbags. Why, the ranchers ask, aren't farm laborers happy to do the same? As one rancher puts it, "There's enough money in California for every man in the state to earn *more* than just a decent living. Why isn't everyone as well off as I am? Too damned lazy, that's all there is to it."

Meanwhile, possibly to counteract the cities' superior attitudes toward the farm towns, the Valley communities indulge in the sort of local boosterism that would have made Sinclair Lewis' George F. Babbitt proud. Local chambers of commerce are untiring in their efforts to get even the smallest towns on the map, and each community is characterized by at least one if not several superlatives. Fresno is the "richest" county in the world. Castroville is advertised as the "Artichoke Capital of the World." Entering Modesto, the visitor is greeted by a huge arch spanning the wide main street, proclaiming * MODESTO * WATER * WEALTH * CONTENTMENT * HEALTH *. Up in Chico several "unique attractions" are vaunted. First, there is the twenty-four-hundred-acre natural park where the original wilderness of the northern Valley is carefully preserved. The park was donated by General John Bidwell, who founded the city. "He was mixed up with Sutter and all the rest," one local resident explains, "and his wife was big on Christianizing the Indians." Chico residents proudly point out that Bidwell Park was the setting for the original *Robin Hood* film, with Errol Flynn, because its thickly clustered live oaks, festooned with ancient grapevines, were considered the closest thing to Sherwood Forest. Hidden in Bidwell Park are two natural lakes, along with what Chico used to boast was the "World's Largest Oak." In 1963 the World's Largest Oak was split by a lightning bolt, and so now Chico's chamber of commerce advertises that it has "Half of the World's Largest Oak."

North of Sacramento is the pretty river town of Colusa. A few years ago Colusa enthusiastically celebrated the hundredth anniversary of its incorporation, and visitors to this event were invited to tour California's second-oldest courthouse (1861) and the Will S. Green mansion (1868). Will S. Green founded Colusa and is venerated as this part of the Valley's "Father of Irrigation," as it was he who first surveyed the Grand Central Canal in 1860. Colusa also has a mini-mountain range all its own, called the Sutter Buttes. Remnants of some long-ago volcanic activity, the Buttes spring up surprisingly from the otherwise flat Valley floor to jagged peaks more than two thousand feet high. Besides giving Colusans something to look at other than an empty horizon, the Buttes allow Colusa—with typical Valley pride and its fondness for superlatives—to declare that the town contains the "World's Smallest Mountain Range."

Still, for all their self-pride and self-promotion, the moneyed residents of the Valley towns remain acutely aware that they are not, and never will be San Francisco—that in San Francisco's eyes they will always be outsiders, visitors, part of the routine supply of tourists. San Francisco remains "the city," and the Valley remains the Valley, committed to a way of life that is agricultural, not citified. Joan Didion's novel *Run River* is set in the rich Delta region, at the confluence of the Sacramento and San Joaquin rivers, where life is always somehow regulated by the rise and fall of water, the floods and ebbs, and where in every mind there was "a file of information, gathered and classified every year there was high water. . . . At what point had they opened the Colusa Weir. When would the Bypass reach capacity. What was the flood stage at Wilkins Slough. At Rough and Ready Bend. Frémont Weir. Rio Vista."

Miss Didion, who comes from the region herself, also portrays how carefully Valley families study the subtle nuances of San Francisco society. At one point in the novel two young Valley women, Martha and Lily, are discussing the social credentials of a third female character, Nancy Dupree, whose engagement has just been announced in the *Chronicle*. Nancy Dupree is from Piedmont, a wealthy suburb of Oakland, across the Bay from San Francisco. Nancy's father's money was made in the construction business. After World War II.

Martha supposed that Nancy Dupree had probably come out at the Fairmont in a white dress ordered from Elizabeth Arden.

Lily was not sure. Those construction people were a little different, particularly if they lived in the East Bay. It was not as if her name were Crocker or Spreckels or something like that.

No, Martha agreed, it was not. It certainly was not as if her name were Crocker or Spreckels or something like that. What a revelation, Lily's sudden grasp on the San Francisco social scene. Was it possible that Lily had at hand a copy of the 1948 San Francisco *Social Register*?

Though San Francisco remains the Valley's role model—laying down the criteria for fashion, interior decoration, entertaining, club life—and though Valley families faithfully subscribe to the *Chronicle* (which publishes a special Valley edition) in addition to their local papers, to most of the old Valley families, with roots going back into the black Valley soil for three, four, and even five generations, back to the days of the earliest pioneers, whose ancestors crossed the isthmus on muleback to get to where they are, the fact that San Francisco still does not quite accept Valley people as ladies and gentlemen is merely a minor annoyance, a familiar but not painful thorn in the side. Most of these families, who certainly could afford to do so if they wished, would not dream of living anywhere else. They go to San Francisco for the shopping, the restaurants, the theaters, the opera, the museums. Then they go home to the towns they know and love the best.

One such person is Mr. C. K. McClatchy, the fourth generation of his family to operate the *Bee* chain of Valley newspapers (a fifth generation is waiting in the wings). The chain includes the Sacramento *Bee*, the Modesto *Bee*, and the Fresno *Bee*, and for years the *Bee*s were run by Mr. McClatchy's doughty maiden aunt, Miss Eleanor McClatchy, who expanded McClatchy Enterprises to include a string of radio and television stations throughout the length of the Valley.* Miss Eleanor was a Valley woman through and through, a pillar of Sacramento society, active in local political, civic, cultural, and charitable affairs, as much in command at the helm of her communications empire as at a cocktail party down in the Delta. Despite her activities, however, her biographical paragraph in *Who's Who in America* was one of the shortest in the book. She supplied no data on her date of birth, her parents' names, her club or church affiliations, her honorary degrees. She merely noted that her newspapers had won a Pulitzer Prize in 1935 for exposing corruption in Nevada. Miss Eleanor had little use for people who tarted up their lives with trimmings. She liked square dancing.

Her nephew is also very much a Valley person. Sitting in downtown Sacramento's elegantly paneled, leather-chaired Sutter Club— Sacramento's answer to San Francisco's Bohemian and Pacific Union clubs—C. K. McClatchy is a pleasantly handsome, well-tailored, urbane and witty man who, nonetheless, like all true Valley men, has a special feeling about the place and what it means: the struggle for land, for water, for success against a landscape that was in the beginning inhospitable to humans. He smiles at a mention of San Francisco's toplofty attitude toward the Valley and its people. "San Franciscans look down their noses at everybody," he says. "They

---

* In 1979 the McClatchys expanded outside California and purchased the Anchorage, Alaska, *Daily News*. Within six months, circulation doubled.

look down at the East, the South, the Midwest, and the Southwest. They look down their noses at Berkeley, Oakland, San Rafael, and all of Marin County—everything that isn't part of their precious Peninsula. They don't want to understand the Valley, and so they probably never will. San Francisco has turned its back on its own history, but the Valley hasn't. There is a sense, here in the Valley, of the continuation of history—of the gold rush, of the opening up of the West by the railroads, of the growth of California from the earliest pioneer days to where it is now, the most populous state in the Union. And you get a sense here of how history has moved—swept, been carried into the present in less than a hundred and fifty years, and of how the present has maintained the integrity of the past."

McClatchy points to the little Delta town of Locke, not far west of Sacramento—small sturdy houses lined up along the levee, with truck gardens on the reclaimed river bottom below—which is actually a rural Chinatown, whose population consists largely of the descendants of the Chinese laborers whom men like Charles Crocker imported to help him build his railroad fast and on the cheap. Today Locke's Chinese American families operate small restaurants, bars, groceries, a laundry or two. "The Valley has *kept up* with its history like no other place I know of," McClatchy says. "Just go and stand on the rim of the Shasta Dam"—called "the Keystone of the Central Valley Project"—"and see the thing that is the source of so much that has happened in the Valley, and beyond it, and you'll see what I mean, why I find this Valley—plain and flat and conservative as it is—one of the most thrilling places to be alive in that I know."

CHAPTER TWENTY-ONE
O Little Town

IF ANYTHING, Santa Barbarans are even prouder than Valley people of constituting a world of their own, independent of San Francisco and Los Angeles. They are even prouder of their special earthquake.

Earthquakes are peculiar and, of course, unpredictable. They are measured on the Richter scale of 1 to 10, as ground motion is recorded on seismographs (presumably a quake registering 10 on the scale is the most violent ever recorded). And yet the reading on the Richter scale often bears little relation to the amount of damage done. The "great" San Francisco earthquake of 1906, which brought on the great fire, measured 8.3 on the scale, and that, admittedly, was a mighty temblor. Five years later, in 1911, San Francisco experienced another quake, measuring 6.6 on the scale, which did little damage, and in the summer of 1979 a quake registering 5.9 caused tall buildings to sway but inflicted no significant harm on people or property. And yet, on June 29, 1925—a date that is engraved on the memory of every true Santa Barbaran—an earthquake registering 6.3 on the scale, or just slightly higher than the 1979 quake, virtually changed the face of Santa Barbara.

Trees thrashed about, the towers of All Saints' Church swayed, and the ground heaved in great waves. At least one Santa Barbara dowager, old Mrs. Cunningham—a Forbes of Boston—was killed. (One of the wealthy Santa Barbara residents had a psychic butler who foresaw the quake and warned her in time to save her collection of costly antique vases.) The aftershocks of the great Santa Barbara quake continued for the rest of the summer, and before it was over, most of what had been old Santa Barbara had been destroyed.

Nowadays, in retrospect, the 1925 quake is usually referred to as "a blessing." Until that time the city had developed somewhat haphazardly, without zoning. After the quake Santa Barbara found itself faced with the challenge of rebuilding from scratch, and it was a challenge it embraced with enthusiasm. When the earth finally quieted, an architectural board of review was formed by a group of local citizens. Its purpose was to supervise the reconstruction of the town and to see to it that this was done in such a way that it would be pleasing to the eye and would also have a certain architectural uniformity. The architectural theme chosen was a vaguely Mediterranean mixture of Spanish Colonial and Mission Revival, considered appropriate to southern California's history. Walls were of beige or yellow stucco, and roofs were of red or yellow tile or terra-cotta. Bell towers and balconies and grillwork abounded. Santa Barbara's acres were strictly zoned. For obvious reasons, high-rise buildings were prohibited. These architectural, building, and zoning codes have been observed until this day and have become a matter of great city pride. Not long ago Santa Barbara found itself in the middle of an intense dispute over the design of a new wing for the art museum, which proposed to depart, ever so slightly, from the traditional Spanish Mission style. Though structural architects have found Santa Barbara's elaborate building regulations somewhat inhibiting, landscape architects have flocked to the area and have prospered creating the town's many pretty parks, malls, and private gardens.

Partly because Santa Barbara was able to rebuild itself so artfully out of the dust of the earthquake, Santa Barbarans consider themselves very special people. They do not identify at all with San Francisco, to the north. Nor do they feel much kinship with Los Angeles, to the south. As for the Valley towns, they might exist in some other part of the globe. In fact, Santa Barbarans often seem to feel no real relationship with the state of California. "Santa Barbara is an *international* city," says Mrs. Michael Wheelwright, the wife of a prominent landscape architect, and many Santa Barbarans would agree with her. Santa Barbara is not merely a city with a permanent population, it is also a resort with a transient one, and many Santa Barbarans maintain other homes elsewhere—beach houses in Hawaii, farms in Vermont—and are always jetting from one part of the world to another. As a result, many Santa Barbara families do not feel California-*based*, as the older families in other parts of the state do. The peripatetic nature of wealthy Santa Barbarans helped account for the fact that when Santa Barbara attempted to publish its own edition of the *Social Register*, the enterprise collapsed after four editions; much of social Santa Barbara was already listed in *Social Registers* of other cities.

Santa Barbara first came into existence in 1850, when it was incorporated by an act of the California legislature, a few months before there actually was a state of California. But it was not until the late 1860s, in the post-Civil War days, that it had its real genesis. It began, much as San Diego did, as a winter resort for families who, rich from the war, were casting about for new ways to spend their suddenly acquired leisure time and money, and were encapsulating themselves in luxurious redoubts where they would encounter only their "own kind." In Santa Barbara, furthermore, most of this overnight gentry came from the East and the Middle West—members of the Armour family (meat), the Mortons (salt), the Fleischmanns (yeast), and the Hammonds (organs), to name a few—attracted by the subtropical winter weather, the beaches, the sailing, and other water sports. The early migrants built imposing winter homes in the hills above the little mission town, and many of these rich easterners were (or so Santa Barbarans like to boast) the black sheep of their respective families and were encouraged to go to California by relatives who were eager to have them transplanted several thousand miles from home. This accounts, Santa Barbarans say, for the special relaxed and laissez-faire air of the place—less grand and pretentious than Newport, less formal and competitive than Palm Beach. "Here we have always just gone our happy ways," says one resident.

Santa Barbara was first colonized by the rich in the days when golf and tennis and polo were becoming popular rich men's pastimes, the era that saw the dawn of the American country club. The exclusive Valley Club, which became the "old-guard club," was the first one built, and later came the Birnam Wood Club, for a newer guard. A third country club, the Montecito—bought recently by a Japanese consortium—came to stand lowest in the club pecking order, and is considered "commercial." The Little Town Club, founded in 1914, became Santa Barbara's leading social club for women and established its quaint rules, such as "Six to a Susan." (For lunch the club has tables for six, with a lazy Susan in the center of each table; it is against the rules to sample a tidbit from anyone else's lazy Susan.) But it is typical of Santa Barbara's residential-resort beginnings that, socially, the real center of things should long have been a hotel, the elegant Santa Barbara Biltmore. It has long attracted such regular international visitors as Baron Philippe de Rothschild, who winters there and swims daily in the Olympic-size pool of the adjacent Coral Casino (a members-only club for Santa Barbara residents, free for Biltmore guests).

When an architect named George Washington Smith came to Santa Barbara in the 1920s he quickly put his stamp on the place, doing for Santa Barbara what Stanford White did for New York and Long Island and what Addison Mizner did for Palm Beach. He designed mansions in the preferred Spanish Colonial style, with vaulted ceilings and the accompanying bell towers, balconies, and courtyards. His flights of Mediterranean fancy were extreme, and

he thought nothing of going to Spain and Italy to bring back boat-
loads of tiles, lanterns, shutters, and grilles to adorn his creations.
It is said that when Harry K. Thaw, who murdered Stanford
White, was released from prison, he visited Santa Barbara, and,
viewing a George Washington Smith house, commented, "I think I
killed the wrong architect." Still, because there are only twenty-
nine Smith houses in Santa Barbara, to own one has long been a—
if not *the*—major status symbol. And when, as rarely happens, a
Smith house goes on the market, it is certain to bring at least a
hundred thousand dollars more than a house of comparable size by
another architect.

One woman who still lives in the Smith-designed mansion she had
built for herself in 1925 after the earthquake is Mrs. Angelica
Schuyler Bryce. The eighty-seven-year-old Mrs. Bryce, who has
always been known by her childhood name, "Girlie," is one of the
grandes dames who for years have ruled the social seas of Santa
Barbara. She actually worked with George Washington Smith on
her house, traveling with him and helping him collect the antique
hammered-iron hardware that was meticulously copied in Europe
and brought to her California estate. On her fifty-five landscaped
acres, called Florestal, Girlie Bryce maintains what amounts to a
private zoo, including forty-five peacocks and a sixty-year-old
Galápagos tortoise named Gappy, who is fed a diet of watermelon
and fresh fruits imported from Hawaii. Gappy reciprocates by allowing Mrs. Bryce's thirty-eight grand- and great-grandchildren to
take turns riding on his back when they come for visits. For all the
splendor of her surroundings, Girlie Bryce complains, "Santa Barbara has gotten so big. If it gets any bigger it's going to be a horrible
place."

And Santa Barbara has gotten big. Before World War II it was
a sleepy town of some 35,000 souls. By 1950 its population had
jumped to 45,000, and today it is a city of over 200,000. After the
war came Vandenberg Air Force Base, bringing in a sizable military
contingent. Then came the University of California's Santa Barbara
campus, and Robert Hutchins with his Center for the Study of

Democratic Institutions, both of which not only added people but also contributed what Santa Barbara considers an intellectual, think-tank atmosphere to the place which it had never had before. Dr. Hutchins' pronouncements from his lush hillside villa ("Mankind's intellectual power must be developed") are given much weight. Then came General Motors, bringing with it some hundred new families. The General Motors people tended to stick to themselves, which was fine with Santa Barbarans, who adopted the attitude, "If you don't want us, we don't want you."

As Santa Barbara has grown, its more firmly established citizens have spent some time trying to define what, exactly, Santa Barbara really is. It is no longer a resort, it is not like any other city in California, or typical of anything, but what is it? Santa Barbara refuses to be influenced by either Los Angeles or San Francisco—many Santa Barbarans insist they never have need to visit either city—or the East. It is a city that has set about determinedly to develop its own style, architectural as well as philosophical, but the latter is a little difficult to describe. It is a style, furthermore, whose practitioners resent and resist criticism from outside Santa Barbara.

In 1976, for example, Santa Barbara was up in arms; there was only one topic of conversation on everyone's lips. (Normally there are two topics of conversation on everyone's lips: spiraling real estate taxes and the more comforting phenomenon of spiraling real estate values.) The uproar was over a magazine article. In its June issue *Town & Country* had carried an article called "The Santa Barbara Style," consisting of a short text and many pages of color photographs of wealthy Santa Barbarans enjoying their favorite pastime, Santa Barbara. It showed Santa Barbarans in polo outfits and riding habits; in their terraced, Italianate formal gardens, around their colonnaded pool houses and pools, in their opulent living rooms and bedrooms with *trompe l'oeil* walls painted to reproduce likenesses of the views from the Gritti Palace Hotel in Venice. It showed Santa Barbara suffused in sunlight, with views of blue sea and skies and purplish mountains, and Santa Barbarans dressed in pastels of pink and blue and lavender, in Pucci pants and Gucci shoes. "Disgusting!" "Perfectly ghastly!" "Dreadful!" were some of the local opinions expressed about the article. But considering the obvious beauty of the setting which the article conveyed, along with the golden healthiness of the residents, it was hard to figure out what the fuss was all about.

Gradually it emerged. While everyone agreed that the article had been correct in pointing out Santa Barbara's fondness for foreign cars—Mercedeses and BMWs in particular—what everyone objected to was the magazine's choice of people photographed to illustrate the piece. What, for example, did Suzy Parker (formerly a New York model, now married to actor Bradford Dillman and living in Santa Barbara) have to do with Santa Barbara? How did Clifton Fadiman (born in New York, and Jewish) or Barnaby Conrad (a San Francisco transplant) fit into the Santa Barbara scene? Certainly *Hair* producer Michael Butler, sort of a millionaire hippie from Chicago who was once arrested for raising marijuana in his garden, was far from the typical Santa Barbaran; he had once entertained Mick Jagger. Most offensive of all, it turned out, was the woman whom the magazine had chosen to picture on its cover, Mrs. Manuel Rojas, wearing chandelier emerald earrings to match her eyes. What did *she* have to do with the Santa Barbara style, everyone wanted to know. Chandelier emerald earrings were most definitely not the Santa Barbara style. The Rojases, furthermore, were considered *nouveaux riches* (Perta Oil Marketing, Inc.) and originally were from, of all places, Beverly Hills. They had come to Santa Barbara as recently as 1974. A more untypical Santa Barbaran couple could not have been found. It was inconceivable to Santa Barbara that Mrs. Rojas might have been chosen primarily for her beautiful face. As far as Santa Barbara was concerned, a far more acceptable cover girl would have been octogenarian Girlie Bryce.

Santa Barbara is a community in which literally hours can be spent discussing who is "typical Santa Barbara" and who is not. The typical Santa Barbaran, it is agreed, is "conservative." If for "conservative" some people read "stuffy and smug," that is perfectly all right with Santa Barbara. Santa Barbarans feel that they have elevated smugness to an art form. The typical Santa Barbaran goes in for espadrilles and tennis shoes more than for emeralds, which Mrs. Rojas was clearly shown wearing in broad daylight, against even the most liberal rules of jewel wearing.

The typical Santa Barbaran distrusts outsiders and newcomers and dislikes change. When the local Baskin-Robbins ice cream shop discontinued a flavor called pralines 'n' cream, the citizenry, who had grown fond of the flavor, picketed the establishment until pralines 'n' cream was restored to the inventory. Santa Barbara women like to boast that theirs was the last community in America to endorse the pants suit, and even then the fashion did not gain many local supporters. The typical Santa Barbara woman does not support the ERA, admires Ronald Reagan and Anita Bryant, and thinks that if Richard Nixon had just burned the incriminating tapes, the whole business of Watergate could have been avoided.

The typical Santa Barbaran is extremely town-proud and civic-minded. It has been said of Santa Barbara that it is a city of meetings and that nothing can be done until a meeting has been called to discuss all the ramifications of whatever it is. At the same time, Santa Barbara is distrustful of city government, and government in general, and believes that any decisions affecting the city should be made by the citizens themselves, who are believed to know what is good for them and what isn't. When a stretch of freeway was planned between San Francisco and the Mexican border, passing through Santa Barbara, Santa Barbarans decided that they did not want traffic streaming through their community at seventy miles an hour. They went to battle with the California State Department of Transportation and—though it took years—they won. Now Santa Barbara has the only segment of the freeway's six-hundred-mile length on which motorists are kept at a respectful speed by being forced to stop for a series of traffic lights. When offshore oil spills began dirtying their beaches Santa Barbarans met and formed an organization called GOO (for Get Oil Out). They took on some of the country's largest oil companies to get them to clean up their operations and won again.

Typifying Santa Barbara's attitude toward city government was Miss Pearl Chase, who once said, "People won't be inspired to help a community unless they are part of it. Government officials are really temporary. They come and go, and this constant turnover means that citizen organizations have far greater power." For years Miss Chase was perhaps the most typical Santa Barbaran there ever was, along with Girlie Bryce. She was immensely rich. Her family owned the Hope ranch, which several years ago was sold off and subdivided and developed—as the Irvine ranch has been attempting to do—to become one of the town's most elegant and expensive suburbs. In fact, it was Pearl Chase's brother, Harold Chase, who developed the Hope ranch property, along with Girlie Bryce's late husband, Peter Cooper Bryce. For all her wealth, Pearl Chase lived rather modestly in a large Victorian house full of sagging furniture, faded curtains, old scrapbooks of family memorabilia, and genteelly dusty clutter. If she owned any emeralds, she was never seen wearing them.

Change of course has come to Santa Barbara, as it has everywhere else where the rich have tried to isolate themselves behind walls and gates and rolling lawns and gardens. And some developments have thoroughly startled the otherwise orderly and conventionally well-behaved residents. In the 1970s, for example, a rich and social wedding united two old-line Santa Barbara families. Then, shortly after the wedding, the young bridegroom announced his intention of having a sex-change operation. For years the sedate Little Town Club never served alcoholic beverages. Again in the 1970s, a proposal was made that the club offer wine with lunch. This created quite a fuss. In a surprising development, it turned out that all the older women members were in favor of the wine, while all the younger members were traditionalists and did not want wine. Eventually the older group won out, and wine was introduced. Soon afterward came hard liquor. "Now," complains an older member, "it's so noisy at lunchtime you can't hear yourself think."

"Oh, how Santa Barbara has changed!" complains one matron, a Santa Barbara resident for more than fifty years. "It used to be a simple, charming place. All the houses had blue shutters. We would eat at El Paseo, standing in line with trays for the most delicious food. The annual Fiesta was beautiful. Now it's horrible. People used to have lovely parties. Now we hardly go anywhere. There was wonderful dancing at the Biltmore. Now it's part of a big chain."

The change, the dowager feels, began during the Second World War. "There began to be a strong fascist feeling here," she says. "There were a few men who were out-and-out Nazis. I remember one man who called 'Heil Hitler!' across a dinner table, and another who said, 'Let us hope and pray that Germany wins the war.' One of those men is still around. During the war it all became terribly snobbish and anti-Semitic."

But unlike Los Angeles ninety miles to the south, Santa Barbara isn't going to get much bigger—at least for the time being. In recent years southern California has been undergoing periodic acute water shortages, and now each Santa Barbara household is water-rationed according to a complicated formula based on past consumption, number of persons in the household, and so on. If a Santa Barbara homeowner exceeds his water quota, he is charged a penalty, even though there seems to be plenty of water with which to sprinkle golfing greens and fill thousands of backyard swimming pools. It was the water shortage that was given as the reason for declaring a moratorium on new building in Santa Barbara some time back. But another reason for the building stoppage, Santa Barbarans admit, was to keep out more new people. The moratorium has had another pleasant effect as well. With no more new houses allowed to be built, the value of existing properties has climbed enormously.

Best of all, despite its growth from a small town to a medium-size city, Santa Barbara has retained a sense of *place*, a singular identity, a sense that Santa Barbara could happen only here, along this particular curve of Pacific Ocean, against these particular mountains. Los Angeles, in its hectic growth, never really acquired a sense of place, of specificity, or a distinguishing character all its own. Except on rare days when the surrounding hills are visible, Los Angeles has lost its topography, even its geography; driving through Los

Angeles, one lacks a sense of getting anywhere. And if Los Angeles seems never to have paused long enough to acquire a distinctive city personality of its own, San Francisco—at least in the view of most Santa Barbarans—seems to be losing the personality it once had, as the Victorian bow-front houses that clustered along the hills give way to high-rise towers; as a Standard station has appeared right on the top of Nob Hill, across the street from the Pacific Union Club, formerly the James Flood mansion, one of the few great houses that survived the great fire; as more and more downtown streets have given way to porno shops and adult movie houses; and as the large homosexual community has become a political force.

And yet, whatever else it is or isn't, Santa Barbara is still a place, its own place, where, as one woman describes it, "genteel people live—people who don't need to be justified by anything."

CHAPTER TWENTY-TWO
Finisterra

IN CALIFORNIA the approach of winter is not distinct. There is no
true autumn, no real foliage change. Leaves fall, and all at once the
elms and sycamores are bare. But the palm trees remain the same,
and the rhododendron and the boxwood, and except for a damp chill
in the air it is possible to believe that nothing really has occurred.
Winter begins with rain. Suddenly the long dry summer is drenched
with a great downpour. Streets run with water, rivers rise in
their banks, and dry creek beds become slow-moving, muddy
ponds with eucalyptus and poplar trunks standing in the middle of
them. Swimming pools fill up to their gutters and turn murky green
with algae. In the Valley the ditches and canals from the great dams
in the north run swiftly. After this first rain every day seems to
have more rain or heavy fog or cold wind, and for a period the land
of eternal sunshine seems lost in a damp, swirling cloud.

A true Californian respects the rain and this curious half winter. For Californians never lose their awe of water, the water that made the desert bloom with peaches, apricots, artichokes, lettuce, and grapes. This great source of life returns to California each year, sometimes as early as September, sometimes as late as November. The rain will mean snowfall in the Sierras, and the amount of snowfall will affect the amount of runoff in the spring melt. At the same time, Californians are fatalistic about the rain, because it can offer not only a blessing but a bane as well. Too early a rain can damage fruit and vegetable crops ready for harvest. In the south too much rain can spur a lush growth of tall trees and shrubbery in the foothills, which, during the dry summer months, will become as parched as tinder and dangerously flammable. The slightest spark will set it off. The arsonist and incendiary are tempted. It is the easiest trick in the world to set a mountain range on fire: just leave a cigarette smoldering between the covers of a folded matchbook and walk rather rapidly away.

In southern California the rain washes the air of smog, but it also brings down mud slides and causes hillside houses to lose their footing and swimming pools to float up out of the ground, like blue boats, from the hydrostatic pressure in the earth. The rain brings down pollutants in the air—most the result of the internal-combustion engine—in the form of a slippery, oily slick, more treacherous than ice, and there are accidents and tie-ups on the freeways. Secretaries and executives alike phone in to say they will be late for work and meetings because of the traffic jams caused by the rain. Californians have grown cynical about the rain, because the water of life is also the water of death. It was bad weather, along with the effects of the Great Depression, along with the effects of Prohibition, that caused the father of Julio and Ernest Gallo to conclude that all was lost and end his life.

Land and water, life and death—these paired themes recur in any account of the California rich. Violence is never far away when life and water are at stake. Land and life, animal or vegetable, are insupportable without water. Our bodies are composed largely of water, and yet water plays tricks on us: we cannot live three days without it, nor can we survive much longer than three minutes underneath it. No wonder our feelings toward water are irrational, almost paranoid. Brigham Young, arriving in a waterless valley in Utah that supported, according to the legend, only a single scrubby pine tree, is said to have declared, *"This is the place."* It must have looked to him like nowhere at all. But Young was tired and ill, too weary to cross the next flank of mountains, and it was as far as he wanted to go. He may well have meant to say, "All right, this place is as good a place as any." To the California pioneers, who went farther, the inhospitable landscape of their destination also must have looked like nowhere. But like Brigham Young, they decided that Nowhere could be a place.

And after so much violence over California's land and water, it is perhaps not surprising that violence has become a habit, that it has followed a number of California fortunes down to the present day and generation. The children of the rich, of course, are often notoriously rebellious. Patricia Campbell Hearst, W.R.'s granddaughter, refused to be a debutante at Mrs. Tucker's ball. Later she refused to continue to attend the Roman Catholic mass. Later she was expelled from the Santa Catalina School for Girls in Monterey, allegedly for possessing marijuana. Still later she went to live with a young man named Steven Weed, and from that *ménage* she was violently removed—either by kidnapping or through her own complicity (one will never know which)—by a bizarre group dedicated to violence, which called itself the Symbionese Liberation Army. There followed a long litany of disorders, including rape, gun-slinging, armed robbery, murder, and a fiery, bloody shoot-out in Los Angeles.

All the incidental ironies were noted in the press, which brought out the almost incestuous relationships existing within the perfumed circle of San Franciscans. Miss Hearst's best friend had been Patricia Tobin, a great-granddaughter of Michael H. de Young, William Randolph Hearst's archenemy. Patricia Tobin's father, Michael Tobin, was president of the Hibernia Bank, which Miss Hearst helped rob. During the lengthy period when Patty Hearst was at large she apparently traveled extensively throughout the United States. And yet, with that curious homing instinct so peculiar to native Californians, she was within a few blocks of her parents' home when she was finally apprehended. (Interestingly, when she surrendered to the F.B.I., one of the first things she asked for was a glass of water.) The jail in Pleasanton, in which Miss Hearst was ordered to spend part of her sentence, was not much more than a stone's throw from the great villa where her Great-grandmother Hearst had once given extravagant entertainments.

Most ironic of all, perhaps, was the fact that throughout her prolonged escapade Patty Hearst managed to create the kind of lurid front-page copy that her grandfather liked best. William Randolph Hearst might not have been flipping in his grave at all. He had never cared much about conventionality or even respectability. He would have loved the story.

The Hearst affair turned California into an armed camp. Telephone numbers were quickly changed and taken out of the directory. Addresses were removed from the *Social Register*. Children were escorted to and from schools by bodyguards, and the two fashionable San Francisco girls' schools, Sarah Dix Hamlin's and Katherine Delmar Burke's, stopped printing student lists. Plainclothesmen mingled with guests at debutante balls; debutantes' names were for the first time withheld from the press, along with the names of opera box-holders; electronic surveillance devices were installed throughout the Peninsula, and an additional guard was stationed at the gate of the Burlingame Country Club. Everywhere the California rich gathered there was fear, and kidnap threats proliferated throughout the state. People in the East had trouble relating to and rationalizing these events. It seemed easier to conclude that everyone in California was crazy.

The same conclusion was drawn at the time of the Charles Manson "family" murders at the home of actress Sharon Tate in Los Angeles when one of the victims turned out to be Abigail Folger, a beautiful Radcliffe-educated heiress to the Folger coffee fortune and a niece of Mrs. Robert Watt Miller, one of the grandest of San Francisco's *grandes dames*. It seemed unbelievable that a proper San Francisco society girl had apparently become involved with the swinging drug-and-sex culture of Hollywood. For months after the Manson murders the rich of southern California went into hiding.

In the summer of 1976 the California rich were jolted again. A busload of Chowchilla schoolchildren were kidnapped and, with their bus driver, buried alive in a moving van that had been sunk in a dried mudhole. The newspapers were filled with harrowing accounts of how the driver was able to dig the children out and save them from suffocation. The motive behind the crime was unclear and seemed senseless; none of the parents of the schoolchildren was wealthy. But one of the alleged perpetrators of this nasty business, it turned out, was. He was twenty-four-year-old Frederick Newhall Woods III, a descendant of one of California's oldest and proudest families. The Newhall ranch had once rivaled the Irvine ranch in size and productivity. One of young Woods's relatives, Margaret Newhall, had married Atholl McBean, the largest shareholder in Standard Oil of California. The Newhalls had been prominent in affairs involving youth and education. It had been old George Newhall, according to one of many legends, who had first suggested to Leland Stanford that he build a university in memory of his dead son.

OF COURSE, by the late 1970s not all the descendants of California's founding families were coming to bad or peculiar ends. A number of Floods, Mackays, and Crockers remain in California leading quiet, sedately moneyed lives. Down on the Peninsula, Michael de Young Tobin and his wife, the former Sally Fay, live not far from his Aunt Phyllis Tucker, the surviving de Young sister. As a hobby, Michael and Sally Tobin collect fine wines, which they store in a specially built heat-and-humidity-controlled cellar. As an oenophile, Sally Tobin says, "I think it's almost *insulting* not to serve wine with meals. Even to people I didn't really want to meet I'd serve wine— and not a California wine either. As for food, we simply won't serve the ordinary. Steak is for butchers." As a San Francisco society person, Mrs. Tobin is as discriminating and traditionalist as her husband's aunt. "Frankly, I'm a snob," she says. "So many unattractive people have come to California that I determined to see to it that my children mingle only with their own kind." Mrs. Tobin also points out the subtle social distinction between Burlingame and the somewhat amorphous town of Hillsborough that Burlingame abuts. Of the two, Hillsborough is the better address, and the Tobins live in Hillsborough. "But," says Mrs. Tobin, "we always say we live in Burlingame. If you hear people say they live in Hillsborough, you can be certain they are parvenus or climbers."

Many of the current generation of the California rich have remained active in the community. Gordon Getty, for example, a grandson of J. Paul Getty (once called "the richest man in the world" and a sometime Californian), is interested primarily in music and opera and in seemingly little else. Others remain active in the business community. Adolph Spreckels' grandson, John Rosekrans, rather than relax with a large inherited fortune, developed a lively and successful business of his own, manufacturing and marketing water-sports equipment—a popular body-surfing board, a floating pool lounge chair, even a floating transistor radio. His brother, Adolph Spreckels Rosekrans, is a prominent San Francisco architect. Though John Rosekrans is now capable of living independently of his Spreckels money, he remains proud of his family's history in California. It saddens him that when Kay Spreckels Gable's son (by "bad uncle" Adolph Spreckels, Jr.) died in an automobile accident, leaving no offspring, there were no more Spreckelses in America to carry on the family name.

Still others, after a taste of city life, have turned back to the land, where their forebears got their start. John D. Spreckels' great-granddaughter Alexandra Kelham married a handsome Stanford-educated stockbroker, W. Robert Phillips, Jr. Several years ago, after a number of years in San Francisco, the Phillipses decided to move permanently to the country, to a spacious and sprawling Napa Valley ranch that had been Mrs. Phillips' mother's summer place. Here on some hundred and eighty rolling acres of the Valley's flank, the Phillipses have been growing wine grapes. "The soil here," Bob Phillips points out, "is very similar to that of the Burgundy and Champagne districts of France, and the Moselle and Rhine areas of Germany. So is the climate. The days are hot and dry and the nights are cool. Wine grapes don't need much irrigation. Wine, they say, needs to 'struggle' to grow."

Wine has become the Napa Valley's biggest business, and nearly seventy bonded wineries operate throughout the Valley's twenty-five-mile length. Unlike the Gallo family's operation in Modesto, where the emphasis is on mass production, the Napa Valley wine-growers—whose collective output amounts to less than 5 percent of California's annual production—stress quality. In 1976 two of the Valley's smallest wineries—Château Montelena and Stag's Leap Wine Cellars—produced wines that were judged better than some of the greatest wines from France's Bordeaux and Burgundy vineyards in a European competition. To be sure, a number of the winegrowers in Napa are gentleman farmers, wealthy Californians who operate at a loss as a tax shelter. But Bob and Alexandra Phillips are determined to turn a profit with their grapes. Both work long hours in the vineyard during the harvest season. For her own table Alexandra Phillips maintains a vegetable garden and fruit trees. Though her house is large, she does her own cooking and housework. "After all, Claus Spreckels was a farmer," she says. "He raised sugarcane and beets. He was my great-*great*-grandfather, though he only died in 1908, just twenty-six years before I was born. Time gets tele-scoped in California. Our history is really very short. The distant past was really only yesterday. Everything today has a direct bear-ing on and relationship to our past."

Alexandra Phillips can remember that in 1940, when she was a little girl, a mysterious tunnel was uncovered, leading from the base-ment of the James Flood mansion—by then the Pacific Union Club—into the basement of the house of her grandfather, Alexander Hamilton, on the other side of California Street. The tunnel was high enough for a man to stand in. She often wonders what the purpose of this tunnel was, what the "direct connection" between her family and the Floods might have been. At the time the tunnel was discovered, the *Chronicle* commented that the Floods and the Hamiltons "supposedly were no more than casual neighbors."

One thing that worries such winegrowers as the Phillipses is the fact that the suburban sprawl from San Francisco, Berkeley, and Oakland has been slowly but steadily encroaching on the Napa Valley, only about ninety minutes by freeway from the San Francisco–Oakland Bay Bridge. A number of well-heeled city folk have discovered the pretty little valley, with its climate much clearer and crisper than foggy San Francisco's. They have begun buying and handsomely restoring the valley's charming Victorian gingerbread houses. Napa, once a drowsy cattle-ranching town, has become chic. A former general store has become a gourmet food shop that sells, among other things, fresh beluga caviar. Trendy new boutiques and restaurants keep opening. So do new communities of mobile homes. As the land in the Napa Valley becomes more attractive to developers its price keeps going up, providing owners with increased temptation to sell. Today even a mediocre acre of grape land goes for as much as sixteen thousand dollars. The fate of the Napa Valley may one day be the same as that of the Irvine ranch: development, housing, shopping centers, office towers, a Sheraton hotel with a revolving cocktail lounge on the roof. Growers such as the Phillipses of course hope that this won't happen and that the valley will be able to cling to some vestiges of its agricultural past.

IN SOUTHERN California, Bernardo Yorba is the great-great-grandson of Don José Antonio Yorba, who came to California with Gaspar de Portolá and Father Junípero Serra in 1767 to expel the Jesuits. Today the early Spanish families, many of whom were originally Catalans, are intricately interrelated through marriages, and Bernardo Yorba's cousins are Peraltas, Carillos, Sepulvedas, Serranos, and a great many other Yorbas, as his great-grandfather, also named Bernardo, had twenty-three children. Mr. Yorba himself has ten, fecundity being a Yorba family trait. Bernardo Yorba, however, is unique in the fact that his house in the Santa Ana Canyon stands on land that was once a part of the great Yorba rancho—some sixty-two thousand acres, *mas o menos,* which the original Yorba was granted by the King of Spain. Like other great ranchos, Don José Antonio Yorba's Rancho Santiago de Santa Ana supported many thousands of head of cattle until the Great Drought, at which time much of the land was lost to gringo moneylenders. Later, reduced in size, the Yorba rancho was given over to groves of Valencia oranges. Bernardo Yorba still grows Valencia oranges on his canyon-side estate, but, he says, "Only enough to squeeze into my vodka." The Yorbas are also notable among the old Californianos in the fact that through the generations they managed to remain quite prosperous. Bernardo Yorba is a real estate developer and owns several large shopping centers in Orange County.

Bernardo Yorba is a large, handsome olive-skinned man in his forties, and he is proud of his heritage, which he prefers to think of as Mexican. "My mother used to say, 'We're not Mexican, we're Spanish,' " he says. "But I'd point out to her the wording of the original grant, which says it was granted to 'José Antonio Yorba, a *Mexican.*' " Yorba works in an office in the Bank of America Building in Anaheim, an office filled with family photographs and other bits of memorabilia, including a collection of antique saddles, some of them trimmed with sterling silver. He is a proud member of the Congress of Charros, a patriotic-historic Mexican American group that puts on elaborate cowboy costumes and performs on such occasions as the Rose Bowl Parade. Yorba and his family, who all speak flawless Spanish—and even speak English with a trace of a Spanish accent—make frequent trips to Mexico, retracing the past, keeping track of their heritage. "I feel a great obligation to my heritage," Bernardo Yorba says. "We must show the rest of the world that we continue to build on our heritage. We have to make a contribution. We have to participate." In a drawer of a filing cabinet Mr. Yorba has collected ten fat folders of heritage—family trees, old documents, deeds, letters, chains of title—one folder for each of his children.

Among the contributions Mr. Yorba makes to the Orange County community are the various school projects he has headed. He is also executive vice-president of the children's hospital and is a director of the Angels Stadium Corporation. "We Yorbas are still doing our share, pulling our weight," he says. "My wife and I want to set that kind of example for our children."

Though more than a hundred years have passed, Bernardo Yorba still speaks bitterly of the cupidity of the gringo moneylenders at the time of the drought, when much of the Yorba rancho became part of the Irvine ranch, and of the federal government's concurrent insistence on challenging the Spanish land grants, which had been established a century earlier. Had it not been for these two forces, Mr. Yorba points out quite correctly, the history of California would have been quite different, and the state would consist of many Irvine ranches, at least one of which would belong to Bernardo Yorba. "Now everywhere you look in California is government land," he says. "We need to produce off this land, but we can't."

Yorba also blames the United States government for fostering the notion that Mexicans are a shiftless, corrupt, lazy, and ignorant people. "Mexicans are an ancient, sophisticated, and hardworking people, with deep roots in both the Spanish and the Indian cultures," he says. "When Spain conquered Latin America, it didn't try to drive the native Indians out the way the English colonists did in North America. Spain converted the Indians, yes, but conversion is an assimilationist move, which is the opposite of expulsion and killing and forcing the Indians onto reservations. If you ask me, the real destiny of California is contingent on our relations with Mexico. We've stomped all over Mexico for years, and the American oil companies have exploited the Mexicans from old Doheny on down. Now, of course, when Mexico has made some new oil discoveries, we suddenly want to get all friendly with Mexico. Talk about cynicism. Naturally the Mexicans want to get a good price for their oil, but we seem to expect them to give it to us. That idiot Schlesinger went down to Mexico, and when the Mexicans mentioned their price he called them bandits—*banditos*—and then couldn't seem to understand why López Portillo felt insulted!"

Like many other Californians, Bernardo Yorba freely admits that he has often employed Mexicans as laborers who are illegal aliens. "They're hard workers, and they're good workers because they love and respect the land. After all, this is land that my great-grandfather Bernardo first irrigated by diverting water from the Santa Ana River. The Mexicans are honest, they're religious, they're never drunk. The Mexican will always make arrangements to have the major share of his money sent home to his family. Of course every now and then I'll get a phone call from the Immigration Office and someone will say, 'Sorry, Bernardo, but we've got your boys.' "

"FINISTERRA"—land's end, the edge of the world—is the name Linda Irvine Gaede and her husband gave to their spectacular home high on a bluff overlooking the Pacific Ocean in a walled and heavily guarded enclave called Irvine Cove. (Like other wealthy families, the Irvines have had to cope with their share of kidnap threats.) From the many westward-facing terraces and patios of Finisterra one can watch seals and dolphins and whales go by, and swarms of pelicans fishing among the rocks. In the garage hangs one of a matching pair of monogrammed, custom-made, hand-tooled sterling silver saddles that J.I. had made for Big Kate and himself by Visalia, the great California saddlemaker. This was Big Kate's saddle. The one belonging to J.I., with his initials carved in silver, has disappeared, along with a number of other treasures, including most of J.I.'s pen-and-ink drawings that were stored in the old Irvine mansion.

In the hills behind the house, deer and possum still run, and a family of roadrunners has established itself in a wind-bent cypress tree. There is indeed a sense of the finite here, of coming to the end, at Irvine Cove. One could not really call the landscape beautiful—dramatic, yes, but the vistas are too stark and demanding for beauty. This of course is true of much of California, and newcomers are often disappointed to find that much of the state is not prettier than it is. The rocky hills are too tough, dry, and implacable; they fail to soothe the eye. The valleys are too broad and flat and mean. It is no wonder that so many Californians use the word "respect" when they speak of the land. Though the Irvine family is far richer than the Yorbas—and became so, one might well conclude, at the Yorbas' expense years ago—Linda Irvine Gaede and Bernardo Yorba are good friends. Bernardo Yorba also expresses great "respect" for Linda's cousin Joan, who, in her long battles with the family company, was defending her heritage too. Linda also respects Joan, even though the two women no longer speak. Linda does not agree with Joan's motives at all, but she respects them. "She has her rights too," Linda says.

When the Irvine Company was reorganized in 1977—along lines that it was hoped would satisfy Joan—Linda Gaede and her husband bought back into the new company: "It was too hard to let go. There were all the emotional attachments to the land and to the family." Though Linda Gaede spent her early childhood on the San Francisco Peninsula, when her grandfather died the family moved to southern California. At first Linda's mother resisted the idea of living in the little ranch town of Tustin, and the family settled in Pasadena, from which Myford Irvine commuted to the ranch. But soon he too was drawn back to the ranch, where Linda grew up and went to school and, with her bicycle and her horses, rode back and forth between her cousins' houses. "I'm not a city person," she says. "I never will be. This is home."

This attachment to the land, which often seems so irrational, might provide a further, final insight into the haunting circumstances of Myford Irvine's death. To begin with, Mike Irvine was a tough man—healthy, hard as nails and, like his father, a bit autocratic. In fact the family often commented on how Mike's brother, Jase, had inherited their mother's gentle, soft-spoken, humorous nature. Mike's tender side displayed itself only in some of the songs he wrote, such as a romantic ballad called "Do You Remember?" Otherwise, like his father, he was all business, an outdoorsman and sportsman. He and his wife liked to take hiking, camping, and riding trips into the mountains; on one trip they spent several weeks living with a remote tribe of Indians. Mike was also a conservative, conventional man. He joined the Kiwanis Club and attended meetings faithfully. In Orange County he was liked for his lack of pretension. He never comported himself like a rich man, and he was often teased because his favorite golfing sweater had a large hole in one sleeve. He was frugal, hated to lose a golf ball, and in the golf games he played with friends, the stakes were never higher than fifty cents or a dollar. (Which makes the argument that he was involved in high-stakes gambling in Nevada seem a bit implausible.) At the same time, he could be philanthropic. In 1953 he spent more than $250,000 to host the International Boy Scout Jamboree on the Irvine ranch.

Blessed with hindsight, a number of people after his death said that Mike Irvine had just not been "cut out for" ranching, but this is unfair. In the eleven years he headed the Irvine Company a number of important steps were taken by him in his role of guiding the ranch's shift from agricultural to urban development. Along the coast he headed the development of such key areas as the expensive housing tracts of Irvine Terrace and Cameo Shores. Under his administration the Irvine Coast Country Club was built and the search for the site of the University of California at Irvine was begun. Under Mike Irvine's leadership the first water from the Colorado River was delivered to the ranch, giving the area the capacity to sustain a larger population increase. While he was in charge, the stage was being set for the master-plan development scheduled for the 1960s and 1970s. Years later Thelma Irvine would recall driving with her husband in 120-degree heat through the well-named Fireball Ranch he had acquired in the Imperial Valley, with a cowboy sitting on the hood of the jeep taking random shots at what seemed like a living sea of dog-size wild jackrabbits. Mike Irvine turned the Fireball into cotton. He developed still another ranch in the Napa Valley. To friends he often expressed his greatest wish, which was, he said, to run the ranch operations just as J.I. would have done. To those who knew him, and to whom suicide is considered an act of cowardice, Mike Irvine was no coward.

In 1950, Mike Irvine asked his wife for a divorce. This came as a great shock to Thelma Irvine, who had then been married to him, more or less happily—or so she thought—for twenty-eight years. It was an even greater shock when she discovered who the woman was whom Mike wanted to marry. She was a pretty blond divorcée named Gloria Wood White, somewhat younger than Mike. Thelma Irvine had considered Gloria White one of her closest friends; long after Gloria's divorce from William White, Thelma had continued to send Christmas checks to Gloria's children. Furthermore, Gloria White was practically a member of the family. Her first husband had been Big Kate's son by her first marriage; in other words, Mike Irvine wanted to marry his stepmother's former daughter-in-law. Mike and Thelma were divorced, and later that year Mike and Gloria White were married.

Today, at eighty, living alone in a large apartment overlooking the Pacific, Thelma Irvine is bright, chipper and healthily tanned from a daily four-mile walk. She no longer harbors any real resentment toward the woman, now dead, who replaced her in her husband's affections years ago. But she is convinced that her husband's second marriage was not a happy one. She and Myford Irvine, for example, had never bothered to be listed in the San Francisco *Social Register*. Gloria, on the other hand, wanted a listing and saw to it that her husband got one for her. She was demanding in other ways, particularly in terms of money. Others who remember the couple agree that there were frequent money arguments. In 1953, Gloria Irvine gave birth to a son whom the couple named James Myford Irvine.

On Sunday morning, January 11, 1959, Mike Irvine awoke at 7:30, as usual, had breakfast, and spent the morning pottering about the house in his usual fashion. According to Gloria's later account, at one o'clock she, Mike, and five-year-old Jimmy, whom his father adored, sat down for lunch in the dining room, and Mike Irvine had a can of beer. He then announced his intention of going down to the ranch office to do some work. This in itself was odd; it was Sunday, and the office was closed. Gloria said that it was time for Jimmy's nap, and Mike Irvine said, "Goodbye, son, I'll see you when you get up." Gloria Irvine said that she also wanted to take a nap. Nothing, according to Gloria, seemed wrong.

At three o'clock, in Gloria's account of the day, she awoke from her nap, roused her son, and drove with him down to the ranch office to visit her husband. This, she said, was a customary practice. That, at least, was what Gloria Irvine told Deputy Coroner James Pond, but this is even odder than the fact that Mike Irvine should have gone to his office on a Sunday afternoon. The ranch house and Myford's Irvine's office were next door to each other, barely a hundred feet apart. No one ever *drove* between the two places, and Thelma Irvine remembers that she often used to carry bowls of flowers over to the office from the house. Why would Gloria and her son have driven to the office? To collect him and drive him home? He always walked the meager distance. In any case, as Gloria's account to the deputy coroner continued, she arrived at the office, found no one there, and then drove home.

As she walked with her son from the garage to the house she noticed that the sky had darkened with a half-winter threat of rain, and Jimmy pointed out a light that was burning in the window of a basement storeroom. The two went down into the storeroom to investigate, and there they found Mike Irvine, slumped in a kneeling position, his right side resting against several cases of liquor and his head a few inches from the floor. Gloria Irvine screamed, seized her son's hand, and ran upstairs to telephone her doctor, Thomas B. Rhone, whom she told, "My husband has shot himself!" In less than twenty minutes Dr. Rhone was at the ranch house and telephoned the Orange County coroner.

On the left side of Mike Irvine's body, with his hand resting on the barrel, lay a 16-gauge Belgian Browning automatic shotgun, and on the other side of the body, beside a cardboard box, was a Smith & Wesson six-inch .22 caliber blue steel six-shot revolver. The shotgun had one expended shell casing in the chamber, and another expended casing was found on the floor about three feet away. On top of a case of liquor was a partially filled box of .22 caliber long-rifle cartridges; one cartridge was lying on the box, one on the floor, and one expended casing was in the chamber. One live round remained in the chamber, and the other chambers of the cylinder were empty.

The two shotgun blasts had entered Mike Irvine's abdomen. The bullet from the revolver had entered his right temple. There were powder burns there. There were also powder burns found on the index and middle fingers of his *left hand*. But Mike Irvine was not left-handed. And to have fired a bullet into his right temple with his left hand would seem to have required the skill of a contortionist.

In concluding that all three gunshot wounds were self-inflicted, the coroner reasoned that Mike Irvine, holding the shotgun near the muzzle, had triggered the first shot into his abdomen with his right hand. Then, since the gun was an automatic, a second shot into the abdomen, directly into the first, had been caused by the gun's recoil against a concrete wall and the corresponding weight of Mike Irvine's body. Then, still conscious, Mike had reached for the revolver with his left hand and had finished the job with a bullet in his temple. Medical tests were made for both alcohol and barbiturates. No trace of either was found. The house was thoroughly searched for a suicide note and, as we know, none was found.

The coroner placed the time of death at two o'clock in the afternoon while Gloria Irvine and her son were supposedly peacefully asleep upstairs. The Irvine mansion was old, uninsulated, full of creaks. It was a big white-shingled place, much added-to over the years until it eventually contained some thirty rooms; like Topsy, the house "just growed." It had been renovated at least six times to suit the tastes of a series of Irvine women, but it was still an old house. Much of its plumbing was also old, and periodically a toilet in an upstairs bathroom would flush all by itself; its erupting geyser could be heard all over the house, and the family would laugh and joke about ghosts. (In 1968, not quite ten years after Mike Irvine's death, some faulty wiring sparked and the mansion was all but destroyed by fire; the marquetry floors, hand-carved balustrades of the staircases, and other rich details were deemed irreplaceable, and the charred remains of the house were razed.) By 1959, J.I.'s pack of yelping hounds no longer shared the house with its human occupants, and the house was a quiet place. Yet no sleeper on the second floor had been disturbed by the angry sounds of gunfire. On the first floor the Irvines' cook, Opal Johnson, was in the kitchen, but heard nothing. Neither did a maid, Lois Doak, who was gossiping with Opal Johnson at the time. The two servants testified that they were aware of no signs of marital discord between Mr. and Mrs. Irvine.

Gloria Irvine could offer no real explanation for her husband's suicide, nor could she say why, when telephoning Dr. Rhone, she had immediately leaped to the conclusion that he had killed himself. She did say, however, that since Christmas her husband had seemed depressed, though she apparently had not considered his condition severe enough to inquire into its cause. True, there had been his near-frantic efforts to raise a large sum of money in the few days preceding his death and his remark to the family that he was "sitting on a keg of dynamite." But the family, while apparently perfectly willing to help him raise the money, had for some reason not bothered to inquire as to what the keg of dynamite was. At one point Joan Irvine's stepfather, Judge Clarke, had asked Mike Irvine why he didn't borrow the money he needed from a bank. Rather airily Mike had replied, "I've never had to borrow from a bank before, and I'm not going to start now."

The mystery deepened when the details of Mike Irvine's estate were revealed. He died worth well over $10,000,000 and had an income of over $500,000 a year. Why should he have had such a pressing need for cash?

In a book on organized crime called *The Grim Reapers* the author, Ed Reid, speculates that Mike Irvine had somehow got involved with the underworld and gambling and in the building of Caesars Palace Hotel in Las Vegas. But Mr. Reid produces no hard evidence to support this and, admitting that he is merely guessing, concludes, "The answer may lie in the sands of Las Vegas, under dunes flattened by the weight of Caesars Palace and the pressure of unhappy and unholy memories." It does seem that Mike Irvine would have been too thoughtful a man, too considerate of his family, to have destroyed himself in a basement storeroom, in such an untidy way, while his wife and young son were asleep upstairs. There is also the illogical fact of the two guns. Mike Irvine was an expert hunter, familiar with firearms and their various capabilities, well aware that the simplest, neatest way to dispatch a life is a bullet between the eyes. Would he have ended his own life so clumsily? Had he, in preparing for his suicide, actually brought two guns into the basement with the thought that if the shotgun into the belly didn't work he would have the pistol handy as insurance? Finally, there is the impossible-to-answer question of why the pistol was held in the left hand and fired into the right temple.

Thelma Irvine did not attend her former husband's funeral, reasoning that there was already "too much notoriety" surrounding his death. But considering that she had been married to him for twenty-eight years, that he had courted her for three years before that, and that she had known him throughout college, she feels, with some justification, that she knew the man better than did any other person. She gives no credence to either the suicide theory or the talk of Las Vegas connections. "He never went to Las Vegas," she says. "He hated to gamble. He was a terrible poker player. When he played golf with me he refused to play for money, because, with my handicap, it would mean that I would probably win. He was not the suicidal type. He never suffered from depressions. I remember once at a dinner party, not long afterward, Linda asked a doctor friend, Dr. Monaco, if he thought her father could have been a suicide. Dr. Monaco simply shook his head and said, '*Impossible!*'"

Thelma Irvine also finds it impossible to credit Gloria Irvine's account of what happened that fatal afternoon. "He *never* went to the office on a Sunday. The office was *closed*. The shooting *had* to have taken place somewhere else. I knew that house like the back of my hand. I knew that storeroom where he was found. I'd remodeled it myself. It used to be a photographic darkroom. But my husband *never* went into the basement for any reason. The room was directly underneath the kitchen and the servants' quarters. Why didn't any of the servants hear three shots? I knew the bedroom where Gloria supposedly was sleeping. It had been my bedroom. She would have heard the shots." Later there were stories in southern California that Myford Irvine had been drinking heavily in the months before his death, and Thelma Irvine finds this also difficult to believe. "He wasn't a strict teetotaler, like his father," she says, "but he didn't really like to drink. Now and then he'd have a drink just to be sociable, but that was it. Can a man's personality change so completely in such a short time? I just don't see how.

"I know he was under tremendous pressure after his brother died. It was an awful strain. After all, he wasn't trained for the ranch. He was trained for the city. But he bore up wonderfully under the strain and never complained about anything." In Thelma Irvine's opinion, Mike Irvine's death was somehow connected with the family, the company, and the land. At the time of his death he was in the process of building a new ocean-side house at Corona del Mar. He was not building it for himself, however. He was building it for Gloria. It was something Gloria wanted. She hated the old ranch house and wanted a house that was big and modern, with lots of glass. The house was going to cost $325,000 in 1959 dollars.

In the weeks before his death he had complained to friends that he had misgivings about building this house for Gloria. He had gone to see his personal physician, Dr. Horace Leecing, who had also treated J.I. before him, and had complained of nervousness and insomnia. Today Dr. Leecing, a retired country doctor in his late seventies—who remembers when he charged two dollars for an office visit and three dollars for a house call at the Irvine ranch— recalls Myford Irvine telling him that he thought the new house was "too pretentious" and that he had had second thoughts about giving in to Gloria and moving into such a big, expensive place. He said that he frequently lay awake at night worrying about this project, regretting that he had committed himself to it, and said that he would prefer not to move but to remain on the land of his fore- bears, on the traditional Irvine ranch. "He told me that living in that house would be like living in a fishbowl," Dr. Leecing says. "He said he would feel like a fish out of water living there." Dr. Leecing also received the distinct impression that Mike Irvine's marriage to Gloria had become a very unhappy one. Dr. Leecing prescribed a variety of sleeping pills and tranquilizers, which Mike Irvine had been taking, and entered a diagnosis of "acute depression."

On the afternoon of his death Mike Irvine was seen at the construction site of the new house, walking around on an open sea-facing deck as though inspecting it or, perhaps, saying goodbye to it. So possibly he had not gone to his office at all.

Thelma Irvine does not go so far as to suggest that Gloria Irvine hired someone to kill her husband so that she wouldn't be prevented from having her house; Gloria, with a large inheritance from her husband, did indeed eventually move into it. "But," Thelma says, "there was a man on the ranch who did commit suicide not long after what happened to Mike. And I've always wondered whether there might have been a connection." The man, a company electrician, had been among the first at the scene of the tragedy, and Thelma wonders whether he knew something that might have "weighed on his mind." Thelma also questions whether Mike Irvine's death might have been connected with Brad Hellis, the man who had been with J.I. on his final fishing trip and who had resigned from the Irvine Company rather than face Joan's threatened lawsuit for financial wrongdoing. "Brad Hellis and Walter Tubach were in charge of buying land for J.I.," says Mrs. Irvine, "but they were cheating J.I. They were buying the best land for themselves and only letting J.I. have what they didn't want. At one point my husband offered to make Brad a vice-president of the company, but Brad turned it down. Why? Because he knew he couldn't get away with that sort of thing with Myford." Had Myford found out too much about Brad Hellis' speculations, and had Hellis arranged for Mike's murder to silence him? Neither Hellis nor Gloria Irvine is alive to answer these dark allegations.

Interestingly, Dr. Leecing—who remains firmly convinced that Mike Irvine's death was a simple suicide (Leecing's testimony was an important deciding factor in the coroner's verdict)—also connects the death with Brad Hellis, but for a quite different reason. "Brad was like another son to J.I.," says Dr. Leecing. "He was Mike Irvine's best friend. But Brad was another one of the causes of Mike's depression. At the time of Joan's lawsuit, and Brad's falling-out with the company, he offered to resign, and it was Mike, as president, who had the deciding vote in accepting his resignation.

Later he said to me, 'I feel I've betrayed my best friend.' But of course he was being forced to decide between the demands of his family and the demands of friendship. Mike had to decide in favor of the family, but he felt terrible about it. Brad Hellis was tops, and so was Walter Tubach. At the Rotary Club everybody loved them. Brad was a man of the highest integrity. I would trust Brad as much as I would my own father."

And so we are left with the unsolved riddle of Mike Irvine's death, a riddle that has a tantalizing number of possible solutions, interconnected, and yet none quite plausible. Perhaps the true villain was the land. Had the land taken hold of him too, as it had done to so many others? Had it possessed him, the way it appeared to possess his niece Joan? Did he take his own life rather than risk the shock of moving off the Irvine land, even though Corona del Mar was only a few miles away? Perhaps. If so, the secret does not lie under the sands of Las Vegas. It lies with Mike Irvine in the land, in the plot of Irvine ranchland where the others of the family are gathered, in the ashes of the old mansion and along the brown hills and among the mesquite clumps and the old canals and levees, in the orange groves and sheep trails and horse paths, all the dusty roads that lead to Finisterra.

Or perhaps the secret was revealed long ago in *Peck's 1837 New Guide to the West:* ". . . the real Eldorado is still further on."

FURTHER ON . . .

And o'er his heart a shadow
Fell as he found
No spot of ground
That looked like Eldorado.
EDGAR ALLAN POE

CHAPTER TWENTY-THREE
The Gilded Nomads

THE FUTURE of California will be written, unquestionably, in the south, where the little town that no one took seriously fifty years ago is now loosely defined as "metropolitan Los Angeles" and continues to eclipse San Francisco in size, economic importance, and attractiveness to the very rich. Los Angeles, furthermore, has lured an entirely new breed of rich, and against the gaudy backdrop of this glittering new city the "old" American pioneer families—the Crockers, Huntingtons, de Youngs, Spreckelses, and even the Irvines —seem like creatures from another, more naive era.

It was not until the summer of 1978 that anyone in Beverly Hills really noticed it—the fact that many of the sleekly dressed denizens of that particular enclave of California superwealth had a decidedly foreign look about them, with swarthier complexions than ordinarily result from a California tan. That was the summer when a twenty-three-year-old Saudi Arabian sheik, who no one realized had moved to the community, revealed the renovations he had had made on his Sunset Boulevard mansion, hard by the Beverly Hills Hotel. He was Sheik Muhammad al-Fassi, and his house, which had hardly been a modest residence to begin with, was now surrounded by a wall imbedded with glittering mother-of-pearl. This wall was surmounted by dozens of large stone vases filled with plastic flowers. The house itself had been painted a bilious shade of green, and fan-shaped windows had been overlaid with gilt scrolls. At night, huge opening-night spotlights, also green, illuminated the house and its extensive grounds, and green and orange lanterns were suspended from the trees. Most startling of all was the curving front terrace, facing the street, which had been decked out with a parade of male and female nude statues. The statues had been painted flesh color and were explicit right down to pink nipples and black pubic hair.

Beverly Hills was accustomed to a certain amount of vulgarity, but this was too much. The neighbors were outraged. Even more disturbing was the fact that the house, and the nude statues, quickly became a local tourist attraction and created traffic jams on Sunset Boulevard as gawkers lined up in their cars for a closer look at the sheik's new house.*

It was at this point that Beverly Hills realized that it had been undergoing an invasion of moneyed foreigners for the past ten years —Latin Americans, Israelis, French, Chinese, Koreans, Japanese, and, most notably, Iranians and Arabs. Foreigners had purchased the Harold Lloyd estate, the J. Paul Getty mansion, and other properties in Beverly Hills at cost of up to $4,000,000 apiece. "Foreigners will pay almost anything to live here," a local real estate man reported, revealing that in 1978 the median price for a Beverly Hills house was

---

* Not long after the sheik's seven-million-dollar renovation was completed he returned to Saudi Arabia—summoned home, it was suggested, because of official embarrassment over what he had done in Beverly Hills. Early in 1980 two mysterious fires broke out simultaneously in two different parts of the untenanted and unguarded mansion. Arson was suspected, and *Newsweek* quoted one of the sheik's neighbors as saying, "We're kind of happy about the fire," though the nude statues remained unsinged.

$500,000. Princess Shams, the sister of the deposed Shah of Iran, had relocated herself in Beverly Hills, along with others of her expatriated friends and relatives. Perhaps the reason why the steady migration of foreigners to Beverly Hills had gone unnoticed had something to do with the fact that Beverly Hills itself was a community of immigrants from elsewhere—New York, Philadelphia, or the Middle West—a nomadic population that had come to southern California in search of fame and riches, or, having already achieved these, to partake of Beverly Hills's famously easy and luxurious lifestyle. Now, it seemed, strangers from other lands were also coming to California in search of El Dorado.

Though no one knows, in this community of about 32,000 residents, exactly how many have come from abroad, some of the results of the influx can be seen in the growth of the Beverly Hills School District's English-as-a-second-language program. Early in 1979, *The New York Times* reported that there were 187 elementary-school children enrolled in these classes—101 more than the year before. Fifty-three percent of these children were from Iran, 12 percent from Israel, 11 percent from China, Korea, and Japan, 6 percent from Spanish-speaking countries, and 5 percent from Italy. The remaining 13 percent were from countries in which French or Russian was the primary language. At the high school level the increase in the use of the program was just as dramatic. In the 1977–78 academic year there were 85 students enrolled in it; by 1979 the number had more than doubled, to 177. By that year 7 percent of the Beverly Hills school population were taking part in the program, and, of these, 79 percent were Iranian.

The foreign influx has also made itself felt along Beverly Hills's celebrated monument to consumerism, North Rodeo Drive, where one strolls not only to marvel at the goods and price tags displayed in the expensive shops but also to be dazzled by the exotic array of foreign and custom-built automobiles parked along the curb. In addition to the traditional foreign-owned fashion and jewelry establishments, such as Gucci, Bally, Battaglia, and Buccellati, there are some impressive newcomers. In 1978, for example, Pietro and Margo

Fallai, wanderers from chilly Sweden, where they had operated a successful chain of boutiques, came to Beverly Hills, where they opened the Yves St. Laurent Boutique and have continued to prosper happily. Another successful venture has been that of Bijan Pakzad, a thirty-six-year-old Iranian who spent more than a million dollars to transform a parking lot into one of the town's most fashionable boutiques for men.

The newcomers, furthermore, have had no trouble fitting in socially with the eclectic Beverly Hills mix of rich: movie and television stars, producers, agents, rock stars, psychiatrists, retired corporate executives, hairdressers, divorce lawyers, and restaurateurs. Within weeks of his arrival on the Beverly Hills scene Mr. Pakzad had been invited to fifteen black-tie dinners and was having to turn down invitations because they were interfering with his six-day-a-week business schedule. The Fallais, who came to this glittering melting pot to escape both the Swedish winters and the crippling taxes, were apprehensive that they would have trouble making new friends. They need not have worried. Soon after their arrival they were being entertained everywhere and were giving large parties of their own in their hilltop house. Part of the easy acceptance of outsiders in Beverly Hills has to do with Californians' traditional wish to appear outgoing and hospitable. But, more important, social acceptance in California is easier because society itself is so new, unlike society in older eastern cities, where there really is an Establishment and where social lines demarcating who is who have been more rigidly and carefully drawn for several generations. "Beverly Hills is not a place where one group controls all the power bases," its New York–born mayor, Joseph N. Tilem, has said. Also it is harder to adhere to the stiff formalities of social ritual in a community in which the style dictates gold chains, designer jeans, and Gucci loafers.

As Mr. Fallai puts it: "Maybe residents of Beverly Hills are hospitable because they know what it is to be strangers. Very few people I've met are native Californians." Mr. Pakzad says it even more succinctly: "If you are successful, it is very easy to be accepted in *any* social circle in Beverly Hills." Success, then, is the Beverly

Hills criterion for aristocracy, not the schools one went to or the maiden name of one's grandmother. Success of course means money, and part of the California dream is that in California success and money are easy to come by. Southern California, in other words, has abandoned every form of snobbery except the one dealing with the bottom line: one's bank balance. But even that is assumed to be expandable. A young psychologist, visiting from the East, was chatting at a party with a young woman he had met just a few minutes earlier and was asked why he didn't move to Beverly Hills. He mentioned something about the difficulty of establishing a practice in a new city. "But that's simple!" she cried. "I'll just have a luncheon for you, and that will be your practice." He is not at all sure that the young woman was not absolutely right.

STILL, THOUGH all the new Californians have arrived more or less successfully at the continent's brink, the nomadic urge persists in curious ways—the urge to continue the illusion, at least, that one is willing to uproot, to move on to some farther, undisclosed place. The quickness with which California has come to be appears to have lent a certain transience to the quality of California life; no one seems to be completely settled in. In southern California in particular—and especially in Beverly Hills—addresses change quickly; these are still migratory birds, drifting and circling, looking for some more nearly perfect place to alight. ("Are you still on Mulholland Drive?" "No, I've rented Cliff Robertson's place at Malibu.") Every resting place is somehow temporary and, quite literally, shaky, but if, as some oracles of doom have predicted, California will one day shake itself into the Pacific Ocean, Californians, one feels, will be philosophical, ready to move on, outward, somewhere.

Nowhere is this illusion, this mobile frame of mind, more apparent than in the miles of mobile-home parks that stretch along the Pacific Coast Highway and elsewhere. (When Linda Irvine Gaede gives driving directions to Finisterra, one of the nearby landmarks is a trailer park.) Many of these parks are quite sumptuous, such as one at Dana Point, where Mrs. Norman Chandler, publisher of the

Los Angeles *Times*, keeps a mobile weekend mansion. Nowhere but in California—not even in Florida—has the mobile home been able to achieve the status of a Correct Address. True, many of California's largest and most lavishly accoutered mobile homes are planted firmly in the ground and are clearly homes that will move no more. But the *mood* is mobile.

Out in the desert, some hundred miles east of Los Angeles, lies yet another enclave of sudden (or very recent) wealth—Palm Springs. In spirit Palm Springs is not at all unlike Beverly Hills. Indeed, it is one of Beverly Hills's favorite weekend playgrounds. Palm Springs is purely and simply about money, nothing else, and it is also a place where mobile-home living has come to a kind of glorious climax of extravagance. Even more so than other California cities, it is a place of superlatives and has its heady statistics backed up by an extraordinarily enthusiastic chamber of commerce.

Palm Springs has "more swimming pools per capita than any other city in the world"—roughly one pool for every four residents. Periodically the chamber of commerce makes a nose count of prestigious automobiles so that Palm Springs can continue to boast more Cadillacs, Lincolns, Bentleys, and Rolls-Royces than can be found assembled on any other 41.6-square-mile area on the planet. At various times Palm Springs has also advertised itself as the home of "the world's most luxurious thermal baths," "the world's only flying great-grandmother," and "the world's wealthiest tribe of Indians." No Palm Springs resident can escape for long his own personal, identifying superlative. A Seattle retailer has been pointed out in local promotional literature as "the owner of one of the largest department stores in the West." A Milwaukee restaurant owner was identified as "the head of one of America's biggest chains of steak houses." Clearly bigness is what counts in Palm Springs. A Pebble Beach woman named Laurena Heple was identified as "the world's largest manufacturer of remote-controlled gates."

If a superlative can be attached to a slogan, so much the better as far as Palm Springs is concerned. Depending on the mood of the chamber of commerce, Palm Springs is either "The Winter Movie

Capital of the World" or the place "Where the Sun Shines on the Stars." The chamber publishes a periodic list, "Hollywood Personalities with Homes in Palm Springs," and a similar list, "Prominent Business People," is also available. Palm Springs, with its physical and emotional proximity to Hollywood and the motion picture industry, has had little difficulty accepting wealthy Jews into the community. But it was less sure how to handle the arrival of moneyed blacks, as was evidenced with the appearance of John H. Johnson, the publisher of *Ebony*, as a new winter resident a few years ago. The problem was solved, however, when the chamber of commerce was able to announce that "the wealthiest black in America" now owned a home in Palm Springs.

In Palm Springs, rich folk and the public relations business have merged, or at least they have come to a working agreement. Everyone is a booster. Conducting a tour of "society mansions" in the low hills around Palm Springs, a resident delivered the following information: "Here is the house where Debbie Reynolds and Eddie Fisher spent their honeymoon. Over there is the house where Eddie Fisher and Liz Taylor spent *their* honeymoon. I forget which house Liz Taylor and Michael Wilding spent their honeymoon in, but the house where Liz Taylor and Mike Todd spent their honeymoon is over there . . ."

The town is touted as "The World's Friendliest Place" as well as "The Winter Golf Capital of the World." Golf, which may have become a middle-class sport elsewhere, is the required upper-crust game here, and it goes without saying that there are more golf courses per capita in Palm Springs than anywhere else on earth. Furthermore, Palm Springs is either "The Birthplace of the Golf Cart" or "The Site of the Development of the Golf Cart," depending on which handout you read. In any case it undoubtedly has more golf carts per capita than it has golf courses and can go so far as to make this dizzying claim: "More homes with specially built, semi-attached golf cart garages than any other resort area." Recently, too, Palm Springs has become "The Playground of the Presidents." It started with Dwight D. Eisenhower, who used to spend a part of each winter in a cottage on the grounds of the Eldorado Country Club. John F. Kennedy and Lyndon B. Johnson also spent time in Palm Springs, and Harry Truman and Herbert Hoover visited there, though not while they were in office.

Most recently, Gerald R. Ford enjoyed a sojourn in Palm Springs, and of course Richard Nixon is a frequent visitor at the Palm Springs home of his friend Walter Annenberg, who maintains Sunnylands, the area's most sumptuous estate, which has its own private golf course. (Though it has only nine holes, the course is laid out in such a way that a total of twenty-seven holes can be played.) There are eight Annenberg golf carts with blue-and-white hoods, thirteen man-made lakes, and a swimming pool that cascades down on various levels like a natural stream. Sunnylands requires a staff of forty-five to run it, and to make sure that his golf course would always have water, Walter Annenberg bought the local water company. The place has guesthouses, equipment houses, and a main house with a fountain copied from the one at the Museum of Natural History in Mexico City. The entrance to the house is a room with a high vaulted ceiling through which sunlight pours down into a reflecting pool. Beside the pool Rodin's "Eve" is placed. All the rooms of the house are so located that they overlook the huge, rare beaucarnea tree which Annenberg purchased from Estelle Doheny's estate and had transplanted from Los Angeles. There is a sculpture garden, a cactus garden, two hothouses—one just for orchids—and Mrs. Annenberg's private meditation garden, a simple affair: a circle of white chrysanthemums enclosed in a square of Japanese pebbles set in grout, the whole surrounded by a holly hedge. Gardeners make sure that Mrs. Annenberg's chrysanthemums are always fresh. Guests at Sunnylands go on picnics with insulated hot and cold picnic baskets and are driven about in a Mini-Mok, a housewarming gift from Frank Sinatra.

In the years since World War II—when the developers first "discovered" Palm Springs—the population has doubled every ten years, and in the next ten years the population will at least double again. The winter, or "in season," population climbs at an even more alarming rate, and on winter weekends as many as a hundred thousand people a day pour into the city, mostly from Los Angeles. These figures would dismay the inhabitants of a traditional eastern resort area, but they delight the wealthy who have made Palm Springs their winter home; the popularity of the place assures them of the wisdom of their original investments.

Palm Springs is also proud of its main street, Palm Canyon Drive, which is a serious contender with North Rodeo Drive for the title of "World's Most Elegant Shopping Street." But the sight that visitors to Palm Springs are most often taken to see is Blue Skies Village. The development was originally backed by the late Bing Crosby, along with such investors as Jack Benny, Claudette Colbert, William Goetz, Phil Harris, and William Perlberg, and it can only be described as the mobile-home park to end all mobile-home parks or, as the chamber of commerce puts it, "The World's Most Sumptuous Mobile Home Park." The original scheme was to lease trailer space, to which the lessor would add a trailer and would also spend at least $7500 on "improvements." This modest commitment, far from discouraging the original tenants of Blue Skies Village, spurred them on to greater, more competitive spending. In one eight-month period Blue Skies trailer owners spent a total of $750,000 on terraces, porches, gazebos, cupolas, ramadas (a superstructure covering an entire trailer), and other adornments. Several Blue Skies residents went off, unaccountably, on Oriental flights of fancy and enclosed their trailers in strange pagodas. One man, in an Egyptian mood, surmounted his trailer with a replica of the Great Portal of the Temple of Karnak, complete with exterior friezes and frescoes.

Mr. Richard E. Bishop, a retired president of a chemical company, spent "in the six figures" turning his 55-by-18-foot trailer into a facsimile of Mount Vernon. "I'm not quite sure how we got started on Mount Vernon," he said at the time, "but we put on the big porch across the front with the white columns, and one thing sort of led to another." For good measure, though the original Mount Vernon didn't have one, the Bishops' version was given a rooftop sun deck. The Bishops' maid was then given a separate, smaller mobile version of Mount Vernon alongside. Because they require less care—in fact no care at all—plastic flowers and shrubbery were set out for landscaping, and a number of other Blue Skies residents quickly copied this clever idea.

"People in other trailer parks around here call us 'the Blue Skies snobs,' " one trailer owner says, "and frankly, we're proud of that label. We're the richest mobile-home community in America. Almost all of us are corporation presidents. We're also a more international group than you'll find in other parks, and we're more social too. We hire professional entertainers for our shindigs. We have fifty-dollar-a-plate- dinners. We have cocktail parties. And, sure, we're exclusive. We're like a private club. No Tom, Dick, or Harry can move into this place. We want *nice* people living here. We check on every-body. We even find out if they snore."

Though Palm Springs is a mid-twentieth-century creation, it did for a while have an old guard. It consisted of exactly one woman, Mrs. Austin McManus, and even she was not a native. Still, Mrs. McManus, who was known throughout the Coachella Valley as Auntie Pearl, was for many years easily the First Lady of Palm Springs. She was a cheerful-faced woman who, even in her eighties, managed to look considerably younger than her years and who used to say, "My heart is bound up in the desert." So, it might be added, was her considerable fortune. Her father, Judge John Guthrie Mc-Callum, arrived in 1884, having sought out the desert air for the sake of a tubercular son. Palm Springs was a sleepy Indian settlement called Agua Caliente, named for the warm mineral springs that bub-bled up through the sand and are now the site of the Palm Springs Spa and "the world's most beautiful bathhouse." Judge McCallum became the area's first white settler. He bought up between five and six thousand acres of land, built an aqueduct to carry water down from the mountains, constructed nineteen miles of irrigation canals, and began growing citrus, fig, and other fruit trees. He never lived to see his investment become a success. At the time of his death an eleven-year drought had dried up his canals and aqueduct—this was before Palm Springs was discovered to rest on a series of under-ground lakes that made water plentiful and cheap—and his fruit orchards had withered and died. "Father died of a broken heart," Mrs. McManus used to say.

But his considerable land passed on to his daughter, who managed her properties with a shrewdness that won her the admiration of every real estate man in town, which is to say a large share of the population. She also exercised a good deal of taste, and the buildings for which she is responsible show style and restraint in a town not noted for architectural distinction. It was she who built the handsome Tennis Club—which has been called with customary Palm Springs excess "the most beautiful two acres in America"—as well as a number of the better-looking commercial buildings downtown.

By the late 1960s, widowed and childless and without collateral heirs, Mrs. McManus began to think in terms of foundations and other beneficiaries of her money and properties. She had become interested in the newly founded College of the Desert, a junior college outside Palm Springs, only to discover that this institution too seemed to have become afflicted with the curious logy-mindedness one occasionally encounters in southern California. She had sent the college a check for seven thousand dollars. The president had called to thank her for the gift and had suggested that the money might be spent to purchase new robes for the college choir. "Now, wouldn't you *think*," Mrs. McManus said to a friend at the time, "that the college— *any* college—could find something better to spend that money on than choir robes? Why not *books*, for example? *Choir robes!*"

It was real estate fever, Mrs. McManus freely admitted, that kept her young. She would stand on the veranda of her comfortable but unpretentious pink stucco house overlooking Palm Springs and the acreage her father had bought and talk, rather the way Joan Irvine still talks, of "whole new cities, whole new communities" being carved out of far-off mountains and hidden canyons and arroyos beyond. In her eighties she was taken on a private helicopter tour over some of those wild, lost ridges, and immediately became excited about their development. "You see," she said with a smile, "I own some of those mountains."

Auntie Pearl McManus is gone now, but the mountains are still there, as they are all over California, waiting to be developed, waiting to turn into money. And the California dream—riches, riches everywhere, endless possibilities opening up in the empty hills—goes on. To the plop of tennis balls, to the chug of golf carts, the swish of designer jeans and the chink of gold chains, it goes on.

After all, El Dorado is just over there, beyond the brow of the next hill.

BIBLIOGRAPHY

Adams, Austin. *The Man John D. Spreckels*. San Diego: Frye & Smith, 1924.

Altrocchi, Julia. *The Spectacular San Franciscans*. New York: E. P. Dutton, 1949.

Amory, Cleveland. *Who Killed Society?* New York: Harper & Bros., 1960.

Berkman, Leslie. "The Winning of Irvine Co.—and What Lies Ahead," Los Angeles *Times*, Aug. 14, 1977.

Chambliss, William H. *Society as It Really Is*. New York: Chambliss & Co., 1895.

Cleland, Robert Glass. *The Irvine Ranch*. San Marino: Huntington Library Press, 1962.

Dillon, Richard. *Fool's Gold*. New York: Coward, McCann, Inc., 1967.
———. *Humbugs and Heroes: A Gallery of California Pioneers*. Garden City, N.Y.: Doubleday & Co., 1970.

307

Eliot, Elizabeth. *Heiresses and Coronets.* New York: McDowell, Obolensky, 1959.

Freedgood, Seymour. "88,000 Golden Acres Waiting for the Dust to Settle," *Fortune* (Nov. 1963).

Harris, Leon. *Merchant Princes.* New York: Harper & Row, 1979.

Lewis, Oscar. *Big Four.* New York: Alfred A. Knopf, 1938.

———. *Silver Kings.* New York: Alfred A. Knopf, 1947.

Lyman, George D. *Ralston's Ring: California Plunders the Comstock Lode.* New York: Charles Scribner's Sons, 1937.

Moffat, Frances. *Dancing on the Brink of the World: The Rise and Fall of San Francisco Society.* New York: G. P. Putnam's Sons, 1977.

Myers, Gustavus. *History of the Great American Fortunes.* New York: Modern Library, 1936.

Peterson, Larry. "Jumping Joan Is All Alone," *Orange County Illustrated* (Sept. 1976).

Purtell, Joseph. *The Tiffany Touch.* New York: Random House, 1971.

Reid, Ed. *The Grim Reapers: The Anatomy of Organized Crime in America.* Chicago: Regnery, 1969.

Robbins, Mildred Brown. *Tales of Love and Hate in San Francisco.* San Francisco: Chronicle Books, 1971.

Robertson, Wyndham. "The Greening of the Irvine Co.," *Fortune* (Dec. 1976).

Taylor, Frank J., and Earl M. Welty. *Black Bonanza.* New York: McGraw-Hill Book Co., Inc., 1950.

Treadwell, Edward F. *Cattle King.* New York: Macmillan Co., 1931.

Werner, M. R., and John Starr. *Teapot Dome.* New York: Viking Press, Inc., 1959.

INDEX